AND THE
Day
Came

AND THE

Day Came

DR. LYNNETTE SIMM

WITH MICHELLE HOFFMAN

WESTBOW
PRESS®
A DIVISION OF THOMAS NELSON
& ZONDERVAN

WestBow Press books may be ordered through booksellers or by contacting:

WestBow Press
A Division of Thomas Nelson & Zondervan
1663 Liberty Drive
Bloomington, IN 47403
www.westbowpress.com
1 (866) 928-1240

Because of the dynamic nature of the Internet, any web addresses or links contained in this book may have changed since publication and may no longer be valid. The views expressed in this work are solely those of the author and do not necessarily reflect the views of the publisher, and the publisher hereby disclaims any responsibility for them.

Any people depicted in stock imagery provided by Thinkstock are models, and such images are being used for illustrative purposes only. Certain stock imagery © Thinkstock.

This book is a work of non-fiction. Unless otherwise noted, the author and the publisher make no explicit guarantees as to the accuracy of the information contained in this book and in some cases, names of people and places have been altered to protect their privacy.

ISBN: 978-1-5127-5215-1 (sc)
ISBN: 978-1-5127-5216-8 (hc)
ISBN: 978-1-5127-5217-5 (e)

Library of Congress Control Number: 2016914319

Print information available on the last page.

WestBow Press rev. date: 10/7/2016

Contents

For My Beloved Family
My journey would never have been possible
if not for your love and devotion.
You all make my life worth living and sharing.
Madison, MacKenzie, and Alexandra
My Parents, Bob and Louise
And My Brother and Sisters

DON'T FORGET, LEARN

I'll never forget. I've tried, but I simply can't. People have begged me to forget, to let it go, but some things become part of you. These events are etched into my memory, and they have formed the foundation of who I am today. The good and bad memories of my childhood have molded, cursed, inspired, haunted, and strengthened me. To forget my past would mean forgetting who I am and where I came from. Forgetting my past would erase the lessons I've learned, lessons from the pain and hurt and the healing and love. So I refuse to forget. I refuse to live a life hiding in silence, even if my remembering and sharing my lessons makes some people uncomfortable.

We all can learn valuable lessons from our past, especially from the memories that came from hurt and/or hard work. I had never viewed myself as valuable *because of* the pain I endured or mistakes I made; rather, the value and wisdom I've garnered comes from processing the pain and continuing to learn how I can use my life lessons to shape me for the better. And, I hope, impact the lives of others as well.

These days, I'm amused by mainstream, romantic tragedies—Danielle Steel-like stories where the heroine finds peace, understanding, and, of course, true love after many adversities. But life isn't a three-hundred-page romance novel, nor is it a Hollywood, made-for-TV movie. The last twenty minutes of our real-life stories never erases or repairs a lifetime of pain. Some people may only remember people's lives for the pain they endured, but if we're lucky, those of us who have survived, healed, and prospered will be remembered for how we overcame, in spite of those unforgettable events. I believe God uses our true-life pain to help others process, overcome, heal, and flourish. He redeems the pain that overshadowed our lives or nearly destroyed our families and us for growth, for good, for ourselves and countless others. So we can't and shouldn't forget. Instead, we should share our life lessons with others. We should share the depth and origin of pain. And, if possible, as it is in my case, we should share the journey from despair to true forgiveness and healing.

Pearls form only through pain or adversity. A tiny grain of sand, which settles in a crevice of the shell and creates hardship for the oyster, causes the creature to adjust, to defend, and to protect itself by covering the sand with a less-abrasive finish. Nacre, better known as mother-of-pearl, covers the grain of sand layer by layer like thin coats of paint. In much the same way, the hardships of life teach us valuable lessons that result in pearls of wisdom. The pages of this memoir contain many of mine.

Chapter 1

TIME TO SHARE

$\mathcal{I}$ have broken every commandment. My childhood left me feeling beaten, broken, and worthless, and as a result, I was on a terrible path. My life was damaged, yet I am here to tell my story of full restoration. This miracle began when I came face-to-face with angels, miracles, and the grace of God. I faced the demons that haunted me for decades in therapy, worked diligently to learn who God made me to be, and answered the calling to share this story.

Sometimes a calling gnaws at you, especially when you don't believe you're up to the task. In spring 2013, my husband, Madison, and I were relaxing near the bay windows in our master bedroom. Generally speaking, life was going well compared to the depression that nearly engulfed me following our move to Texas nine months before. The partially drawn Roman shades allowed the spring sunshine to gently filter into the room, and the light matched our moods as we talked about the week's events, our daughters, and life in general.

Madison looked so comfortable in his cargo shorts and graphic T-shirt, his usual weekend attire. After listening, he asked, "So what plans do you have for the summer? You said you don't have another class to teach, so what are you and the girls going to do for the next three months?"

"Well, this may sound lame, but I was thinking about *actually* writing my story." I bit my lower lip and waited for a response that didn't come. "I don't know if I can do it. Just talking about Dad is going to be hard because I don't remember much, and what I do remember is awful. My relationship with Mom has been so convoluted with need, anger, and hate, yet intermingled with incredible love, that it could be a book by itself." An uncomfortable chuckle followed by a deep sigh was my way of cueing Madison to chime in.

"If it's something you want to do, go for it."

"It would be extremely personal and possibly embarrassing. And the girls! I cringe inside just thinking about how I'm going to tell them everything that happened. And what if they hate me once they know what I've done?" My heart began to race and my eyes fill with tears. I looked out the window and tried to envision myself explaining everything to our beautiful daughters. At that moment, MacKenzie, a high school freshman, and Alexandra, a sixth-grader, were safely tucked away from our conversation, their noses probably buried in books. Wonderfully mature and grounded young ladies, they itched for school to be over and our backyard pool construction to be finished for summer.

Madison's tender gray-blue eyes looked straight into my warm brown eyes. "Listen to me. I'm here with you. You can do this if you want to. Just take it one memory at a time. You have an amazing story to share. Sure, the girls will have questions, and they might be shocked at some of what they hear, but they love you! You're a strong, loving mom who will be there for them like you always have been. Plus, they've reached an age where they'll be able to understand the truth and still see you for who you are. They'll recognize the hurt little girl you once were and the awesome woman you've become, *Dr. Simm*."

Madison always knew just what to say. Throughout our life together, he has been my biggest supporter. Once again, he was talking me through my fears and logically laying out the possibilities. But talking to Kenzie and Alex about my past felt like more than I could handle. Just the thought of it brought tears sliding down my cheeks. I slowly wiped them away with the back of my hand.

"Learning about my past might change how they see me. They'll have mental images that … well … that they should never have. Knowing about my abuse could hurt them and damage relationships. I'm struggling with the risks and the fear." My mind raced with the secrets I'd have to reveal. I winced at an especially touchy topic between Madison and me. Knowing it would eventually have to come out, I decided to see if it would sway Madison from encouraging me to tell our little secret.

"Talking about Bowen will be a shock. I'm still so ashamed of what we did, and you don't even talk about it, even though you say you have no regrets." Wiping my cheeks more, I attempted one final excuse for not writing. "And we haven't even mentioned how I've hurt you. I don't know how the girls will be able to respect me once they learn about my betrayal and the hurt I've caused you. Our marriage saw some really dark places because of my actions—actions that could have destroyed our family— not to mention the depths of my destructive emotional ups and downs that continue to haunt us. There are things I don't know if want to share or even *can* share, for that matter. I don't want to humiliate or embarrass you, our families, or myself. I don't want to hurt my parents, my family, the girls, or you. I'd have to talk to Mom and Dad, not to mention Mary, Robert, and my stepsister about my writing a book. What if they don't want me share all our family secrets, for the world to judge? I—"

"This is *your* story—about *your* life." Madison's face contorted with a look that said he would protect and defend me if anyone tried to hurt me. "Besides, you talked to your parents years ago about possibly telling your story, and they seemed okay with it. I don't see why they would forbid you now. I know Mary loves you and would support you. Robert may not like it, but I think he'll go along if you talk to him. He loves you too. Your stepsister, well, you'll have to figure that one out." His voice softened as he leaned toward me. "Regardless of what they say, I believe writing this story will help you, and it might help others. You're not going to write a tell-all book. If some family members don't agree to the book, write them out!" Relishing his mischievous grin, I couldn't help but feel blessed as his words of assurance continued. As he leaned toward me, he continued. "Look, I know you're afraid of hurting your family, but—you'll see—this book will help a lot of people. You and I both know you would be writing your story for the right reasons. Go for it! Don't be afraid. Just write. Edit later."

I turned my head and looked to the delicate rose bushes outside our bedroom window. Once I began to understand and agree with his logic, I started thinking about my faith and God's enormous part in the journey. I wouldn't be able to write without detailing how God helped my family and me through the abuse, anger, and forgiveness, or explaining how He had become an integral part of our lives. These days, writing about God can be like walking a tightrope between religion and faith, but the fact remains that my faith simply was and is a part of my life that can't go unrecognized.

At nearly forty, Madison's face had begun to show signs of wisdom—soft wrinkles around his eyes, his hair nearly completely gray and white, yet still as boyish as when I first met him over twenty years ago. He nodded just a bit and lifted his eyebrow ever so slightly. "What are you thinking about now?"

Knowing Madison's conservative approach to religion, I took a breath. "I know without a shadow of a doubt that Jesus saved me. I also know that the devil got a hold of me at several points in my life and almost ruined our family and me, and all who I love was nearly destroyed in the process. I can't write my story and not explain that, but I have no idea how to encompass it all. I'm afraid I won't be able to do Him justice."

"You're right. Writing about God may kill it for some readers, but not writing about your experiences, *all* of your experiences, would be a fraud. You have an authentic and gripping story. Talk about the negative stuff and how bad it got. Write it all. Describe how your healing process went and how things have changed. Be real, and then let God handle the rest."

My eyes widened with shock. Madison had never commented about God like that. *What a man I have. He surprises me all the time and always knows just what to say!* Nearly laughing amid the dissipated tears, I stood to hug him. "Madison, how am I going to talk about you and not make you look like a saint?"

"I don't know, but have fun trying!" He grabbed me around the waist, pulled me into his lap, and whispered, "I love you."

"I love you too." I kissed him and then nestled back in my chair.

"So, doctor and soon-to-be author, how are you going to start the story?"

"I guess from the beginning. I'll start with Ernie. If I'm going to tell my story, it should start with his departure." Quietly, I sat back and began to recall the stories I had heard several times over the years.

Chapter 2

OUR FAMILY BEGINS

Trembling, I sat between my two siblings—Steven, my older brother, and Mary, my younger sister—in the judge's chambers, every nerve on edge. Steven, with his straight, dark-brown hair and tan skin, easily cultivated over days of playing outside because we were half Hispanic, was to my right. Mary, her hair the same dark brown but filled with ringlet curls pulled into two adorable side pigtails, was to my left. My hair was a lighter shade of brown, and my curls were tighter than Mary's. The unruly curls had been wrangled into a ponytail for the occasion.

As we sat together in our Sunday best, I didn't know what to do with my hands, so I quietly twisted them together in my lap. The little girl inside of me wept, though my cheeks stayed dry. I felt like my father had abandoned me, again and forever. At not quite eight years old, I simply couldn't process the notion that my biological father would just give his kids away. My heart ached beyond words. The man I would later come to love as a father, Robert, or Bob, would formally adopt the three of us that day, but I still longed for my real daddy, and would for years.

LOSING MY FAMILY

The pain and confusion in my life began even before I was born. It's somewhat comical how that happens. A baby is delivered into the world to two people trying to navigate the muddy waters of their own lives. My parents, Ernie and Louise, were doing just that when I was conceived. They attempted to run from and deal with their painful childhood memories, all the while contemplating their futures with a son and a new daughter. When my mother was merely seventeen and my father twenty-one, they had my brother out of wedlock. Four months after his birth, they married. Roughly five months later, Mom was pregnant again—with me.

All children want to be loved and treasured. Sadly, sometimes one or both parents are simply incapable or unwilling to sacrifice their own lives for the sake of their children's well-being. Whatever the reason, repercussions of parental shortcomings can pierce the very heart of a child, causing damage long before the child is old enough to realize it.

Throughout the years, my parents' story repeated itself. He left. She begged him to come back. He came back. She kicked him out. He went, though he wanted to stay. He was right. She was wrong. She was right. He was wrong. Though my parents might have tried to make their marriage work, they continually failed. From what I've been told, this cyclical insanity occurred a few times before my mother discovered she was pregnant for the third time. As the story goes, she asked God to give her a sign about whether she should continue try to make her marriage work. Her decision? If she had a boy, she would stay; if she had a girl, she would leave. Whenever I heard this story growing up, I felt less valuable, less important. Internally, I would say to myself, *I'm a girl too. I guess I'm not worth fighting for either.*

After Mom gave birth to my younger sister, she followed her prayer-agreement with God. My dad moved out—this time forever. All of us fumbled our way through life amid the torrential destruction of our family. When parents separate before children are old enough to remember, the kids must rely on stories to piece together the family history. In many situations, perspectives and feelings distort those memories, especially with the passage of time. As a little girl, I remembered only two things—my dad was gone and I wanted him back. Mom said I asked about him on a regular basis and cried when he didn't pick us up for scheduled visits. Steven, Mary, and I waited, all dressed up, for our father to arrive. Each time left me feeling sad and confused at the least and sometimes utterly devastated. He never showed up, not once.

As I grew up, I developed a fantasy about Ernie. *Maybe he will pick me up at school this afternoon. Or maybe he'll drive by the house, see me playing, and decide to stop and play with me.* Despite repeated disappointment, I did my best to be good. I prayed and begged God on a regular basis, especially around holidays and my birthday, for Ernie to come and see me. *Maybe he'll come for Christmas this year. Please let me see him. Please let him surprise me on my birthday!*

In the end, there was nothing. No cards. No calls. No visits. His absence led me to assume that when a couple divorces, they also divorce their kids. I wasn't old enough to understand what was going on, but the message came through loud and clear: my dad doesn't want me. The emotional upheaval left me feeling lost and lonely—feelings that began to fester into insecurity and anxiety. I blamed my mom. I blamed my dad. I blamed God. Most of all, I blamed myself. Negative self-talk flooded my mind often. *If I were a good girl, my dad would come see me. I must not be good. My real dad doesn't want to see my pretty clothes. He doesn't want to hug me or see my curly hair and big brown eyes. I'm not worth his time.*

In 1975, my parents separated and divorced. Later that same year, my mom met and began dating Robert (Bob). Mom fell in love, and we did too. We loved what Bob added to our fractured family—structure, security, fun, laughter, and love. Over time, Bob became the dad I'd always wanted. My brother followed him everywhere. Mary and I loved to play tickle with him. He was a good dad, and we all grew to love him rather quickly. On October 22, 1977, Mom and Bob married. I was five and a half years old.

With his Elvis-like sideburns, Bob looked like the rebel James Dean. Everything about him personified masculinity—his dirty, dust-covered blue jeans; stained, tight-fitting white T-shirts; and big hands, rough and nicked from his long, blue-collar workdays. When he dressed up, he wore pressed pants, Western button-down shirts or seventies velour sweaters, and always a splash of Brute cologne.

I remember us kids laughing when we saw him in the morning before he dressed. Though his face and arms were deeply tanned, his sleeping shorts revealed blinding white body and legs. We loved to watch him fix his hair. After he slathered on Dippity-do and meticulously ensured every strand was in place, he gently placed a hairnet atop the goo and blew it to a crisp dry. I was always amazed that by day's end it looked the same as it did when he left that morning.

Bob lived with us before he and Mom married, so things didn't change much after their wedding. He established rigid household procedures, and we understood the unyielding nature of his rules. Though he wasn't afraid to use his belt if needed, he genuinely liked us and regularly spent time with us. Oftentimes, he would cook or help cook for the family before settling in to watch a John Wayne or Elvis movie. Though he worked long, hard hours, he always engaged with us when he arrived home. With his bloodshot eyes, crooked smile, and lit cigarette, he frequently told me how beautiful, smart, and lovable I was. His hugs were never superficial; rather, he gave big bear hugs that made me feel very loved and secure. It didn't take long before we took to calling him Dad.

The biggest adjustment from the marriage was learning to live with our new stepsister. Two and a half years my senior, she played nurturer to Mary and me. She was the oldest sibling in the house, which carried with it a level of authority over the rest of us. But what bothered me the most was she spent time with her biological mother every other weekend. I quickly developed feelings of jealousy and envy toward her. After getting all dressed up, she would take off on an adventure with her mom. Plus, she always returned with delightful treasures—new dolls, toys, and clothes. But when the visit was over, she always came back to us.

I became obsessed over the contrast between our absentee parents. *Why don't I get to go on such adventures with my father?* But deep down, a voice reminded why. *I'm not good. I'm not pretty. I'm not loved.* I felt it only fair that I should have both my dads too. It was painfully obvious that my biological father didn't want me, but I believed with all my heart that, in time, he would come to love me. I just had to remain patient, ready, and as pretty and good as possible. *I'll get good grades and be a good girl. You'll come for me once I'm truly good. I promise I'll try harder so you'll want me.* Still, nothing changed. Ernie never visited.

Over the next two years, I continually longed for my absentee father, yet I felt grateful for the blessing of a loving step-dad. Still, Bob could sound and look mean if he got mad or frustrated, and we saw that side of him from time to time. But he was also a joker, and he loved to sing. He worked extra-long hours to provide life's little surprise luxuries: new bikes or a one-thousand-piece Barbie dollhouse that took him hours to put together. Always full of energy, our new dad was always doing something with or for us. I never doubted that he loved us, and the feeling was mutual.

Over time, Mom and Dad started discussing with us four kids the idea of becoming a "real" family. Initially, I didn't understand what that meant. Once I grasped what they were saying, I panicked. *What do you mean adopt me? I already have a daddy. I love Bob, but I still want my real dad too. He won't give me up, will he?* But as time passed, the hope that Ernie would return slipped further and further from my grasp. I grew resigned to being adopted, and a part of me looked forward to it, just not the little girl inside.

The day we talked about finally arrived—the six of us would formally become a "real" family. No matter what my mom and my soon-to-be new dad had said in an effort to soothe our fears and assure us, I was still riddled with conflicting emotions—excited, happy, and apprehensive, yet blanketed with a sense of terrible loss. I wondered if Ernie would show up at the courthouse, to the point that my mind raced with questions and pleas. *Would he see us and refuse to sign the papers? Would he cry and beg us not to leave him? Oh please, be there and fight for me.* Upon our arrival, I frantically searched for him in the parking lot and in every passing corridor. No sign of him. My heart broke yet again, as I my mind dealt with that final, ultimate rejection. *Can you really just give me away? Why? What did I do wrong? Why am I not lovable?*

We entered the judge's chamber, and I turned to take one last look back to see if Ernie was behind us. Nothing. As the big wooden door pivoted on its hinges, the only thing I heard was *click*. I spun back around and stared at my feet, clad in my best, Sunday shoes, as the judge led us to our seats. Dark, rich wood paneling added a masculine feeling to the judge's chamber. An assortment of large matching books filled his floor-to-ceiling shelves—just like you see in the movies. Three leather club chairs were purposefully positioned in front of his meticulously arranged large wooden desk. The judge told us we were there to sign the papers and make the adoption official. I choked in a breath of stagnant, musty air.

The judge asked each of us, "Would you like Robert to be your father?"

One by one, we replied, "Yes."

"Do you understand that each of you will now have a new last name?"

"Yes."

"I want to change my whole name," Steven blurted out. "I don't want to be Steven Jr. anymore. I want to be Robert Jr."

My proud parents looked on, not surprised by my brother's announcement. Following a slight hesitation, the judge offered a cordial smile and said, "All right then." He looked at Mary and me and asked, "Do either of you want to change any other part of your name?"

Having mulled the question over since the home visit, my mind immediately raced with thoughts of Natalie or Samantha—anything other than Lynnette! But the words simply would not escape the prison of my lips. I was too shy, too sad, and too worried. Still holding out hope, I thought, *What if Ernie tries to find me? I need to have the same name so he can find me. I know you're going to come looking for me someday. I just know it!*

I quietly shook my head and whispered to the judge, "No, sir." In similar fashion, Mary said no as well. Following three short, one-syllable answers, the judge nodded and scribed his official signature on several papers. When that gavel came crashing down, one might think it was a day of celebration—an opportunity to move forward from the abandonment, but my little girl heart simply sank. I couldn't stop repeating well-worn tapes in my head. *Why didn't Ernie fight for me? I guess I'm not worth fighting for. Has my real daddy already forgotten me? I'll never be good enough.*

To celebrate, Mom and my now-official dad took us four kids out to dinner. My brother, now named Robert, delighted in his new name and status. Mary never had memories of Ernie, so she seemed oblivious to our loss. As for me, I entertained a jumble of feelings from happiness to sorrow, but mostly I felt conflicted. I was happy. Bob was a great dad. Mom was happy. I had a new stepsister. Robert and Mary were elated. Yet I struggled with what seemed to be my unique reaction to the events of the day. *Why am I the only one who's not feeling overjoyed? Aren't Mary and Steven—oops, I mean Robert—thinking about our real father?* I had a big empty hole in my heart that I thought would never be filled.

Chapter 3

WRITING IS HARD

I began the writing process in early April after Madison and I talked; now it was almost May. I felt certain that after more than eighteen years as a college student and teaching college for over a decade—seven of those years in the English department—I could whip out a book with my eyes closed. After all, I'd know where every comma belonged. I couldn't have been more wrong. Academic writing—researching journals and books, analyzing information and creating a twenty-page paper with all the proper APA formatting—may run through my veins, but inspirational or storytelling writing is another beast entirely.

I took my complaints to Madison. "I've realized that what little I had written reads like an instruction manual. Dry, boring stuff no one will want to read."

"Why don't you try using dictation software? Just tell the story. Stop worrying about spelling, grammar, and structure. You can edit later."

While his suggestion succeeded in my getting the words on the paper, what I'd written still lacked inspiration. I prayed, "God, how am I going to write this? I have the story, but I don't have the skills. Please show me what to do."

Just then my friend Michelle came to mind. Michelle and I had become very close over the last year. When I think back on how we met, I can't help but smile. I have no doubt she was God sent.

After moving into our Texas home, Madison and I decided that window coverings were first on our purchasing agenda. Madison contacted a company he found online and set an appointment for the following day. The window company representative arrived, and I immediately knew she was not the person I wanted to do business with. Aside from the industrial/track-home product line, she had an uninviting personality. I politely explained that she just didn't have what I was looking for. I wanted blood-red fabric Roman shades, just like I had back at home.

I miss Colorado. I miss all my friends. I miss knowing where the dang bank is! I'm tired of nearly crashing as I try to navigate the unknown roads. Yes, I know it's important for Madison, but I'm so alone. Why, God? Why did you take away all of my support? Why did you leave me so utterly alone with Madison working long hours and the girls at school all day? Ugh!

"What? I'm sorry. What did you say?" I asked the sales rep after returning from my internal pity party.

"Well, I do know someone else who carries custom window coverings," she replied.

"You do?"

"Yes ... um, but it's kind of a strange situation."

"Why is that?"

"Well, it's my husband's ex-wife." Any shred of doubt I had prior to that day that I was in the backwoods south was immediately obliterated by her proclamation. "Yeah, I know. I told you it was strange. But if you want, I can give her a call."

Stunned, I said, "Yeah, sure." With that, she collected all her window covering books and left. Madison and I began to laugh. We doubted she would call anyone, and every window was completely naked, exposing us to the world. So it was off to Home Depot for some temporary paper shades.

As I was calling out the navigation directions for Home Depot to Madison, a call came in.

"Madison, it's an unknown number. Should I answer it?"

"Yes," he replied dryly.

Giggling, I hit the accept button and swiftly handed the phone to him. Madison was introduced to the original sales lady's husband's ex-wife. She explained she had received a call and was wondering if we were still in need of window coverings. By the end of the conversation, we had an appointment. "Well, let's see what shows up this time," Madison said with a grin.

On Saturday morning, the woman, Michelle, arrived as promised, and from the moment I laid eyes on her, I felt as if I had known her for years. Her short, spikey hair, eclectic manner of dress, and unique personality immediately transported me to a place of comfort and familiarity. Twenty minutes into our consultation, Madison and I were standing upstairs with her when I looked at Madison and said, "Who does she remind you of?"

"Nonnie," he responded.

"Yes!" The mental image of Nonnie flooded in.

With a look of surprised confusion, Michelle asked, "Who is Nonnie?"

"She's my godmother," I responded. "Her real name is Linda, but we call her Nonnie."

Looking at Michelle was like seeing Nonnie twenty years earlier. I was immediately taken in by her resemblance, and aside from carrying the products we were looking for, there was no doubt Michelle was the person I wanted to do business with. The following week, I asked her if she would like to have lunch. I had already explained that I was new in town. Thankfully, she accepted. With frequent lunches and even some couple's nights out, it didn't take long for our relationship to go beyond business.

It made sense to me to work with Michelle again. So after talking with Madison and then Michelle, she agreed to help me write my story. Working together sounded fun, but what followed was anything but exciting. I had great difficulty expressing the details that would make the story readable. Michelle suggested an interview-like process, so we tried it. In the beginning, recalling some of my childhood was fun.

Chapter 4

ENJOYING OUR FAMILY

After the adoption, our family engaged in all the wonderful things that normal families enjoy. We lived in the main house on a piece of property my maternal grandmother owned. Grandma Mary's property, on Francis Avenue in Chino, California, also had a smaller guesthouse and six apartments behind the main house. Grandma rented five of the side-by-side apartments to various tenants, and she and Grandpa lived in the first apartment closest to us. An extremely long driveway for the apartment tenants' use went by the left side of the main house. This driveway, lined by a chain link fence with alternating green and white slats, delineated the property line. At the back of the property lay an enormous field, which hosted an abandoned bus and a small corral where we kept our horse. The main house driveway stood to the right side of the property nestled against a long rectangular lawn where we had a swing set and plenty of room to run and play.

Parties, family gatherings, and weekend activities were regular occurrences. Given the property size, we became the default hub for family gatherings. Almost every birthday and holiday we were surrounded by extended family, which brought with the occasions a sense of belonging. All the kids had bikes, roller skates, or skateboards that we rode up and down the long driveway. Childhood friends visited regularly, and we played outside until the sun went down. Dad even installed an aboveground pool and tetherball in the yard. When we had exhausted every avenue of playtime, we could grab a garden hose, make mud pies, and get dirty to fill the gap.

Though my parents liked to entertain, many times we just had fun as a family. One of our favorite activities was to crank up the radio and dance around in the living room as our parents bombarded us with their laughter and delight. In addition to dancing, we played hide-and-seek, ate ice cream sundaes for dinner, attacked one another with ice cubes, rode our horses, and played with the dogs.

Just before the start of my third-grade year, Mom and Dad bought a house on Norton Avenue in Chino. Aside from geography, nothing really changed. We still hosted barbecues and holiday gatherings, just as we had when living on Grandma's property. I recall with fond memories my ninth birthday party, an all-out Strawberry Shortcake-themed event. We were a normal family; we had ups and downs, laughter and fights. Because our family was good, I was happy. I finally had a dad who loved and wanted me.

Mary started kindergarten that year at Newman Elementary. Robert was in fourth grade and my stepsister in fifth grade. We had fun being together in the same school. The older two and Mary were dismissed later than I was, so every afternoon I walked home alone. I cherished those precious moments because I had Mom all to myself, even if for just a bit.

I worked especially hard in Mrs. Harrison's third-grade class. With unyielding determination, my grades went from less-than-satisfactory to outstanding by the end of the school year. To celebrate my accomplishments, Mom and I spent an afternoon together, just the two of us. She took me to the mall where we had pictures made in a photo booth and ate lunch at Farrell's, a restaurant with an old-time ice-cream-shop feel. We even told the waiter it was my birthday so he would give us free ice cream! This ranks as one of the fondest memories I have with Mom. I felt so special and worthy of her time and attention.

With three siblings, this focused level of parental interaction on a regular basis wasn't an option. The reality of day-to-day life was much different. Like any other woman, my mom had her moods. Some days, caring for four children on a daily basis left her tired, frustrated, and overwhelmed. Oftentimes, cousins were dropped off at the house, which merely added to her responsibilities. More often than not, when she wasn't cooking or doing laundry or whatever else needed done, she stayed in her bedroom. She tried to watch television and smoke cigarettes in peace and quiet. She sent us all out to play in an effort to minimize her interaction with the abundance of children. I assume she did this to maintain her sanity. One by one, we kids meandered into her room with complaints, requests, or injuries, which meant we constantly interrupted her much-needed downtime. She had a lot heaped on her—as disciplinarian, housekeeper, cook, homework teacher, chauffer, and more. My parents limited our daily chores when we were young, but as we got older, the chores increased, which at times created more work for Mom. She was generally quieter than Dad, but her anger and frustration sometimes spewed forth in the form of yelling and cursing. We knew when we pushed her buttons, but we also knew that a nicely colored picture, well-prepared mud pie, or a simple "I love you" warmed her heart. In spite of all she had to do, she was a loving mom.

When we were quite young, Dad worked out of town Monday through Friday. But after we moved to the house on Norton, he and Mom decided that while he would be losing money, it was important that he be home more. So he secured a local job that required no travel. He still worked away from the house most of the day, but when he arrived home, he was fun and loving. Having Dad home every night revealed what we thought was only a weekend occurrence: he drank. A lot. Every night. Still, he never failed to make it to work or to nurture us kids. Mom drank, too, but not as much as Dad. When they drank, it seemed like he got louder and Mom quieter. Yet they tended to us all, regularly bandaged our scraped knees, or pulled out our loose teeth. Dad liked animals and provided opportunities for us to experience and enjoy animals as well. We had horses, cows, goats, rams, turkeys, bunnies, and dogs—it was like a mini zoo! Mom sewed us some summer outfits, helped us with school party treats, planned and managed every play date, and even led my Girl Scout troop.

Chapter 5

INTERVIEWING CHANGES

*A*s Michelle and I continued to lay the groundwork for the book, the interviewing process progressed fairly well—that is, until we got to the hard stuff.

"Okay, we've covered the early years, so tell me about your dad when things began to get bad." Regardless of how gently Michelle asked, it still felt like prodding. My insides churned at the thought of sharing the details. My mind screamed, *I'm not ready for this! I don't want to talk about it. It hurts.* So I tried to avoid answering. "I don't remember," I said. "He drank all the time."

"Where was your mom?"

"Around, I guess."

"Just relax. Start with what you do remember."

"It's just that I'm scared, worried, and a bit hesitant to write all this down."

"That's totally understandable. Let me ask you first—why are you scared?"

"I've told people about the abuse but never in such detail. Reliving it is harder than I thought. The other part is the effectthat writing is having on my family now. I'm going through all this, which means they have to go through it with me."

"Anyone in particular?"

"Right now, Madison and the girls. They've already dealt with my problems far more than they should have, and now I'm causing pain and disruption again."

"I'm not saying it's a cop-out, but you know you have their support in this. So who else are you afraid of?"

"Pretty much everyone. I have no idea what other members of my family have said or not said and to whom. This will be out there for everyone to read and judge, and I don't want to hurt my family."

Michelle's smile reassured me. Then she stood and crossed the room to hug me.

She whispered in my ear as she did so. "You know the ending of the story. It will all be worth it. Trust Madison and me; we have your back on this. And trust yourself. You're stronger than you think. More importantly, trust God. He knows what He's doing."

I couldn't help but smile, inside and out. I took a deep breath and recalled Madison's loving words of encouragement. I allowed them to wash over my heart once more. "You can do this. Just take it one memory at a time. Writing this story will help others and you."

Although I still felt like I was cocooned in fear as I tried to recall the abuse, I also felt lifted. I summoned the courage that only God can give to step into the forbidden darkness of my childhood and remember, explain, and detail the lifelong tentacles of childhood emotional and sexual abuse that had once nearly strangled the life and love out of me.

Chapter 6

DRINKING AND PARENTING

As I mentioned, when Dad changed jobs, he stopped traveling out of town. That was when we noticed that he drank. Every night. By today's standards, Dad was a functioning alcoholic. As time passed, Mom began to drink right along with him. Her drunkenness marked the start of an erratic home life. The amount of booze dictated the household atmosphere, which made discipline and daily life unpredictable. While the rules remained the same, you never knew if you'd be struck for the first offense or after the tenth. It all depended on how much they'd had to drink and what mood they were in. If called by name, we were to immediately acknowledge by responding, "Coming!" and rush into the room they were in and await further instruction. Failure to do so would result in discipline. If we did something wrong and lied about it, punishment would be significantly worse than if we confessed from the start.

Though my parents did what they deemed fair, we grew

extremely fearful of them. As a child, I felt their heavy hand when it came to discipline, especially when they drank. My siblings and I have countless memories of being slapped across the face, having our heads knocked together, or being hit with a belt across our bare butts. A few times I remember my parents using a tree branch or flip-flops to hit us—really, they used whatever was handy when they were drunk. In addition to the physical discipline—child abuse by today's standards—my parents had sharp tongues. They regularly cursed at us and called us derogatory, hurtful names. "Thunder thighs" and "lazy" whipped out of their mouths on serpent-like tongues.

I have a clear memory of a time when Dad spoke to me in Spanish, and I didn't know Spanish. He pointed toward his bedroom and instructed me to go retrieve something for him. Confused and afraid, I went into my parent's bedroom and just stood in the room crying. I knew he wanted something, but I didn't understand what he'd said, and I was too afraid to go back empty-handed for fear of being hit. Within moments, Mom entered the room.

"Why are you crying?"

Tears rolled down my cheeks. I wiped them away. "I don't know what he wants."

She chuckled underneath her breath. "He wants his cigarettes."

She handed me a pack of cigarettes, which I promptly took to him. Crisis averted.

Our sibling dynamics weren't too different from other families; however, I grew to feel left out and unwanted by everyone. Everyone else had something special about him or her. Stepsister was the oldest and the only child with two families. We never viewed her as anything other than our sister, but on occasion I felt like my parents considered her the special one. Robert was the only boy, so he enjoyed the most hands-on activities with Dad and was treated differently from the rest of us. Mary was the baby of the family—adorable and loved by all.

I had no special identifier. I fell through the cracks. I wasn't the oldest or the stepchild or the only boy or the youngest. I was simply in the middle. I wasn't athletic, but I did shine at school. While my grades didn't always reflect my best, I was a hardworking and determined student, so school become the one area of my life that garnered the most attention. In later years, it would inevitably serve as my safe haven. But no matter how dysfunctional our lives were, I could never have imagined the impending chain of events that would forever alter the trajectory of my life.

Regardless of anyone's special status—or lack thereof—we all got punished. Sometimes my brother's punishment was considerably harsher. The frustration, fatigue, and demands of parenting worsened significantly when Mom and Dad drank. The abusive behavior began to affect our sibling relationships. As we got older, my siblings and I continued the cycle of verbal and physical abuse amongst ourselves. We did to one another what had been demonstrated to us by our parents because we believed it to be acceptable behavior.

I remember times when my sisters and I would fight. Foul language, hair pulling, and hitting were acceptable. If Robert got into a fight with us girls and hit us in his anger, Dad would hit him so hard we girls would cry. At times, we threw one another under the drunken bus that was Dad or Mom's anger in desperate yet failed attempts to save ourselves. Still, there were times when we tried to save one another.

I never knew what was going to happen. Would I be saved, sold out, or just passed over? The unpredictable environment deepened my anxiety and insecurity. I felt alone. Soon the need to save ourselves created more rifts between us children than it brought us together. What God designed as an innocent and carefree time in a person's life simply wasn't in the cards for my siblings and me.

FROM DYSFUNCTION TO ABUSE

I began the fourth grade in September 1981. School did not go as well as the previous year. My nine-year-old body began to show the beginnings of puberty, and I had a hard-nosed teacher. Her cold demeanor only seemed to intensify the aloneness and anxiety from my home life. This teacher offered no hugs or words of encouragement like Ms. Harrison had. No quality one-on-one time during recess to practice my cursive writing. Instead, she imposed rigid rules and angry looks as she yelled at the students to pay attention.

In April 1982, my mother traveled to New Mexico to assist Grandma Mary and care for her ailing father. While Grandpa wasn't Mom's real father, he loved us all. Dad stayed home and looked after us. One evening, we kids watched a TV show in the living room alone while Dad isolated himself in the bedroom. I don't specifically remember what show we were watching, but it somehow prompted the question, "Where do babies come from?" Giggling over the topic, we decided to seek out an authority to quench our thirst for knowledge. After careful consideration and discussion, we reached a consensus that I should be the one to ask Dad. Filled with fear and intimidation, I set out on my assigned mission in search of the answer.

When I opened my parents' bedroom door, I saw him sprawled out on his bed in typical fashion, drunk. I approached and asked the required question. "Dad, where do babies come from?" I don't recall exactly what happened, but I do know that rather than answer my question, he opted to show me. I can't remember extensive details from the violation other than the vivid memory of sitting on top of him. To what extent he "showed" me is unclear, but given the fact I had no frame of reference as to right and wrong, I didn't understand that his actions constituted sexual abuse. Still, I had an undeniable feeling that what took place was incredibly wrong, and shame kept me from telling a soul what had happened. But from that day on, I didn't want to be alone with him, and it would be years before I truly understood why.

Days passed before Mom returned home from New Mexico. Dad never uttered a word to me about what he had done; rather, a continued discomfort rose between us. For a time, it seemed that what had happened that night was an isolated incident. I thought about letting out my proverbial breath a little. But as the weeks passed, my theory would be disproved as the abuse eventually escalated.

One night, several days after Mom's return, I lay nestled sound asleep in the lower bunk. I awoke to the sound of Dad entering the room. Because I knew my older sister slept in the bunk above me, I didn't feel any immediate cause for alarm. His breath reeked of alcohol and cigarettes, and he wasted no time making his intentions clear. He began touching me, putting his hand in my private area, and forcing me to touch him in return. Overcome with anxiety at the thought of my stepsister, his *real* daughter, waking suddenly, I merely lay there and did as he instructed. Harsh consequences for disobeying him loomed in the back of my mind and kept me grounded in silence.

Before my fourth-grade school year ended, we arrived home from school one afternoon to find Mom sitting on the sofa. Her puffy eyes and red nose told us she'd been crying.

We kids surrounded her. "What's wrong, Mom?"

She wiped away fresh tears. "Your grandpa died today."

Our youthfulness lent little understanding or experience in comforting her overwhelmed and emotionally raw state.

She reached for her wallet and pulled out four one-dollar bills. "Here, go to the store, and get yourself some candy." With that, she closed herself off.

We left as directed, but we questioned why she didn't want us around. We felt the sting of pain and loss too. When we returned home, Dad was already there. It was obvious that he had been crying too. With his usual whiskey and coke sitting on the counter, he began to take out leftovers from the fridge. Mom was cocooned in her room with the door shut. None of us were hungry, but we all began to eat what Dad served. He moved slowly toward his bedroom and left us alone for the rest of the evening.

The following months seemed to drag on as summer came and went without much joy. Mom kept to herself, as much as a mother of four could without the aid of a school schedule. Drinking filled most evenings, as both parent mourned. Then the nightly visits from Dad began again.

Every passing night sleep eluded me for fear he might return. While his visits were irregular, his unmistakable agenda was not. Top bunk, bottom bunk, it made no difference to him. As the months passed, the uncomfortable acts morphed into a routine of sorts, though I never knew for certain when he'd come. When he did sneak in, I knew what he expected. Sometimes older sister would invite me to sleep with her in her bed. She positioned herself on the outside rail, which placed me up against the wall. I felt very safe and protected on those nights because Dad never assaulted me when his *real* daughter stood guard. She never spoke to me of anything out of the ordinary, certainly not sexual abuse, and I never mentioned anything about it to her. One might assume she suspected what was going on because her actions seemed more guardianship than that of a typical eleven-year-old sister. Unfortunately, sometimes Mom or Dad came into the bedroom before we fell asleep, and if they saw us in bed together, they'd say, "No, we're not doing that," before making us separate. Each time, my mind begged my mouth to cry out, "I need her! I want to share a bed and have my back to the wall. It's the only time I truly feel safe!"

Our collective living situation worsened. In December, halfway through my fifth-grade year, Dad was forced to close the business he owned. The individual doing the books had embezzled money—a fact Dad didn't discover until it was too late. We had to sell our home on Norton and move into one of the modest apartments on Grandma Mary's property. Though the location provided familiar territory, memories of Dad's sexual advances loomed ever-present. The vast fields provided hours of entertainment, a good thing to occupy us kids while Mom and Dad dealt with the financial crises. They had little time to focus on any of us, but I didn't mind. In truth, I preferred to be left alone.

The two-bedroom apartment was cramped and unwelcoming. With only two windows, it always seemed dark and gloomy, similar to our lives at the time. I still reeled with mixed emotions about the sexual abuse at the hands of my father. Thankfully, the cramped quarters afforded a somewhat safe haven. The tiny apartment allowed for no privacy whatsoever, which prevented Dad from having access to me.

We lived in the apartment for over six months as my parents saved the necessary funds to move to New Mexico. My grandma and Mom's sister's family lived there and convinced my parents it would be a great place for us to be. I didn't want to leave all my friends behind, but the decision was not mine to make. The summer before my sixth-grade year, we loaded up the RV and set out on a course toward New Mexico. Our parents told us little about the move—only that we would be living with my aunt and her family for the time being. Nothing could have ever prepared me for what was to come. It would inevitably prove to be the worst time in my life.

Chapter 7

OVERWHELMED WITH MEMORIES

I'd canceled our interviewing sessions twice. I had legitimate reasons, yet I knew I was avoiding working with Michelle. One day, my cell phone rang. Seeing her name on the caller ID, I knew I would finally have to face her.

"Hi." My voice sounded weak in my ears.

In her soft voice with just a hint of a Southern twang, she said, "I haven't talked with you in a while. Is everything okay?"

"I just can't do this right now," I rasped, hoping it would be loud enough for her to hear.

"Talk to me. What is it?"

"It's—I just can't talk about everything in such detail. You don't understand. The one or two hours of interviewing with you leaves me emotionally drained for a week. I'm not sleeping well. I'm having nightmares. I just don't think I can go on."

"You can do this. I'm here for you, and so is Madison."

"Can't we just go on to a different part of my life?" I choked back tears, unable to utter another word.

"Look, where are you? Are you at home? Lynnette, are you still there?"

Tears streamed down my face. I licked my lips and tasted the saltiness. "I'm here. I'm in the dark … in the closet." Crouched in the fetal position, I began to gently rock back and forth.

"You need to call Diane." Michelle's stern voice felt comforting, not judgmental.

Diane was the therapist I started going to just months after we moved to Texas. Once Michelle and I began our friendship, we talked almost daily, and while my one new friend helped fill the endless, empty hours of the day, it still wasn't enough to thwart the exhausting, anxiety-filled depression from descending upon me again. I knew at some point I had to address it. We had moved into our home in August 2012, and by November, my emotional decline had become overwhelming, so I decided to call Nonnie. As with every instance in the past, her loving wisdom was not without direction.

"I just don't know what's wrong with me."

"Love, you're depressed. You have all this time to yourself, and it's getting to you."

"I knew this would to happen. I hate being alone." I gave a sideways glance and spied my reflection in the large mirror in our living room. Yep, just me. Still alone.

"I know you do. Maybe it's time for you to figure out why you hate being alone."

"Ugh. More therapy! I've had years of it. I don't want to go over everything again. Will I ever be done with it all?"

"No. There are things you will always have to struggle with, sometimes a little, and other times a lot. Your past is part of who you are. Think of it as a tune-up. Everyone needs a tune-up now and then."

More therapy? When will it ever end? If I don't even know where the Costco is, how am I going to find a therapist?

Nonnie made me promise I would fine a therapist, soon. With that, I buried my face in a sea of defeated tears. I knew only one person to ask—Michelle.

In an attempt to hide my embarrassment, I sent Michelle a

text asking if she had a therapist referral. Within seconds, she responded with the name and number of her therapist, Diane. I knew it was time to get back on the couch before things got out of control again. I immediately called Diane's office and scheduled an appointment.

I had been seeing Diane for over nine months, but once I began writing, the therapy sessions became weekly and tended to focus on the unresolved issues that writing my story brought to the surface. So Michelle was spot-on telling me I needed to call Diane. Reliving the past had literally brought me to the fetal position in a dark closet—meaning it was something I obviously needed to address. After I hung up with Michelle, I called Diane for a midweek appointment.

During our session, I told Diane that I loved the way she intertwines scripture into our sessions. Without hesitating, the right words just flow out of her mouth, as if God is speaking directly to me. We've also been using a therapy called Eye Movement Desensitization and Reprocessing (EMDR). Without an overly detailed explanation, it basically means I don't have to tell her every single detail of my past. We just discuss the issues I'm having at the moment and delve into previous experiences only when necessary. Talking to Michelle about that horrible time had proven to be like reliving everything in Technicolor; I was thankful that EMDR didn't require me to have to retell everything, yet again.

Chapter 8

THE RV

I was six years old when my parents acquired the 1970 Allegro RV. They initially purchased it for Dad to live in when he worked offsite during the week as opposed to the flea-bitten, cheap hotels the company provided to out-of-town employees. There was nothing special about the RV except that everything was meticulously miniaturized. I thought it looked like a dollhouse on wheels. Its cream-colored exterior had a large brown stripe down the side, and the interior, along with everything else in my life, was beige. The galley hosted a small kitchenette with mini-fridge, two storage areas, a micro-bathroom, and a dining table that transitioned into a bed barely large enough for two kids.

My parents slept in the back of the RV—an area so small there was just enough room to close the door before you fell onto the full-sized mattress. The RV seemed to break down more often than it was usable, but no matter the issue, Dad always managed to get it running again. When not being used for his residence, we would load up the RV and drive to a nearby lake for a long weekend of camping. Those were good memories for me—splashing along the shallow water's edge and sitting under the stars by the evening campfire. While the RV hosted an array of positive memories in my early childhood, it would soon become my worst nightmare and the place I dreaded most of all.

When we arrived at my aunt's house in New Mexico, I saw a barren and uninviting place. Though there were other homes nearby, it was not a typical subdivision in the modern-day sense. The plain, single-story brown house was nestled in a mountainous development surrounded by numerous trees and expansive land. The small front porch was as dull as the house itself and bore no flowers or gardens to indicate anyone lived there or visitors were welcome. The front door opened into a rectangular living room that boasted a pony wall on the backside. That led into the galley-styled kitchen. An expansive laundry room lay just beyond the kitchen threshold. It had two backdoors—one to the left that led to the master bedroom and one to the right that led to our RV parked outside, mere steps away.

The interior of the house was no different than the exterior. Completely void of décor, the mishmash of utilitarian furniture screamed local garage sales. The couples had bedrooms of their own, the four girls were given the master bedroom, and both boys slept in the living room. As with every other place I'd lived, my surroundings contained nothing but shades of brown hues mixed with the typical 1970s rustic plaids.

To say we were in close quarters was a colossal understatement given that ten of us lived there. By the end of our first day, the adults settled into an evening of drinking and smoking. This quickly became a nightly ritual and typical way of life in New Mexico. Nothing made sense or invoked any level of excitement or even protection. I desperately wanted to be back at Grandma Mary's apartment in California where I felt safe and secure.

We kids spent our summer days outside exploring new

terrain, a safe haven compared to the tiny house inhabited by drunken adults. Being one of six children underfoot, I found it relatively easy to go unnoticed.

Within weeks, Mom secured a position with my aunt's employer working on the assembly line at a local factory. School finally began, which provided a welcome distraction from the otherwise dismal surroundings. Our daily routine cemented swiftly; women went to work, and children went to school. As for Dad and my uncle, neither one of them had jobs, which meant they looked for jobs occasionally but then were home most of the time.

Returning home from school filled me with anxiety because I never knew what to expect from my dad or uncle. If they'd been drinking, their demeanor was consistently unpredictable. After school one afternoon, Dad asked me to come with him. Filled with apprehension, I did as he asked and followed him out the back door toward the RV. Once inside, he wasted no time putting his drunken hands on me, and the rush of familiar emotions came flooding back. He forced me down on the dusty galley floor, partially disrobed me, and began touching me in ways I had not previously experienced. The smell of cigarettes permeated every cell of my nostrils, as the smoke-stained carpet scoured my frozen, half-naked body. With the exception of Dad's shallow breathing or occasional instruction, I could hear no identifiable sounds or noises of any kind. Inside, I longed to cry out, "Why are you doing this to me? This feels so wrong. What if someone comes in? Please, just hurry up, and be done already." Without uttering a word or so much as a groan, he continued his assault. Nothing was in my control, and I lacked the mature defenses to put an end to the unimaginable violation. He directed me to touch him and please him, and he seemed to expect me to enjoy myself as well, but that was far from any reality I could grasp. Instead, I closed my eyes and emotionally disconnected, the only way I could escape what was happening to me and still manage to survive. I lost a little more of my innocence—and my very soul—that day.

Because the abuse was erratic, I never knew when to expect it to try to avoid it. Anxiety filled my every waking moment. From the instant Dad touched me, I knew what was coming and where we were going. I don't remember what he said to get me into the RV, but regardless of his manipulation, there seemed to be no boundaries. Oftentimes, he coerced me to reciprocate the atrocities, which made me feel even dirtier than before. In the midst of the abuse one day, I worked up the nerve to ask, "Can I tell Mom what's happening here?"

Without hesitation, he said, "She already knows."

His words pierced me deeply. My own mother had chosen not to protect me. She didn't care that he did this to me. I wish I'd had the confidence to tell someone—anyone—but my childhood reality was "do as you're told and keep your mouth shut." This familiar understanding of do what you're told to do and don't ask questions rendered any verbal warnings and intimidation unnecessary. I wasn't about to cross Dad's unyielding boundaries for fear of repercussions that were sure to follow. So I reasoned, *Besides, he loves me, and he's not mean to me. Plus Mom knows, and she's okay with it. If I make him mad, he'll leave like my other father did.* The magnitude of his actions was engrained, and I felt powerless to stop his advances. Still, a tiny voice inside me couldn't help but wonder, *With all the people bustling about in this tiny household, how can he get away with it? Where is everyone else while this is happening to me?*

As time passed, Dad's cycle of abuse became undeniably clear—the drunker he got, the more he came after me. It didn't take me long to realize that consuming excessive amounts of whiskey would cause him to pass out, so when told to refresh his drink, I would generally put 75 percent alcohol in the glass topped with a splash of Pepsi. Doing so generally guaranteed at least one night's reprieve from the seemingly endless, vicious cycle.

Dad's actions made me feel dirty and used, but part of me assumed it was happening to all the kids, not just to me. With four children in our immediate family, plus two cousins in the house, you were never made to feel special. So while the attention I got from Dad was negative, at least he noticed me—something I desperately wanted and needed. Too young to truly understand right from wrong, and believing that Mom already knew, I assumed his assaults were normal events that took place in everyone's home. Still, it wouldn't be long before someone discovered what was happening, an unexpected, truth-seeking advocate I never saw coming.

Late one afternoon in December of my sixth-grade year, a friend (who wishes not be named) talked to me about what she believed was happening. She wasted no time in asking if my dad was hurting me. Her probative question left me speechless with a glazed, emotionless expression. Given her authoritative position, I felt compelled to answer her question, but the words would not escape my lips.

She gently pursued her quest for the truth. "Is he touching you?"

Still—nothing. I couldn't bring myself to utter the words.

She pointed toward my private parts and asked again, "Is he touching you here or here?"

I felt sheepish and scared to reveal the truth, but the desire for someone to protect me eventually overpowered my anxiety. Slowly, I nodded. And with every nod, relief and hope swept over me, yet feelings of shame and guilt remained firmly rooted. *Someone knows. What now? Will it stop?* I had finally exposed the secret, and with that, the seed of truth had been planted in my brain that Dad's actions were indeed wrong. Following a tender embrace with my new confidante, I left the room believing the conversation was a secret, one that carried an expectation of her protection going forward.

Later that evening, the house was eerily quiet, more so than usual. I heard Mom call my name, so I scurried off to the living room as quickly as I could. She and Dad were perched next to each other on the couch. Immediately, my legs began to shake and my stomach churned as I stood across from them with a military-like posture. It felt as if my feet weren't touching the ground, an all-too-familiar stance customary to being chastised or punished for some sort of rule violation. Dad's eyes were locked on mine—blank, as if to look right through me yet intimidating at the same time.

"Is Daddy being a good daddy?" Mom pursed her lips and stared at me. I felt blindsided by her question, but this time Dad was present. Her eyes, riddled with pain, almost pleaded with me for the accusation to be false.

Sheepishly, I whispered, "Yes." I didn't have the guts to admit the violation with Dad sitting there. Silence filled the room. Fingers entangled, I began to feel cold and faint. I longed for someone to advocate on my behalf. *Why isn't my confidante standing here with me, telling them I'm lying? Dad, why don't you tell Mom the truth?* I wished I would faint and shock them into reality.

"Then why would someone say something was happening?"

"I don't know." *Mom, can't you see right through me and tell that I'm lying?*

"Is he hurting you?"

"No." *I don't want you to be mad at me, Mom.*

Aside from a few vague questions, Mom didn't dig for the truth. My eyes bore deeply into hers, my attempt to beg her to see right through me. *Please, Mom, can't you see I'm afraid?* A crucial confession opportunity had passed. Had Dad not been in the room, I think my answers would have revealed the truth, but his imposing presence and deafening silence throughout the inquisition left me feeling defeated.

"Go to your room." Mom didn't look at me as she lit yet another cigarette.

Without uttering a sound, I immediately retreated to

the confines of the girls' room, fell onto the bed, and wept, consumed with overwhelming shame, guilt, and fear.

My sisters and cousins returned from their temporary exile and came into the bedroom. The buckets of tears I cried had finally dried, but I hadn't moved an inch since falling on the bed.

They gently tiptoed into the room, stood near the side of the bed, and collectively asked, "What happened?"

"Nothing."

"What's wrong?" Mary stroked my hair.

"Please tell us." One of my cousins sat on the bed near my feet.

"Just leave me alone." I could say and do nothing at this point. I had denied the truth and would now live shackled by my very silence.

They didn't pursue any further conversation or attempt to inquire as to what happened. But underlying tensions became ever-present in our home after that evening. Nothing more was said or asked of me regarding Dad, but questions had been raised and allegations levied, thus the seed of doubt had been planted. Dad avoided me completely. No eye contact whatsoever. No conversations of any substance. *Now I get nothing. Either I do the sex stuff Dad wants and get some level of attention or he refuses to come near me.*

Parental moods in the house shifted to anger and bitterness. *This is my fault. I caused this. Does Mom believe me? Does she know the truth? I said what she wanted me to say, but she's still mad at me. Everyone is mad at me. Do the others know? How would they feel if I had told them the truth? It feels like the spotlight is on me all the time.* I merely kept my head down and hoped I would go unnoticed.

By the end of the month, Dad decided to return to Chino with Robert in tow. They loaded up the RV with their personal belongings and left for California. I managed to feel guilty about that too. *It's my fault that the family broke up. I know what's really happening.* Mom and Dad explained that things weren't working in New Mexico, so Dad and Robert would head home to start on some new opportunities there. I knew we would move back at the end of the school year as well, but for the first time in as long as I could remember, I felt safe and protected.

Chapter 9

FREE FROM IRRATIONAL GUILT

The Fourth of July was days away—Independence Day. How perfect is His timing, as my therapist and I continued to work through all the hidden compartments of my memory. I could already feel the sweet freedom coming as we finally broke through the irrational guilt I'd carried for decades for breaking up my family and hurting them.

Recently, Diane and I had been working on the guilt I felt for the financial burdens my parents had experienced ever since I told the truth. In my mind, I understood the abuse was not my fault and my parents' choices were not mine. In my heart, however, I always felt guilty for Dad losing his job, Mom having to support us all, and my siblings doing without. My dad did get a job after jail, but with so many people to support, our finances never seemed to recover. We were poor, and it was my fault. Even after we kids moved out, my parents continued to struggle. Having a record makes finding good-paying jobs hard, especially in the blue-collar industry my dad worked in.

During our last therapy session, I recalled a conversation I had had with my brother, Robert, a few years earlier. We lived in Colorado at the time, and he and his family were visiting for the holidays. My family and I lived in the south Denver area, and our parents were in north Pueblo. They were trying to keep the current stagnant housing market from wiping out their retirement plans by getting the equity from selling their home. They shared with us that they planned to purchase a fifth-wheel trailer and travel more, visiting their children and their families around the country. With Robert in South Carolina, my older sister in California, and Mary in Louisiana, my parents had lots of traveling options available.

It had been a wonderful visit. Christmas cookies were made, Hanukkah candles had been lit, and laughter filled the house. After the gifts had been unwrapped, the big dinner eaten, and everyone headed home or to bed, I had a moment to connect with my brother. We chatted about our families and lives, and then we talked about our parents and their big move.

"I'm excited for Mom and Dad, but I'm worried about how they can afford to move about."

Robert nodded.

"I've always had a sense of responsibility for them."

"Why? All of kids help Mom and Dad when and if they need it."

"I know. It just that things have never been the same since— you know. All of that chaos hurt their finances and Dad's job opportunities. I just can't help feel responsible."

Robert grabbed my shoulders firmly and brought me closer to him. "You should never ever feel responsible! It was their mistakes, their fault, *not yours*." His voice was firm like a dad's should be.

Tears flowed down my face. I felt grateful for his support. I knew he was right. From that day forward, whenever I talked to Madison about any financial help, we discussed whether I felt obligated to do it or felt like we gave out of love. With the passage of years, the obligation left, and only the sense of caring for my family remained. My parents always helped others, and now I could honor that by doing the same.

After the Fourth of July celebrations, Diane and I continued therapy the following week. We began to concentrate on self-image, an issue that has plagued me most of my life. We agreed that the root of my self-hatred began with the abuse, but we delved deeper to discuss the betrayal of my body as puberty magnified the abuse.

Chapter 10

FEELING UGLY

The remainder of my sixth-grade year felt incredibly awkward. Though I liked certain boys at school, I never felt comfortable being anything but friends. Ultimately, I didn't know how to act around them. Nothing about me was like any other girls. They were skinny; I was pudgy. They had long, straight hair; mine was a kinky-curly, ragtop mess. My clothes were conservative, mismatched, and screamed of hand-me-downs, while they wore new, store-bought designer outfits. I constantly felt like an outsider, alone in the crowd because of a secret that weighed more than my chubby body and heart could handle.

I did my best to act like a normal kid, but there was nothing natural or normal about how I felt. I longed to be skinny like my stepsister and the popular girls in school, but I didn't have the discipline to help myself achieve that look. I regularly consumed anything I could get my hands on—a coping mechanism and soother of sorts. As my food intake increased, so did my waistline. As puberty continued, I felt betrayed by my own body, fueling the low self-esteem and negative body image I already suffered from.

Life at home hardly improved following Dad and Robert's departure. Nightly alcohol consumption continued, and Mom became despondent. She isolated herself daily and made little to no attempt to integrate with the rest of us. She struggled to manage life's bare necessities—work, home, isolate … work, home, isolate. We kids took on more and more of the household responsibilities, including laundry and general cleaning. Dinnertime consisted of plopping down on the floor in front of the television with a paper plate. It felt as though everyone knew something was wrong, but no one talked about the elephant in the room. Day after day the endless cycle repeated.

This is all my fault.

BACK TO CALIFORNIA

By the beginning of June, school had come to a close. Mom quit her job and loaded what few personal items we had in the car before setting a course for California. My stomach churned the whole way there as I thought about being near Dad again. *How is he going to act around me? Will he put his hands on me again?* While life in New Mexico the last six months had been less than desirable, it was assuredly better compared to the first six months in the RV with Dad.

We arrived in California and drove straight to Grandma Mary's property. "We're going to live here for now while Dad and I save money to buy a place of our own," Mom explained.

"So are we living in the main house again?" I asked.

"No."

"One of the apartments?"

"No."

"Then where?"

"We're parking the RV in the back field by the old school bus."

"We're living in the RV?" I gasped.

Without any emotion, Mom said, "You girls will sleep in the bus. Robert will stay in the RV with Dad and me."

"What?"

"You heard me."

"But Mom—"

"Hush up! Not another word."

To avoid evicting the family currently living in the main house or any of the families in the apartments, Mom and Dad refused to accept Grandma's offer to live in the primary residence or one of the apartments as we had before. Just as she said, my parents parked the RV in the backfield of the property next to the rusty, rotted-out school bus where we girls began setting up residence.

I could never have imagined life being worse than ten people living in the small, dark house in New Mexico. How incredibly wrong I was! I now called home a place that had once been forbidden territory. Entering the school bus through the emergency backdoor, I immediately noticed that every window had been broken and replaced with heavy gauge plastic. Someone had strategically placed long wooden boards across the seats to cover the aisle space. Three twin-sized mattresses atop the planks formed our beds. Dad had hung a long metal bar near the driver's seat to hang our clothes. The musty smell of rust and mildew nearly suffocated us, but we didn't dare share our thoughts on the matter. Regardless of our discontent, the filthy, smelly bus was now home.

Mutual friends of my parents lived in one of the rear apartments, and they permitted us to shower there every other day. Bathroom needs were allocated to the RV. California nights were generally mild, but Dad set up a small space heater to provide heat when needed.

The bus was a scary place to live, especially with no one there to protect us. But when the rains moved in, the meticulous slapping of raindrops on the metal roof reminded me of a marching band's drum corps, and my troubled soul found a level of comfort and solace. On a few occasions when the storms produced severe wind, thunder, and lightning, Mom and Dad made us join them in the RV. Regardless, neither place was desirable.

Life in general felt more like survival mode. Mom and Dad had their morning routine, we had ours, and the two barely intersected. After Mom left for work, we would go to the RV to eat breakfast. Fairly self-sufficient, we required minimal parental interaction. At times, my parents tried to make the living situations fun, acting as if we were camping. Unfortunately, stress and excessive alcohol consumption took hold, and what had once been bearable became near toxic.

Throughout the summer, we managed to fill our days exploring the field with its countless gopher and snake holes or riding our bikes up and down the expansive driveway. On a rare Friday or Saturday evening, Mom would take us kids to Skateway, the local roller rink.

Skating with extreme caution so as to not make a fool of myself, I took pride in the fact that I could skate backward. Mary was content going round and round in a circle, while Robert, sporting his finest *Miami Vice* look, did his best to garner the attention of young ladies by speed skating past the adoring crowds. I relished these rare moments of blissful childhood fun.

Absorbed in mere survival like the rest of us, I felt my stepsister begin pulling away from the family. Her anger had been building, and she now had an option that none of us other three kids had: her mother.

Throughout the summer, Dad never laid a hand on me or even attempted to spend time alone with me. Mom's distrustful gaze was never far behind. Aside from the mundane nature of endless depressing days, the only constant in my life was Mom repeatedly asking, "Is Daddy being a good daddy?" Over time, I came to despise that question. I never had the courage to change my original answer and merely continued to reassure her that he was.

Almost sixteen, my older sister began challenging Mom's authority on a daily basis, and their interactions inevitably developed into a screaming match. It all came to an end when she ran away and called her mother for help. After learning of our living conditions, her mother took my stepsister with her. I was hurt and angry because I felt my older sister was abandoning me yet was jealous that she, alone, had another option. *Ernie, I wish you would rescue me from this miserable life! Why don't you care about us? Why don't you help?*

TRYING TO HIDE

The start of my seventh-grade year provided distractions to an otherwise problematic life. The New Mexico school I had attended in sixth grade neglected to forward my transcripts, so the new school placed me in standard academic classes versus the remedial reading class I was accustomed to. Eager to be in regular classes, I seized my new, unusual situation and hoped I would finally be viewed as a normal kid.

The majority of my school was Caucasian. Minorities who attended were exceptional students and, based on their attire, had parents who obviously had money. To me, the girls in my class all looked like miniature Barbies, and anyone who didn't fit the stereotypical mold didn't fit in. Given my big eyes, enormous smile with a mouthful of oversized teeth, hand-me-down clothes, and unruly, kinky-curly hair, I was definitely on the outs.

I had never been popular and was repeatedly bullied because of my hair. Never a day passed that I wasn't called Niggy, Brillo-head, half-breed, or some other derogatory name. I had become well versed in ignoring people's negative actions and pretending the pain they inflicted didn't bother me. Regardless of the bullying and educational challenges, school provided the one place where I felt normal.

While it seemed everything about me was different, I

knew I wasn't alone in my struggles to fit in. I connected with my teachers and yearned for their approval. Their words of acceptance soothed my open wounds and helped me to feel worthy. Oftentimes viewed as a teacher's pet, I worked hard and eagerly performed extra duties whenever possible. I made sure to be exceptionally personable with all my teachers and diligently strived to garner their approval. I wasn't sure what my future held, but I knew I wanted to grow up and be just like them.

Weekdays consisted of riding my bike to and from school and doing chores and homework. What free time we had was spent riding our bikes on the driveway or playing in the field at the back of the property. Ultimately, I felt that my job was to stay out of Mom's way. "Go play" or "Dinner" was about all I ever heard from her after she returned home from work. I wanted only to feel loved, accepted, and worthy, but even my own mother seemed incapable of fulfilling my unspoken desire. Whatever her challenges in life, I felt like we kids just added stress and pain. My mother didn't maintain an open dialogue with her children. In fact, most times she seemed cold and rather curt. Still, in spite of the daily challenges, I recall a few special moments—hugs, loving comments, and acknowledgment for my academic work. I clung to them like the very air I breathed.

Early winter arrived, bringing with it a raging case of strep throat, one of many hazards that came from spending night after night in a drafty bus.

"You're not going to school today. Get your pillow and blanket and lie down in the RV," Mom instructed.

I felt absolutely horrible—fiery throat, aching body, and a high fever. Alone again, and angry at life in general, I wondered when the misery would end. Everything and everyone in my life seemed to be falling apart. Robert had been acting up and receiving regular, heavy-handed discipline from Dad. Cathy had moved to her mother's house. Despite having one less kid,

Mom appeared more stressed than ever. I couldn't imagine life getting any worse. Once again, I was sorely mistaken.

Over the next few days, strep throat turned into tonsillitis, rendering me home for more than a week. Mom spoke with what sounded like true concern for my well-being. "I've got to go to work, but Dad will be here to take care of you." With that, she left, and for the first time in months, I was alone with Dad.

All eyes had been on him since our return. He had maintained his distance when it came to me, but all that was about to change. By midday, as if guided by a fraternal, loving tenderness, Dad walked over and began caressing my shoulders. "I'm sorry you're sick, princess."

His inebriated touch was familiar territory I wanted no part of. With every stroke of his hand, my skin crawled, as if carpeted by thousands of venomous spiders. *Why are you looking at me like that? I know that look. You're making me uncomfortable. Please don't do this, Dad. I'm so sick, and you're making me feel worse.*

I knew what he wanted and where this was going. But I was powerless to stop him, and he knew it. With budding breasts from puberty, my body betrayed me by responding to his touch. I couldn't have felt more disgusted and defeated. Physically reacting to his touch repulsed me and made me feel dirtier than ever. No matter what I did, I couldn't stop it, and the cycle of abuse began again.

If God was there, He was there without any recognition from me. Isolation and helplessness filled every sense and left me believing I had nowhere to turn for help. I don't remember how far Dad went that day; my mind simply won't allow it. I vividly remember his advances, but what happened next is devoid. With eyes tightly shut, only my body and subconscious know what truly happened. But do illicit details truly matter in a situation like that? Honestly, I'm thankful to have been spared specifics.

In a short amount of time, Dad's abuse progressed to a point with no boundaries, worse than ever before. It sporadically occurred in the RV, but he generally took me to the marital bed, a disturbing image that will forever be burned in my memory. *He can do what he wants because you didn't say anything. It's what you deserve. You had your chance to tell, so you must want it. Shut up and deal.* I saw no end in sight for my suffering, so I merely resigned myself to a new reality. Since nothing I did or said would to change it, why bother? From the first time, almost three years earlier, the outwardly cheerful girl had been replaced with internalized silence. My emotional constipation manifested itself physically through repetitive stomachaches, which I medicated with an abundance of Pepto-Bismol.

School had become the only safe place in my life, so I plunged into my studies to try and forget or at least mask the disgusting images of Dad on top of me. If I wasn't attending school, tending to household responsibilities, or doing homework, I was being raped—raped by the man who was supposed to love and protect me.

I had a couple of friends at school, but they knew nothing about my living conditions. Shame and embarrassment kept me from inviting them over. I never found the courage to share my pain with anyone—not family, teachers, or even my closest friends. I wish I'd told someone—anyone—but overwhelming fear kept my silence firmly rooted. I needed a friend—someone I could trust to share my burdens. God knew my heart, and His gift to me came in the form of a classmate named James.

James was popular, not in the way of being a jock or social status, but everyone liked him. He had a way about him that attracted friends and laughter. I found him nurturing, tender, empathetic, encouraging, genuinely kind, and a terrific listener—attributes largely absent from typical thirteen-year-old boys. I found his tall, thin build physically appealing, but his piercing blue eyes were what immediately caught my attention. Our casual relationship instantly refreshed me and brought with it a sense of calm and peace. Initially, I shared no details regarding the complexities of my home life, but he knew things weren't good. Rather than probe for details, he befriended me and listened to what little information I seemed willing to share.

Aside from the growing friendship with James, the only event I can remember producing a degree of happiness was my thirteenth birthday. Mom surprised me with my very first supply of makeup. I had never been allowed to wear makeup before, so I was incredibly excited to receive the assortment of Maybelline cosmetics—black mascara in a pink tube with a neon-green cap, a bright blue and dusty purple eye shadow duo, powder base cover-up, and roll-on lip gloss. It seemed I was finally growing up, or at least viewed by my mother as maturing to some degree. After opening the gifts, I dashed into bathroom and immediately began plastering my face with the beloved treasures, making sure to leave no crevice untouched. *I hope this will make me look prettier! Maybe, just maybe, my fellow students will accept and begin to like me.*

Unfortunately, no matter what I did or how hard I tried, no amount of makeup would draw attention away from the unmanageable mane of curls covering my head. *I'd give anything to have straight hair. Anything! Between makeup and straight hair, I'll finally be accepted; I just know it.*

Being the only one in my family with extremely curly hair, no one else could teach me how to manage it. We knew nothing about the array of suitable styling products or ironing options. Recognizing my ongoing frustration, Mom promised to take me to a professional salon for a style consultation. I could barely handle my excitement!

The wait to have my hair done seemed like an eternity, but the day finally arrived for us to go to the salon. Mom made it a special time for just the two of us. We headed toward a side of town that bore no familiarity. The patchwork, bumpy roads were eerily dark, narrow, and lined with intimidating, street-dwelling inhabitants. Since I had not grown up around a variety of ethnicities, I found the unfamiliar sounds, smells, and bustling activities rather interesting but also scary. Mom parked her car directly outside the worn-down salon and ushered me in to meet Riza, a cosmetology peer of Mom's from a decade ago. Riza, a buxom, black stylist, spent the next two hours schooling us on the fine art of dealing with afro-like hair. Her kindness and patience made our surroundings seem less threatening. Strand after strand, she pulled, tugged, and glopped on an array of products traditionally used to straighten African-American hair. Over time, the products burned my scalp, but I didn't care. I was overcome with joy to see how long and straight my hair was. *I feel so pretty and normal, like everyone else!*

Riza's education that night was invaluable and helped me overcome a lifelong struggle with my unruly, ringlet hair. No matter the level of dysfunction that I lived under, I resolved that I could manage one element in my life, even something as menial as my hair. Regardless of the time, effort, and discomfort required, I committed to the process that would follow me every day for the next ten years.

Chapter 11

PASSING THE GIFT OF SELF-LOVE

I can't believe Kenzie turns sixteen in less than a month. Madison and I have talked about taking a family trip to celebrate. MacKenzie is looking so beautiful as she continues to mature into a young woman. Right behind her, Alexandra will be turning into an official teenager, thirteen. Alex is just as beautiful and smart as Kenzie, but so unique as well. Before our family trip, the girls and I need to clothes shop for the trip and for school. I have never felt completely comfortable among the racks of tiny clothes that never fit my daughters or me.

"Nothing looks right. I feel so big and stupid looking," Alex speaks words I must have said a thousand times to myself over the years.

"It doesn't matter the size on the label as long as you feel comfortable in what you're wearing."

"Why can't I be skinny like other girls?"

"Because God didn't make us that way, but that doesn't mean we're not beautiful. We're built to last through the trials of life, like sunflowers. We have a thick stock to survive, and we always point toward the positive things in life. Plus, we're beautiful in the eyes of the people who love us."

"Do *you* think I'm pretty?"

"Alex, my boo, there is no normal. There is only who you are. You are a super genius. You love to dance and read. You're kind, compassionate, brave, unique, loving, loyal, and so much more. You're not only gorgeous on the outside but also on the inside. You pour out beauty and life to everyone you meet. There is only one Alexandra Lynne Simm, and you are perfect to God and to me."

Kenzie chimes. "You're beautiful, Alex. I don't feel pretty all the time, but I am beginning to feel prettier more as I get older."

I couldn't help but laugh. By this time, tears flood Alexandra's eyes, which puts a smile on my face. I hope she knows how amazing she is, the way I didn't for many years. She looks so much like me, but my girls are so much stronger than I ever was. They know who they are and who they want to be.

Chapter 12

BACK TO WHERE
WE STARTED

The end of the school year finally arrived. While some of the bullying had diminished after I straightened my hair and James befriended me, I still didn't belong to any particular group, especially the "it" crowd. It seemed like no matter what I did, I simply wasn't able to fit in. I had no athletic ability and was too shy for drama, not smart enough for academics, too poor to be popular, and not ethnic enough for any crowd. I just didn't fit.

Right before the start of my eighth-grade year, Mom and Dad agreed to move the family into Grandma's main house after the existing tenants turned in their notice. The best thing about moving into the main house was getting my own room for the very first time. I had always shared a room with my sister, so having a space that belonged solely to me was unchartered territory and brought with it inaugural feelings of freedom and maturity. The small white room was nestled on the backside of the house. Accessible only by walking through

Mary's room, it seemed to me a protected cove. Mom and Dad (and Grandma) gave me permission to paint the room any color I chose; I settled upon a robust pink, mimicking Pepto-Bismol. After two walls were painted, I splattered the leftover paint on the closet doors giving them a very 1980's look. Grandma gave me a small glass lamp with a pink lampshade to place on the table next to my full-size bed. We constructed curtains from leftover pink fabric and used delicate ribbon to tie them back. Outside the window was an enormous pomegranate tree bearing fruit within reach. Mary and I could reach out the screen-less window, pick the fruit, and devour it, leaving our hands as pink as my room. My parents gave me a makeup table and chair that I used to organized my makeup and store my curling iron. I felt incredibly girly, grown-up, and somewhat protected in my new pink cove.

I lay in bed one night, safely enveloped in my blanket. I had tucked it completely around me, exposed only from the nose up, and I felt safe and happy for the first time in a long time. Not only had we moved out of the rotting, dangerous bus, but I had a place all my own. I sighed contently and closed my eyes.

In what seemed like only a few moments, I heard footsteps tiptoeing through Mary's room. My body involuntarily stiffened in response. My eyes adjusted to the soft moonlight, and I quietly squirmed, a desperate attempt to tighten the cocooning covers. I trembled with dread and fear as Dad approached. This time I had no sibling present to thwart his advances, not that the presence of anyone in the room ever seemed to matter in the past. I could smell the alcohol on his hot breath as he leaned in close to stroke my hair. He wasted no time unwrapping my protective swathe like a long-awaited Christmas present. It was all I could do to keep from vomiting when his skin met mine.

Just as every time before, it didn't take long for me to emotionally disconnect. I took my mind to a luxurious pink palace that reflected a way of life completely opposite my immediate situation. I just couldn't bear to be intellectually present. I fell away, thinking, *God, where are You when I need You? Do You even know I exist?* Then … nothing. All memories of that night are wiped away. Just the disgusting feelings and hatred of my betraying body remained.

Nothing changed throughout the summer. Fearful of the night and what might or might not occur, I methodically swaddled every inch of my body every night, but Dad erratically imposed his drunken assaults at will. *I just want to die. Just be gone. No one would even notice.*

AMELIA'S STORY MIMICS MINE

Throughout my eighth-grade year, nothing changed. It had been over four years since Dad first touched me, and I saw no end in sight. I knew his actions made me uncomfortable and felt very wrong, but in those days, no one talked about sexual abuse—not the way they openly do in society today. Everything that happened to me felt wrong, but nothing had a name—that is, until the evening of April 21, 1986.

As with most nights after dinner, my parents retreated to their room to watch TV and left us kids to our own devices. I went into the living room where I plopped down on the sofa and began flipping through the channels, looking for something of interest. Mary sat beside me. As the oldest one in the room, I controlled what we watched. Since we didn't have cable TV, viewing choices were limited. I opted for the ABC Monday Night Movie, *Something about Amelia.*

The main character of the movie was a thirteen-year-old girl who lived in a beautiful home with parents and a younger sister who adored her. Amelia was very different—unusual in a way I related to but couldn't initially put my finger on. Fully engrossed, I connected with Amelia's character and anxiously waited for the storyline to unfold. *Why do I feel like I know her?* The story didn't capture Mary's attention like it had mine; she got up and left the room, leaving me there alone to journey into Amelia's life.

Amelia's parents were moderate drinkers, and her father smoked two packs of cigarettes per day—both points I definitely related to. When she arrived home on her bicycle after babysitting, she saw her father gardening in the backyard. Amelia continually shied away from him; she even carried a notebook binder across her midsection as if to serve as a barrier between them. After gulping his beer, her father attempted to engage her in conversation, but Amelia was reserved and obviously intimidated. *I feel that way, too, when Dad looks at me like that. Yuck!*

Throughout the first part of the movie, I noticed deep-seated sorrow on Amelia's face and body language that felt exceedingly familiar. I don't know why, but I felt like I walked in her shoes and lived her life. But how could I? Her father and mother adored her. They told her how pretty she was, and her father repeatedly called her Princess. They never hit her or called her ugly names. They spent time talking to each other, going to church, bowling, and watching football together. *How could I possibly relate? Our family doesn't do those things.*

But one scene in particular changed my life. Amelia arrived at school and immediately reported to her counselor's office, as instructed.

The counselor, Mrs. Bennett, met her at the door. "Come on in, honey. Close the door."

Amelia entered the office, closed the door, and took a seat in the brown wooden chair across the desk from where Mrs. Bennett sat down. "Well, we meet again. So how ya doing?" Mrs. Bennett asked. The counselor seemed to care. She seemed genuinely concerned about Amelia's well-being—like she knew something was going on with her.

I stayed riveted as the scene revealed ... something about Amelia.

Amelia looked puzzled and scared at the same time, as if she wondered what Mrs. Bennett might know. "I thought all you had to worry about was my schoolwork."

"You used to be on the honor roll. Your grades have been going down. And I think the reason you're doing so poorly is because you're feeling so poorly." The counselor paused to allow Amelia an opportunity to interject. When the girl didn't speak, Mrs. Bennett continued. "Can you talk about it at all? Have you talked to anybody else about it—your mother or a friend?"

"No." Amelia's soft whisper morphed into stammering, as if to correct herself. "I mean, it isn't anything. There isn't anything to talk about."

Mrs. Bennett gave Amelia a look that seemed to say she didn't believe what the girl was saying; I had seen a similar look on my mother's face. Mrs. Bennett stood and walked over to Amelia. "You know, Amelia, you happen to be one of my favorite people around this place." She gently offered a comforting smile and slowly sat in the open chair next to the frightened student. "I think there is something you want to talk about. I mean ... if there was something you felt you couldn't handle yourself, I'd certainly want to help you out."

Amelia looked down at her hands in her lap. "It's not as if you could do anything about it."

"Well, if I couldn't, I'd find somebody who could. Please tell me what's going on." Mrs. Bennett face had a pleading look.

Amelia looked defeated and hopeless. She struggled to say the words that were screaming to come out.

My mind reeled. She won't say it. I know. I was there. It's too awful, and they won't believe her. I couldn't, and she won't either.

"I can't. I can't tell anyone."

I knew it!

"Maybe it isn't as bad as you think it is, ya know." Mrs. Bennett tilted her head lower in an attempt to make eye contact with the girl.

Amelia shook her head. "No … it is."

"What is?"

She forced out the obviously painful words, "My … my … father's been messing around with me."

She did it! She said it out loud. She told someone her awful secret. Tears ran down my face. I wept for Amelia—for her bravery and the hint of hope I saw in her eyes. I wept for her loss of innocence as well for as my own. I wept because I felt weak and horrible.

Mrs. Bennett looked deep into Amelia's cowering eyes and knew the student was telling the truth. Neither needed to say another word.

At that moment I realized I wasn't alone. Other girls, other daughters, like me had endured abuse and violation at the hands of those who should have protected them. For the first time in my life, my emotions had names. Everything I'd been feeling for over four years was now labeled and validated. I wasn't crazy. I wasn't alone. I hadn't done anything wrong. My nightmares of being touched became very real. They had a name—incest. I longed to have the guts to tell someone like Amelia did, but years of torment, confusion, and shame anchored my speech, so my heart cried in silence. Amid flowing tears, I could think of only one person in my life I truly trusted: James.

Once James and I had time to talk, away from everyone at school, I told him about the movie I'd just watched. He saw the hurt in my eyes and listened to the words pouring out of my quivering lips as I explained that my parents didn't love me. I shared some horrible stories about living in the bus and RV and all the drinking. At fourteen years old, I'm sure this horrific information overloaded James, but he never told anyone or made fun of me. He just continued to be my friend.

By the end of my eighth-grade year, James had morphed into my greatest confidant. However, I couldn't explain the true horrors that were happening to me to James; I was afraid of what might happen to our friendship if he knew the truth. *He would be disgusted and leave me too.* Still, his emotional support with regard to my other revelations validated me and set the stage for things to come.

Chapter 13

TRUTH REVEALED

It was late July in Texas, and the freezing air-conditioning in Chick-fil-A drove the girls and me to the outside patio. Thankfully, a nice breeze kept the heat at bay. As we began to enjoy our chicken, waffle fries, salad, and the now-customary half-sweetened tea, Michelle called.

"Are the girls within earshot?" she asked.

"I can talk, but the girls are with me," I explained.

"I just have a couple of questions."

"Ask away. I'll do my best to answer."

Through carefully chosen words, I give Michelle what she needed to continue writing the details of my story. After I hung up, I was filled with shame from hiding and fearing that my girls would finally know my horrible secret.

Years ago, in a conversation with Nonnie, I asked her opinion about talking to my daughters about the abuse in my past. "When would be the right time to tell the girls the truth?"

As always, her tenderness and precise response perfectly met my needs and covered my insecurities. "As a mother, you'll know when they're mature enough to handle it. As a woman, you'll recognize when they need to know."

Just then, a flash of advice from my mother came crashing in. "Never write anything you don't want the whole world to know." This valuable piece of advice came on the heels of a peer, sibling, or teacher finding a personal note. Writing the book would be no different. Though substantially more than just a passing note, I knew the girls would eventually learn the truth. I had to tell them before they accidentally or purposefully discovered my work in progress or figured out the coded whispers between Michelle and me or Madison and me. With all this swarming in my mind, I decided to take advantage of this opportunity—alone time with the girls, free from other distractions—to tell them the first part of my story.

"As you know, I'm writing a book about my life."

They both nodded and continued eating their lunch.

I forced a smile before I continued. "Well, there are some parts that I need to tell
you both before the whole world knows."

This got their attention.

"You both know that Grandma and Grandpa used to drink a lot."

"Yeah," they responded in unison.

"And you remember how I've taught you that hurt people hurt?"

More nodding.

"Well, when I was a young girl, Grandma and Grandpa were different people. They drank a lot. When they got drunk, they called us kids names or they hit us. Now, of course, every child needs proper discipline. I know that. And we were no different. But when people drink a lot, their behavior becomes unpredictable. That means that their punishment was unpredictable because they reacted out of emotion. So I never knew if I would be punished for the first mistake or the tenth. This made for a very unstable environment." *Breathe, Lynnette, breathe.*

"Yeah, Mom, we know about this." Kenzie popped a fry into

her mouth. The look on her face told me she knew I was trying to stall.

My hands began to shake under the table and my insides churned, but I continued. "Yes, I know you knew that, but I needed to remind you that people don't always know what they're doing when they're drunk. In addition to the unpredictable discipline, Grandpa ..." *Just spit it out. You've told others; you can tell the girls. Dear Lord, please put Your hand on me as I try to explain this. I need You, Father. Comfort me.* "Grandpa sexually abused me."

Time stood still. I tried to interpret the looks on their faces as they processed what I'd just said. Kenzie's eyes welled up with tears, and Alex quietly lowered her gaze to her lap.

"Oh, Mom. I'm so sorry." Tears rolled down Kenzie's face.

Alex remained silent.

"I know you may have some questions. And you can ask me anything. Or you can talk with Dad or Nonnie. We are all here to help you."

Alex finally broke her silence. "Did Grandpa hurt Auntie Mary or anyone else?"

"No."

But one of Kenzie's questions caught me off guard, bringing with it many of the old feelings and insecurities from my childhood.

"Did Grandma know what was happening?"

Instantly, my mind went back to that day—the day our family was torn apart.

Chapter 14

FAMILY BROKEN

The summer before ninth grade passed quickly. As with most summers, we kids played, watched TV, or visited friends. We did our best to steer clear of parental paths, but fights erupted and siblings got annoyed, which caused our parents to do the same. Regardless of my attempts to isolate, Dad still managed to make his way to my room occasionally. *This is never going to end. I don't even know how many times this has happened. It's like my brain is just blocking it all out. I must be going crazy.*

School finally began in August, bringing with it the ever-welcomed distraction. On the weekends, the family scattered, each person doing what he or she wanted. Dad worked outside or walked next door to talk and drink with friends. Robert stayed in his room listening to music or escaped to a friend's house. Mary spent her days playing or watching cartoons. Mom watched her favorite TV shows, which she had recorded on VHS tapes during the week.

One afternoon in August 1986, I quietly walked into Mom's room and settled myself on the floor next to the bed. Watching her soaps used to be a daily ritual, but now that she had a job, it was sacred time for her when she finally had a day off. The room-darkening curtains were customarily closed, but the light from the television readily reflected the smoky haze from the multitude of cigarettes previously consumed. Amid the smoke, I could see her drink on her bedside table. It was impossible to know if it was just soda pop or a mixed drink. How many had she already had? She didn't seem drunk, so I sat down quietly. I felt safe in her presence and knew no one would hurt me while I was with her.

During one of the commercial breaks, she looked over at me and asked, "Is Daddy being a good daddy?" Fear and confusion immediately infiltrated every fiber of my being. It certainly wasn't the first time she'd asked this question, but it had been a long time since she had last asked it. I wondered why she brought it up again now. *Does she suspect something's going on, or has someone said something to her?*

I didn't utter a word; instead, I merely sat and stared at her. *Does she have some indication that my answer will be any different from what it was over two years ago when asked? Things are actually going well for our family now.* We were finally living in a real home, not a rusted-out old school bus. Life felt relatively secure, more so than it had been for as long as I could remember. While I heard what she asked, I sat crippled by years of fear and shame. *Why, Mom, why? Why are you asking me this now?* Before looking down, I blinked and quietly said, "What?"

"Is Daddy being a good daddy?" She repeated, her words now laced with concern and empathy. She waited patiently for my response.

"No," I whispered. I felt pain in my gut from shame at being exposed and fear of hurting my mom.

As if she hadn't comprehended the magnitude of my response, she asked me again, "Is Daddy being a good daddy?"

The commercial break ended, and her soap had resumed playing, but her maternal focus did not waiver in the least. It took every ounce of strength and courage I could muster to lift my head and look her in the eyes before tears began welling in mine. I didn't have to answer the question again. The way her eyes bore into me, I knew that she knew I was telling the truth. Without warning, the flood of emotions I had bottled for over five years came crashing in and overwhelmed my sense of reality. *What will Mom say? What will she do?* There was no turning back now.

She reached down and pulled me into her tender, loving embrace. I let out a long, ragged breath. I knew in my heart Mom believed me and felt a sincere, deep compassion for my pain. Had I known what her reaction would be, I might have had the courage to tell her long ago. But pain, guilt, and shame continually silenced me. Without delving too deeply, she asked just enough questions to fully understand that my dad had been molesting and raping me for years. She even asked why I didn't tell her the truth years before. I explained that I was so scared because Dad was staring at me that day and I felt like I was in trouble. After I shared with her the years of abuse, I crumbled and was cradled in the safety of her bosom. The truth had finally come out, and I knew without a doubt that she would do something about it. Little did I realize that this conversation would start a firestorm that would rage through our entire family.

TRAUMA TO RESCUE

It was the first time in my life I recall feeling so protected, something I valued deeply. By my revealing years of sexual abuse, Mom felt compelled to act on what she now knew. The time we spent together that afternoon seemed like an eternity, but in truth it was probably no more than thirty minutes. After she dried my tears and made sure I was relatively stable, she left the room in search of my dad.

Curiosity of their whereabouts overrode my fear, so I quietly walked out of the bedroom to see what was going on. I spied them standing right outside the backdoor in the midst of a heated confrontation. Her arms and head thrashed about and words spewed from her lips as she cried with such anguish that it still haunts me to this day. Dad's slumped posture screamed guilt. He listened to her accusations without interruption; he merely nodded. As with any other adult conversations that took place in our home, my parents shielded me from the details of their exchange, but Mom's anger and Dad's surprise were unmistakable. I've no recollection of how much time passed, but the conclusion of their conversation brought with it Dad's immediate exit. The only thing Mom allowed him to do was enter the house long enough to gather some personal belongings. In those few moments of conclusion, Mom's stance was firmly rooted—a lioness posture, ensuring her body remained positioned between Dad and me. She wouldn't allow him to come anywhere near me. With his clothes and toiletries in hand, he looked our way with tear-stained cheeks and said, "I'm going to fix this. I love you, Louise. I love our family. I love Lynnette." With incredible remorse etched on his face, he walked out the door and left us to grapple in the chaotic wake.

Evening arrived, and the trauma from the day's events gripped the entire house. Mom couldn't stop crying, and everyone in the house, except me, was confused by what was going on. Robert and Mary only knew that Mom was a wreck and Dad was gone. Desperate to understand, their inquiries went unanswered, which rendered them upset and fearful. I wanted to forget the conversation with Mom ever happened or somehow retract my words, but I could do neither. While I desperately wanted Dad's actions to stop, I didn't imagine that the truth coming out would require his exit. Our family dynamics had instantaneously shifted from dysfunctional to trauma and conflict. I laid my head on the pillow that night and saturated every square inch of its fibers with tears. *I've done this. I'm to blame. Everyone's upset, and it's completely my fault.*

We didn't know it at the time, but Dad slept in his car in one of the garages on the property behind the main house because he had nowhere else to go. We never saw him or even knew he was there. He drove away before we woke and returned to the garage after we went to bed.

Within a week, the entire family was scheduled to see a counselor. Arriving at the appointment in separate cars, Mom and Dad entered the therapist's office first, leaving us three kids in the waiting room. Still clueless as to what had transpired, Robert and Mary waited patiently. I worked hard not to squirm in my seat, hoping and praying my nervousness and guilt would go undetected.

Later, through secondhand accounts, I learned what initially transpired in the room between Mom, Dad, and Paula, the therapist. Dad immediately divulged to Paula how he had sexually abused me. He left no details to the imagination. Though cowering, he freely admitted his transgressions and took full responsibility for them. He spoke about his desire to fix the impulse and restore his family to a place of health and unity. Paula listened intently to his story, and then told my parents she would have to speak to the children and determine if I was the only victim. Mom and Dad understood her request and respected her authority in the situation, so they knew they would have to reveal to Robert and Mary why we were really there. They exited the private office, sat down amongst us, and shared only the necessary elements of the truth with Robert and Mary before Paula separated us from their potential influence.

Once seated in the small office with Robert and Mary, I felt as if all eyes were focused on me. With carefully chosen words, Paula shared Dad's confession with us before she asked a series of questions to determine if I was the sole victim over the years. Learning Dad had confessed to the abuse brought a sense of comfort to my weary heart. I knew then that he wanted to stop hurting me. In the end, having Dad back home and reestablishing our family life was my heart's desire. Once Paula seemed satisfied with the answers she received and realized that no one else had been harmed, she dismissed us and asked my parents to return.

As is the case with many additional conversations, my parents filled in the gaps of places and things I couldn't possibly know.

Paula immediately began to speak. "I am grateful for your willingness to come in and seek help. It's very commendable of you to take ownership of your actions, Bob. Based on my conversation with the children, it is obvious to me that Lynnette was the only victim, but I need for you to understand something. What you did is a crime. It is a criminal offense, and I am required by law to report you to the authorities."

Mom and Dad were stunned. They believed Dad had committed immoral acts but not criminal ones.

Before Mom and Dad left her office, Paula said, "I strongly encourage you to get involved with Parents United, a support group for parents of children who have been sexually abused. The program is for nonoffending and offending parents. They offer free counseling not only to you but also to the entire family." She handed them a pamphlet, and they agreed to contact the organization immediately.

After we left her office, we had a family conversation about what had taken place. Our parents reassured us that Dad would get the help he needed to get better. Mom and Dad registered for Parents United that afternoon. With legal action imminent, they decided to voluntarily report Dad's crime to the authorities. Dad drove to the police station alone and made a full confession, fully expecting to immediately be taken into custody.

"Mister, a formal complaint must be provided by your wife and a statement from your daughter before placing you into custody. You're free to leave," the investigator told him.

"Okay, I understand. When should I come back?"

"You don't need to come back. Once the evidence is

gathered, a warrant will be issued for your arrest, and we will pick you up."

"Just give me a call, and let me know when that happens. I'll meet you wherever you want to surrender myself."

"We will be in touch."

Over the next few weeks, Dad did everything in his power to make things easy on the officials. He knew Mom planned to take me to the police station soon, so he scrambled to make as much money as possible to help support our family. Once arrested, he would probably lose his job, which would render us destitute almost immediately. My father's behavior was never self-serving; in fact, his actions proved his devotion to the overall welfare and future of his family. *Why did it take him so long to finally see that I was worth so much more? Am I more worthy of your love and sacrifice today than I was yesterday? What's different about me today that wasn't there before the truth came out?* I didn't have answers to the questions that plagued my mind and heart, but I was grateful for the newfound security my dark, dusty pink bedroom now afforded.

In the weeks that passed since our visit to the therapist, Robert became withdrawn and isolated and Mary became exceedingly angry with everyone around her—especially me. She simply couldn't understand why I had lied about *her* dad.

"You're a liar! Why would you do this to Dad? Why are you lying?" she spat, terror and anger filling her eyes.

Mom heard the commotion and came to clear up the situation. "She's not lying. Lynnette is telling the truth. Dad did this." Still, no amount of maternal words would lessen Mary's anger toward me. No matter what I did or how hard I tried, I was now the sibling outcast. *This is my fault. Everyone is mad at me. If I had just kept my mouth shut!*

Later that week, Mom drove us to the police station where I was scheduled to make a formal statement. *There's no turning back now.* Arriving at the station felt overwhelming. Without knowing it, my all-too-familiar mode of self-protection took over in the same way I had always done when Dad abused me. I emotionally checked out. Of my five primary senses, the only thing I remember is what I saw—comfortless, sterile shades of gray. *What will I have to say? Will they make me tell them everything? I just want this to be over with so Dad can get the help he needs and come back home. Then maybe everyone will stop being mad at me.* Thankfully, I had to answer only a few questions; this made the process easier than I had anticipated. I felt relieved and thankful when I walked out of the police station. It was over!

Unfortunately, unbeknownst to my mother or me, things were far from over. In reality, the legal nightmare was just beginning.

Four days after we gave our statements to the police, officers unexpectedly showed up at our house. "Ma'am, we are here to take your daughter, Lynnette, down to the station for a deposition."

Shock and fear washed over my mother's face. "Why? We were just there a few days ago. We both gave complete statements."

"I understand, ma'am, but I've been instructed to bring her to the station immediately. You will be notified when we're finished with the interview."

Mom grabbed her purse and keys. "That won't be necessary. I'm coming with her."

"I'm sorry, ma'am. That's not permitted. We are required to take her alone."

Enraged by their rigidity, Mom's defiance escalated. "I won't allow it. I am coming with her."

The officer whipped back, "Ma'am, if you do not cooperate with us, we can take her away and put her in protective custody. I don't think that's what you want, is it?"

Oblivious to our rights to have a child advocate or lawyer present, Mom succumbed to their pressuring demands. Without further confrontation, the security of my mother's shield was stripped from me and placed in the perceived safety of the Chino police.

As instructed by the officers, I climbed into the back of the squad car. My surroundings felt surreal. I looked at Mom crying only to see Mary watching me get in the car. *I thought only criminals rode in the back of a police car. What did I do wrong? I'm telling the truth, I promise. So what did I do wrong?*

On our way to the station, the officers stopped at McDonald's, bought me a meal, and asked a few questions while I ate. I didn't understand what they wanted from me. I had already been to the station and told the other officer what Dad had done. Within minutes, we were back in the squad car heading to the station.

With the exception of bits and pieces, the trauma of being ripped from my mother's protection and taken like a criminal to the police station prevented me from remembering many of the details. My mother, who had me recount what had happened upon my return home that day, helped fill in the gaps.

Once we arrived at the police station, I was ushered into a tiny interrogation room that held a rectangular metal table and three uncomfortable chairs. The dingy off-white walls leaned toward gray from years of neglect. A mirrored glass lined one wall, just like you see on TV. As with my previous visit to the station, everything was sterile and scary. Two plain-clothed men entered the room and immediately bombarded me with questions. "What did your dad do to you? When did it start? How many times? Did he have sex with you? How long has this been going on? Did you ever tell anyone?"

Their questions were very specific, seemingly unending, and intimately intrusive, the effect of which made me quite uncomfortable. I did the best I could to answer their questions, but it never seemed to be enough. *Please believe me. I promise I'm not lying. It really did happen, but I just can't remember everything you want me to. In fact, I worked really hard not think about it. I had to take my mind somewhere else when he hurt me, so I wouldn't think about what was happening, so I could escape the reality of what he did to me. It's the only way I could deal with it. But now you want me to tell you everything I've tried so hard to forget!*

The officers pressured me for answers, but I simply couldn't recall the specifics to the degree that would ultimately satisfy them. I was lonely and scared—a heart-pounding kind of scared. *Where's my mom? I need my mommy. Please, I don't want to talk about this anymore. I just want to go home. Please, I just want to go home.*

Their relentless pursuit of the truth continued nonstop over the course of four hours. Completely alone in the grimy room, I did my best to answer their questions, with no adult to advocate on my behalf at any time. At my wit's end and emotionally exhausted, I nearly broke down. They finally decided that they had the necessary evidence and called my mom to come get me. I cried the whole way home, as Mom gently asked what had happened.

Once the police got what they needed, the judge wasted no time in issuing a warrant for Dad's arrest. Rather than calling him so he could willingly turn himself in—as he had politely requested—officers stormed his place of work with an arrest warrant in hand. While placing him in handcuffs, they made it known to everyone within earshot that he was being arrested and charged with fifteen counts of lewd and lascivious acts with a minor.

Within days of Dad's arrest, he and his court-appointed attorney appeared before the judge to enter a plea. Mom and Mary attended the arraignment. I opted to stay home.

The police transcripts confirmed the following:

"Mister, you have been charged with fifteen acts of lewd and lascivious acts with a minor. Do you understand these charges?" the judge asked.

"Yes."

"How do you wish to plead?"

"Guilty."

"Have you conferred with your attorney regarding the evidence against you?"

"No."

"Then I do not accept your plea. You need to seek counsel before entering a plea."

The public attorney spoke up. "Your Honor, I've tried to explain the charges involved. We ask the court for additional time to review the evidence before entering a guilty plea."

Reluctantly, Dad agreed. A plea of not guilty was temporarily entered until Dad had the opportunity to speak with his attorney. But Dad had already decided that no matter the charges against him, he would plead guilty. No amount of prison time would prevent him from protecting me from the pain of testifying in court. He didn't want to hurt me one second more. Dad understood his actions were wrong, and he was prepared to accept whatever penalty the courts handed down. With that, the bailiff ushered him out of the courtroom back to his county jail cell.

Before an official court date would be set, the district attorney's office began the process of building their case. Unbeknownst to Dad, the court notified Mom that a mandatory medical exam would be performed on me. I was utterly mortified when Mom told me what would take place. It seemed I had no voice in anything that happened to me—not then and not now. For years I had been powerless with regard to Dad molesting me, and now I would be at the mercy of the authorities. *Does anyone care what I think or want?*

Within days, Mom took me to a doctor's office to have the physical exam. Every person in that medical practice knew why I was there, which exacerbated my sense of humiliation. The exam took place in a sterile clinical environment and was the most degrading, humiliating thing I had ever experienced. A nurse handed me a thin paper drape along with instructions to disrobe from the waist down. Within minutes, three people entered the room.

"Hello, Lynnette. I know this is uncomfortable, but we will make this as quick and as painless as possible. Please place your feet in the stirrups and scoot down to the end of the table," the doctor said. He positioned himself at the foot of the exam table and repositioned the paper drape exposing every facet of my vulnerability. He then pried my knees apart and inserted a cold metal spreader.

My entire body stiffened at his touch, and I stared at the ceiling, wishing myself a million miles from that cold, impersonal, humiliating place. His exam violated me in ways that exceeded anything I could imagine.

The physician used swabs to collect fluids and dictated various findings to the attending nurse. Removing the instrument, the doctor then inserted his fingers inside of me while his other hand applied pressure to my tender abdomen. I squeezed my eyes closed tightly and prayed it would end. The so-called exam felt like I was being raped all over again, but this time with an audience.

CRUMBLING FAMILY

For years, our family dynamics had been based on hiding the truth through omission, deceit, or lies. Whether we used these tactics for self-preservation, to avoid arguments, or forgo judgment and lectures, the entire family manipulated the truth. Dad's arrest would prove to be no different. Rather than risk having the whole family climbing all over her, Mom lied. Given the amount of stress she was under and the utter embarrassment we collectively felt, she believed one more person offering his or her opinion would be unbearable. So Mom told our extended family and friends that Dad had been arrested for DUI. Given the amount of alcohol he regularly consumed, they seemed to accept the lie as plausible.

Everyone except me visited Dad in jail on a regular basis. Even his parents went to visit him, but I just couldn't. In spite of everything he had done to me, I still loved him. Yes, I loved him. All I ever wanted was for him to stop molesting me. I never wanted him to be in jail, and yet a tremendous amount of anger still brewed inside me.

Regardless of extended family members being in the dark, Mom and Dad faced the truth head-on. They were willing to do whatever was necessary to restore the family. *I'd love to help, but I don't want to see him. I'm still mad at him, but I can't say that because Mom needs everyone to be strong. Plus, Mary hates me already.*

Life had gone from bad to worse, much worse. In addition to the humiliating physical exam, the DA's office forced me to attend weekly one-on-one therapy sessions with Paula, the therapist who had reported the abuse to the authorities. I found Paula to be generally dull and unapproachable, but our insurance plan didn't offer any other options. Her benchmark-style therapy lacked tenderness and a genuine level of concern. The weekly meetings took place in a tiny windowless office that felt sterile, dark, and uninviting, hardly a setting that encouraged my participation. Plus, Paula's bland approach to therapy did little to soothe my wounded spirit. She persistently encouraged me to feel anger toward Dad, but she failed to understand that, no matter what he did to me, my feelings toward him were primarily fear and intimidation—rarely anger. My initial attempt at expressing anger was to boycott jail visitations. Regardless, I knew he loved me and our family.

Paula frequently referred to Dad's actions as rape. Whenever she said that word, it triggered visions of violent, evil behavior I had witnessed only in movies. But his touch was never like that, so associating the word *rape* to what he did proved difficult. He was never harsh or physically overpowering in a way that made me feel threatened. His gentle approach made it nearly impossible for me to be mad at him. I couldn't see anger amid the abuse. So trying to be mad at someone when I didn't instinctively feel that way was challenging. I guess if

I were going to be molested by someone, Dad's tactics could be considered the lesser of two evils. *Maybe I am just too sick and repulsed to understand the depth of his abusive betrayal. I'm so confused and feel horrible, but I don't want to lose my family. I can't stand how everyone hates me. I'll just put my feelings aside and do what I have to do so they don't hate me and pray they don't eventually leave me.*

Life at home continued to spiral out of control. Everything that was wrong seemed to be centered on me. I had no place to hide, nowhere to escape. My family was broken, mad, crying, or yelling all the time. *What have I done? I told the truth, and now it seems like I'm being punished even more.* It felt as if we were all trapped in the same hospital emergency room but behind individual curtains—privy to the sounds of what was going on but unable to see, feel, or help one another through our own personal hells.

Everyone wanted out of the ER, but the problem was our home and the ER were one in the same. Stepsister came by occasionally, but her visits only stirred up the already dysfunctional dynamics of the household. Robert, Mary, and I rejected her attempts to rule as she had in the past because her authoritative posture tended to instigate fights. One of her visits landed the two of us in an all-out fight like never before. I had taken all I was going to take from her. Thunderous name-calling peaked, and I launched toward her petite stature. I had no trouble overpowering her and pinning her to the floor. With raised fists fully prepared to beat up her pretty little face, Mom came from behind and jerked me off her. That proverbial catfight was the final straw that ended our childhood relationship. Our sister bond was destroyed. We were two damaged, hurting children with nothing else holding us together. So I lost my older sister.

Chapter 15

AFTERMATH

My oldest daughter touched my hand, bringing me back to our lunch at Chick-fil-A. I looked into her overwhelmed eyes and did my best to share with them what had happened without giving too many unnecessary details. Kenzie had the most questions and listened attentively as I explained how everyone dealt differently with the disintegration of our family. I understood the repercussions of telling the truth both then and now.

"What happened to you all? Was it hard? Why didn't anyone ever notice what was happening?" Kenzie's rapid-fire questions spilled out. Her face softened with compassion and concern, and her eyes became watery as tears were ready to slip out.

"Our lives were consumed because of the drinking and chaotic environment. Also, remember, my grandpa was deathly ill, and then he died. I think all the hurt just consumed my parents." I knew that wasn't an excuse, but I still tried to explain the complexity of it all. "Um, what happened to us was we fought. Mainly among ourselves out of anger, but my parents did fight for us kids and themselves. Therapy was most important."

"Dad knows about this too?" The words came almost as a whisper from Alex. Her eyes moved quickly, as if she were trying to speed-read the situation. My heart filled with shame, fear, and anguish as I watched my girls try to take it all in. I cringed, knowing there was more to come.

"I told your dad just three dates into our relationship."

"Was he mad?"

"He was shocked and more hurt for me. But like you two, he got to know my parents for who they are now, not for their mistakes. It did take longer, especially because I wasn't done being mad at them myself." I gathered up the trash to indicate that we were leaving. The girls followed me to the car.

"What about Aunt Mary, Uncle Robert, and the rest of the family? Do they all know too?" Kenzie's voice trembled with anxiety. She always worried about everyone else.

"My brother and sisters know, of course, but I don't know about their spouses, and I doubt their kids know. We all handled this secret differently." I turned onto Eldorado Parkway and headed home. The car was quiet, each of us in our own thoughts.

All I remembered was the hurt and sense of being alone. Looking back, I could see that my stepsister must have felt left out, hurt, and alone. To a degree, we all did, but she found herself on the outside looking in. After she finished high school, she tried to reconnect with us, but I think Robert, Mary, and I were all so wounded—barely surviving, really—that we were unable to foster her attempts. Unfortunately, she and I could never reclaim the sisterhood we had once shared. My siblings and I have all struggled with the events and secrets of our childhoods.

Chapter 16

BARELY HOLDING ON

Though Mom did her best, she had innumerable responsibilities heaped on her. It was probably all she could do to keep from losing it, and quietly, I'm sure she did lose it. Between holding down a full-time job, carting every member of the household to and from weekly therapy sessions, and attending weekly meetings with Adults Molested as Children (AMAC), a subsidiary of Parents United, she felt it was important for her to understand what had happened and why Dad had molested me. She recognized that she was ill-equipped as my advocate and resolved to empower herself with as much information as possible. In doing so, she worked to help me and my brother and sisters, as well as eventually deal with Dad when he got out of jail.

To her credit and astounding inner strength, to which she credits all to God, she quit drinking. Unfortunately, it still seemed like she spent nearly every evening sequestered in her room. Sometimes at night I could hear her through the shared wall of our bedrooms. She cried softly or talked to Dad on the phone. Her physical and emotional isolation, along with nightly crying, prevented me from feeling her love. I'm sure she felt physically and emotionally drained beyond all understanding. All I saw and felt was her pain, every day and every night. *I'll do anything to make you stop crying—anything! I'll even let Dad come home if it will make you stop.*

When Mom was at work, our mouths constantly spat cruelties as foul as medieval sailors cussing and name-calling one another. It seemed that we kids never extended a single ounce of kindness or tenderness to one another. Everyone talked or shouted, but no one said anything that made sense. Tensions were so thick; all we knew to do was emotionally, verbally, and physically fight our way through it. At best, life felt like Survival 911, and the mounting stress was about to irrevocably alter the most innocent life of us all.

Mary and I had become very distant. Between transitioning into teenagers and dealing with an unstable home life, our immaturity and pain caused us to fight over everything. Mary's anger toward me continued to escalate, and she launched relentless accusations toward on a daily basis. "*My* daddy would have never done this—ever! I don't believe a word you say!" Life between us was like residing in a hornet's warpath. Our relationship had become as explosive as a boxing match without a ringside referee.

Weeks of her stubborn bullying finally pushed me to the breaking point. In the midst of one her daily attacks, I reached up and slapped her across the face as hard as I possibly could. Stunned by my action, she fled the room. In the past, I might have felt guilty for hitting her, but since Dad's arrest, physical altercations amongst the kids had become common. I guess it was the only way we knew how to expunge the pain and anger.

About a week after our confrontation, Mary, who had just walked in the door from school, looked very different. The left side of her face drooped and her eyelid was down-turned, which prevented her from closing her eye. She couldn't smile, and it seemed the muscle tone on that side of her face was gone.

"What's the matter with your face?" I asked. I had never seen anything like it. She looked as if all emotion was void from the left side of her face. Mary and I went to get Mom, who then began to ask Mary to move her face.

"Close your eyes."

"I am trying."

"I know she's faking." Underlying jealousy was welling up within me. I finally had Mom's attention and now Mary was trying to take it away.

"I'm not." Mary began to cry.

"Stop it, Lynnette. She isn't faking. Go away. Go to your room."

After Mom barked at me, she continued to run down a checklist of things she thought of. Before the day was over, Mom had made a doctor's appointment for the next day. We all woke up hoping to see Mary's face back to normal, but it wasn't. So they went to the doctor's appointment. I went with them, since Robert seemed to be MIA most of the time. He did all he could to be out of the house and away from the drama.

After the evaluation, the doctor told Mom that Mary had Bell's palsy, a facial paralysis to one side of the face, which generally occurs in adults. Though the doctor had a name for it, there was no known treatment, especially for children.

"How ... how could this have happened?" Mom was trying to get her head around what had happened to her baby.

"There is no way of telling. The same herpes virus that causes cold sores is generally thought to cause most cases. It usually comes on suddenly and during the night, causing inflammation of the nerve that controls the muscles in the face. Other causes could be blunt trauma. We just don't know for sure."

"What do we do to fix it?" Mom's voice shook, and I could see her choking back the tears that welled up in her eyes.

"There's no cure, but it usually gets better in a few weeks."

Over the next several weeks, Mom took Mary to several specialists—a neurologist, ophthalmologist, otolaryngologist—anyone and everyone who might be able to help or explain how this happened. Sadly, they all told her the same thing. "There's a good chance it will completely reverse itself in the coming months, but be prepared for the possibility that it could be permanent. There's simply no way to tell but to give it time."

Every time I remembered the fight we had had the week before, overwhelming guilt constricted my airways, making it difficult to breathe. *I'm a horrible person. That's where I slapped her. I caused it. It's my fault. Every bad thing that happens to my family is my fault.*

With one daughter emotionally distraught, the other daughter physically distraught, Dad in jail, and the family barely holding on, Mom finally reached her breaking point and called the cavalry—her mom, Grandma Mary. Mom explained that Dad was in jail for driving under the influence and then told Grandma everything that had happened to Mary.

Grandma said, "Send her to me, Louise. I'll take care of her."

"I can't, Mom. I don't have the money for a plane ticket."

"Don't worry. I'll pay for it. Just send her to me, Louise."

Within days, Mom put Mary, my scared, lonely twelve-year-old sister on a plane to New Mexico. Once Mary got there, Grandma sought the advice of a neurologist, a chiropractor, and various physicians to see what, if anything, could be done.

Following a month of suggested treatment, Mary came home. I stood in the airport, waiting impatiently for her to disembark. Hope that she would be healed filled me. But when she approached, I noticed that her improvement was minimal, and the effects of her Bell's palsy were still obvious. Though finally able to close her left eye, Mary's paralysis never fully diminished, rendering her face forever altered. The doctors diagnosed her with a virus that causes Bell's palsy, but I couldn't help but wonder if the sole responsibility rested on the slap I laid squarely on her face. Another piece of guilt stacked atop an already-enormous pile of self-imposed blame.

Chapter 17

GRANDPA IN JAIL

As I turned into our driveway, my focus returned to the present and my daughters. Alexandra sat in the car, still and quiet. I was worried because she wasn't asking questions; instead, she just listened as Kenzie asked, "Did Grandpa go to jail for what he did?"

"Yes. He served eight of the twelve months he was sentenced."

"Can I go to my room now?"

"Sure, sweetheart. I know it's a lot to take in." Alexandra hugged me, then Kenzie. A tear rolled down my cheek. *God be with them. I'm so sorry.*

There were many more details regarding that time—details I couldn't remember. I knew I would have to ask Mom and Dad to help me fill in those gaps for the girls and for the book. I walked to my bedroom, holding my cell phone to my ear. "Hey, Mom."

"Hey, honeybun. What's up?"

"Well, I just told the girls. It was easier than I expected. They are awesome girls."

"Of course they are. You're doing a great job."

"Thanks. They did have some questions, and I while I know the answers, I realized I don't know the details."

"You know you can ask me anything."

"Yeah, I know. I just need to take notes. Is that okay?"

"Of course. Your dad and I are still planning on coming over this weekend. Write a list of questions, and we will do our best to fill in the blanks."

"I know this isn't easy for you or Dad. I really appreciate it. Now that the girls know, we can chat openly when you two come over."

"No worries. You know your dad and I support you."

"I know. I love you both. See you Saturday, and don't forget we have church at ten on Sunday."

"I'm packing now."

Saturday, out on the patio, I talked to Mom and Dad specifically about the arrest, jail time, and after took notes on a pad. With passion and love, they spent almost two hours filling in the details. I was surprised by how cloudy my memory was. Dad smiled often, surprised by all the details I didn't know, behind-the-scenes stuff.

Dad told me when he attended AA for the first time.

"One of the things I attended before going to jail was an alcohol course. Mom and I decided to go through this alcohol program. It was an eight-week program. That's where I met Tom, the instructor. Tom went through a similar situation, perpetrator and incest survivor himself. He asked, 'Why are you here? What brought you to this program during the one-on-one admission process?' I'm one of these people who when asked, I answer as honestly as I can.

"I'm not perfect though. It was one of the hardest things I had to do. I was embarrassed, ashamed, yet I did what I had to do. I needed help. I learned about all the affects of alcoholism. Tom explained things to me for the first time, and I was both crushed by what I had done to my family and yet hopeful. He saved my life."

I can honestly say all that Dad and Mom did to help me touched me. I had no idea and probably wouldn't have cared back then, but what they went through could probably fill another book. I even asked them if they wanted to write with me, but they both declined. They said they just want others to learn from the book. Learn what to do and what not to do.

Chapter *18*

TAKING RESPONSIBILITY AND SAVING ME

Nearly four months had passed since Dad's arrest. While the drama continued at home, he remained in county jail awaiting trial. The district attorney had acquired all the necessary statements, evidence, medical findings, and whatever else they needed for their case. Days before the trial was set to begin, Dad had his final meeting with his attorney.

"Mr. Gresham—Bob—the DA is seeking thirty years. You need to plead not guilty when we go to trial. We can fight this."

"No, I want to plead guilty. I did this. I deserve to be punished."

The primary bargaining power for Dad's defense was pages of transcripts from the four-hour deposition I had provided. It contained a number of "I don't know" and "I don't remember" responses that the defense attorney used to lessen the number of counts against Dad. Because of the number of questionable areas in my deposition, the DA offered a twelve-year sentence.

Once again, Dad's attorney consulted with him. "Bob, there are holes in the evidence. We can fight if we go to trial. I'm confident I can get you less than twelve years. Please consider a 'not guilty' plea."

"NO! I'm going to plead guilty. I will not cause another minute of pain for Lynnette. If I plead not guilty, she'll have to testify. I won't do it."

"But Mr. Gresham—"

"I don't care what the report says," Dad said. "If she says it, it's true. I won't put her through any more pain. I'm pleading guilty."

At that point, the attorney decided to give up the fight. He returned to the negotiating table with the DA to inform him of Dad's decision. A court date was set.

As instructed, Mom and I arrived at the courthouse for the final court date. Just before court was scheduled to begin, the DA asked Dad's attorney if he could meet with Mom and me. Following a brief conversation with Mom, Dad's attorney escorted us into a private room where the DA was waiting.

The district attorney looked directly into Mom's eyes and asked, "Mrs. Gresham, what do you want to happen to your husband?"

Pausing for a moment, the anger and anguish she felt was undeniable. "He has to pay for what he's done. I don't want it to be twelve years, but he does have to pay."

His eyes softened before looking my way. "Lynnette, what do you want?"

I want my family back. I want Mom to stop crying. I want her to love me. I want a normal family. I want … In nearly a whisper, I said, "I don't want my dad to go to jail. I just want it to stop."

The district attorney folded his arms and settled back into his chair. I believe a moment of clarity came over him as he considered all the factors in this unique case—a case, no doubt, very different from the majority he had prosecuted in the past.

1. The report given by the child was sketchy and riddled with "I don't remember" responses, and the medical report was only able to determine that the child had had sex.
2. The abuse involved only one of four children in the home versus predator-like behavior.
3. The father took full responsibility and was willing, without question or debate to the accusations made, to accept consequences.
4. Regardless of defense opportunities, the father would not allow his daughter to testify for any reason.
5. The parents confronted the situation. Both mother *and* father were present, cooperative, and accountable.
6. Therapist reports stated that, amid the turmoil, the family had been united since day one.
7. The parents put Lynnette and the other children first, at all times.

The district attorney left the small conference room and entered the courtroom where Dad and his attorney were waiting. The judge was notified, and court was called to order. Following a few brief exchanges between the judge and both attorneys, Dad entered a final plea of guilty. Based on his findings and the discussion with Mom and me, the district attorney surprised everyone by recommending a one-year sentence. When the gavel came crashing down for the second time in my life, an enormous sigh of relief escaped from Mom. It was if she had been holding her breath for four months and finally allowed herself to surface for some much-needed air.

Our family was indeed different from others. At no time did Dad fight for himself or his freedom; rather, he fought for me—for his family. How odd it seemed that, regardless of the cost, the one who had hurt me the most was the one who had fiercely protected me. During those times of trial, I remembered one of Dad's greatest life lessons: Own what you did and take responsibility. If you make a mistake, admit it because if you lie about it, the consequences will be significantly worse.

Chapter 19

WORKING ON GETTING BETTER

Memories for me were like a series of short films spliced randomly together, so trying to explain the details about the trial to the girls proved challenging. Kenzie and Alex seemed satisfied with what I had shared that day at Chick-fil-A.

I remember that it seemed as though the girls were experiencing information and emotional overload. I imagined they would need time to digest what they'd heard. When we got home, I hugged them both as I said, "I know this is a lot to process. Just give it some time. If you think of anything you want to talk about or have any other questions, just ask me, or Dad, or Nonnie. I love you both very much."

As I navigated through writing, and before I even started, I had being going to therapy. Diane was my fourth therapist. She had been remarkably helpful, especially when I needed to schedule an emergency appointment. Her calmness was soothing, and her words felt like the Holy Spirit was flowing right through her.

"I am still so filled with anxiety and depression. There are days when having to take the girls to school is about all I can do.

I'm afraid Madison is getting fed up with me and this book, and the girls must be tired of hearing about it."

"The Lord will carry you through this, yet I see why you're anxious. Remember, there is nothing He cannot handle. Scripture shows us that God doesn't choose those who are equipped. He equips those He chooses."

"Then why do I feel so beat down?"

"Hard work takes it toll, and from what you've told me, it sounds like Madison and the girls are your biggest supporters. Lean into God. He is providing you with all you need, and rest. It's okay to take time given all you're trying to do."

I don't know what I would have done without Diane. I don't know what my life would have been without therapy. I had learned from my years of therapy that God has provided us with the tools we need to heal. Therapy is one tool that I think too few people use. I remember telling a friend once that the importance of therapy is we can't see everything about ourselves with our own eyes. For example, I can't see my back or my forehead with my own eyes without the help of a mirror. Therapy is like a mirror, a tool to help us see the things we hide from and fear, and therapists are just people we need to listen to us vent, wail, and analyze what we see in the mirror.

Over the years, I'd counseled the girls about school issues, friend drama, or even dealing with me. I remembered making sure to suggest that they could talk to other people if they wanted to. Once I explained to Kenzie, "Sometimes you need to vent. You need to be heard. I know it may seem like I don't understand what you're going through, so here is a list of safe people to talk to. You can go to them anytime about anything." I gave her the list of names and phone numbers of trusted family members and friends.

A week or so after revealing my childhood to the girls, I explained how therapy had been a part of my life.

"Did therapy help you?" Kenzie's sweet face smiled up at me.

"Yes. I had someone to turn to who wasn't biased, who wanted to help my family and me."

"Like Diane?"

"Yes, like Diane. I had therapy from the beginning."

"Did everyone have therapy?"

"Yes. My mom and dad made sure Robert, Mary, and I all had therapy, some more than others. My stepsister was an adult by then, so my parents couldn't make her go, but I've been told she did. Everyone tried to heal … in his or her own way."

Our discussion went on as I explained the group therapy I was in and some of what my parents did. I also wanted to make sure the girls knew that their grandpa wasn't the same person who had abused me. I went into greater detail about the efforts he and Grandma had taken to learn and grow from this tragedy.

Chapter 20

DAUGHTERS UNITED

*O*n January 6, 1987, I began attending group therapy through Daughters United, a subsidiary of Parents United. Our weekly sessions took place at a local church. Mom's AMAC meetings were held at the same time in a different part of the building. Because I already had weekly counseling sessions with Paula, I was less than excited to spend yet another evening talking to a bunch of strangers, but since I didn't have a choice in the matter, I did as instructed.

The group therapist, Linda, had a very welcoming spirit. Unlike Paula, she provided an immediate sense of safety and comfort—something I lacked in life but desperately craved. I was rather guarded when it came to openly talking, but in time I began to trust and share tiny increments of my story. Though I'd always been a strong-willed, opinionated young girl, years of abuse had nearly muted my voice, which made group therapy a difficult transition.

Generally, eight to ten girls attended each meeting. We started by introducing ourselves and sharing why we were there. Actually speaking aloud the words "I'm Lynnette, and my dad molested me" somehow made the abuse seem more real. I had lived in a shroud of secrecy for so long, but no more. The shroud had been lifted, but I didn't know whether to be grateful or fearful.

Most of the time, Linda suggested a topic or posed a question for the evening. Some I recall vividly, such as the following:

- Do you ever have sudden flashbacks about being molested?
- When you were being molested, did you sometimes try to pretend you were somewhere else or make yourself numb?
- Because they're afraid, most girls don't struggle against their molester, but later they feel guilty that they were too easy. Do you ever feel that way?
- Sometimes girls don't tell about being molested because they are trying to hold the family together. Is that true of you?
- Have you ever been able to tell your molester how you feel about him? If not, what would you like to say?
- How do you think your mother feels about your being molested? Do you think she looks at you differently now?

The questions immediately resonated with me. I felt as though someone had been watching through the windows of my home and knew exactly what went on.

Other times, Linda provided a scenario to the group and then asked each of us how we would respond. In addition to processing our feelings, we were asked to talk about our molester(s) in ways that seemed rather odd. At first I didn't understand why, but ultimately the exercise encouraged us to humanize our abusers.

- What are some nice things you can share about the person who molested you?
- How do you think your abuser felt after they molested you?
- Do you have fond memories of times with your abuser?

No matter her approach, Linda always got the group to look beyond the abuse itself. She wanted us to learn how to protect ourselves going forward—not only from our original abusers but from potential ones as well.

I also liked that group therapy allowed me to be around other girls who had also been abused. Except for Amelia in the TV movie, I thought I was the only one who felt this way. No one in my life could relate to my pain and experiences, but group therapy was like having a room full of Amelias.

The first girl I befriended was Brandy—a skinny girl with red, spikey hair whose eclectic dress screamed rebel. She didn't have a fake bone in her body, and she never missed an opportunity to make her opinions known. What I loved the most about Brandy was that we simply "got" each other. Her father had abused her, too, so we didn't have to explain the various feelings swirling inside of us. We understood each other because we had lived the same pain and shame. It was so refreshing not to have to justify a bad day or elaborate on a rotten mood. Brandy became my living Amelia, and I loved her from the moment we met. Initially, I thought my friendship with Brandy and the strength I garnered from her got me through some hard times at therapy. I considered her a gift from heaven. At the time, I never understood that God had also given me survival skills and a feisty attitude that tugboated me through the murky channels.

In time, I became more and more comfortable talking about the abuse and began actively participating in the various discussions. When new girls came in, I was able to see right through them. While quick to call them out, I also never missed an opportunity to help them. I slowly but steadily developed self-analysis skills, which I would employ again and again in life. Some of the greatest lessons I learned from Linda in group therapy were

- It's **NOT** my fault.
- It does **NOT** define who I am.
- I **HAVE** control my own life and my decisions.
- I **HAVE** to respect myself before others will respect me.
- **BE TRUE**—don't change who I am for others.
- **DO NOT** be ashamed of what happened to me.

Linda was incredibly wise, and her gentle demeanor brought a sense of comfort and security. I shared with Mom my desire to have Linda be my individual therapist as well as group therapist, but there was little she could do about it. Linda was not covered under our insurance plan, and Mom couldn't afford to pay her directly. I was forced to continue seeing Paula, but Linda's presence in my life offered the saving grace I needed to survive.

WORKING ON GETTING BETTER

I wasn't the only one who worked hard to heal. Dad attended Parents United group therapy before he was incarcerated, and when he went to jail, he asked his individual therapist if there was group therapy available as well. When he learned there were no programs in place, he insisted that there should be. The therapist discussed the possibility with other inmates who were in jail for the same crime, and more than ten men agreed to create a group. To Dad's surprise, a neighbor who had been friends with our family joined the group. Dad, his fellow inmates, and the therapist met weekly in addition to their individual therapy.

Dad was moved from the county jail to Glen Helen Correctional Institute in San Bernardino County. Since he had been in county for four months, he had only eight months remaining to fulfill his sentence. He knew why he was there and remained steadfast in his decision by taking advantage of every opportunity provided to him. He willingly took part in individual therapy and did whatever was necessary to make things right. During therapy, Dad confessed for the first time that he had been molested as a child. He learned how sins of the past are often carried from generation to generation, rendering those who are abused as children to usually (but not always) become adult perpetrators themselves.

In therapy, Dad admitted to abusing drugs and alcohol. He began to understand that substance abuse erratically altered his judgment. When he sobered up and realized what he had done, the guilt was so overpowering that it made him sick to his stomach. Rather than face his demons, however, drugs and alcohol served to mask the denial and guilt. The cycle was seemingly endless.

Drunk = Abuse; Sober = Guilt; Guilt = Drunk; Drunk = Abuse

Communication, making amends, and trying to rebuild relationships were all included in his therapy, and Dad willingly embraced them all. When I heard about his progress, I couldn't help but be proud of him. He never avoided talking full responsibility for his actions, which went a long way toward helping me heal.

I never talked on the phone or went to see Dad in prison, but we did write letters from time to time. Mom and Mary visited weekly while Robert visited sporadically.

DAD'S RELEASE: APRIL 1987

Dad fulfilled his prison sentence with exemplary behavior and a willingness to do whatever he had to in order to regain a healthy status. After serving four months in the state prison, he was released for good behavior and would spend the remaining four months on parole. Part of the early release conditions included a separate residence from the family, so Dad secured an apartment not far from the house and immediately began attending Adults Molested as Children (AMAC) with Mom. Upon release, convicted offenders generally attend a group therapy session through Parents United specifically geared toward the perpetrators themselves; however, Dad met and exceeded the perpetrator therapy in prison and was allowed to forgo that condition of his release. In addition to mandatory group therapy, Dad wasn't allowed to come to the house without Mom present. When he first started coming by, I felt extremely nervous, but my desire for life to return to normal and for Mom's stress and melancholy to end trumped my fear. If that meant being around Dad, I was willing. In addition, Dad acted like a different person—definitely the result of a combination of being sober and going to therapy. My fears lessened with each passing day.

Linda recognized the variety of emotions that washed over me during that time. Her approach to communicating these concerns in our group was tepid but extremely empathetic. Her first priority was to ensure my physical safety and emotional security.

Life at home had improved little, and the dysfunction of our family dynamics grew increasingly unstable. Our immediate family tackled the trauma head-on, but extended family remained in the dark regarding Dad's arrest and still assumed he had been imprisoned for drunk driving. Unfortunately, the secret wasn't going to stay hidden for long because not long after Dad's release, Grandma Mary came for a visit. Mom had previously scheduled a doctor visit for me, and to avoid missing more work, she asked Grandma to take me.

The last time I was seen by a doctor was during the state-ordered medical exam. I sat nervously with my hands crammed into my jacket pockets and feet crossed as the doctor began flipping through my chart. Without blinking an eye, the first question out of her mouth was "I see you were molested by your dad." Shocked by her audible proclamation, I turned to look at Grandma. Every ounce of color instantly drained from her face, leaving the whitest of white I had ever seen. She never said a word to me about what she learned that day. Instead of bombarding me with questions, she opted to save the inquisition for Mom when she arrived home from work. As with every other adult conversation when I was growing up, I wasn't privy to what was said, but I'm sure it was laden with anger, sadness, and tears. I felt relieved that Grandma didn't speak with me about it. I had no desire to divulge the humiliating details with her. Realizing that she finally knew the truth was bad enough, and her silence, for once, was golden.

As the months passed, the entire family continued to attend therapy, making every attempt to restore the family dynamics to some semblance of continuity. Occasionally, we visited Dad's apartment or he would come to the house. Still, no matter how hard I tried, being around him always felt awkward.

Group therapy seemed like the only place I truly felt at ease. Being able to relate to the other girls and share similar stories provided an outlet absent in every other aspect of my life. Individual therapy sessions with Paula felt like a waste of my time, however. No matter what I did, I couldn't connect with her. I derived the vast majority of my progress from my time in group therapy with Linda at the helm. Mom recognized the heartfelt connection I had with her and decided to speak with Linda about becoming my individual therapist. It took weeks to process all the paperwork, but in the end, Linda would assume the role of my individual therapist as well as my group therapist. I could not have been happier!

Chapter 21

GODSEND

For years, therapy had been part of my life. The girls and Madison didn't seem surprised when, after moving to Texas, I found a new therapist. As with every therapist after Linda, I compared my new therapist to her. I still vividly remembered the triage-like therapy I had in the beginning and the precious gift God had given me to survive: Linda.

The girls and I continued to have many conversations. After explaining how therapy helped us all, I decided it was time to explain the true nature of Nonnie's relationship with me. The work I did with Linda, aka Nonnie, saved my life, and I wanted my girls to understand how important therapy was to me and how special Nonnie was to our family.

The kitchen was bright with afternoon sunlight shining through the bay windows near the kitchen table. I had just finished making lunch and sat with the girls at the oak table we'd had since Alexandra was born. I was surprised at how the my girls still loved peanut butter and strawberry jam sandwiches as I watched them eat, smiling to myself, as I slowly stirred the leftover chicken vegetable soup from last night's dinner. My eyes fell on Kenzie's beautiful curls springing out of her messy bun.

"Kenzie, you know you're named after Nonnie, right?"

"Yes. She's our godmother. Mom, I've heard the story."

"Indeed she is. But now I want to tell you both the story about how she became your godmother. You know we are not Catholic, so she became yours and my godmother because God sent her to me when I needed her most.

"You know Nonnie was a school counselor, right?

"Yes," they both chimed.

"Well, did you know that before she became a school counselor she had her own private practice as a therapist?"

They both shook their heads as they moved from their sandwiches to the cooling soup.

"Well, based on California laws, a therapist cannot have a personal relationship with a former patient until they forgo communication for two full years." I smiled and took a breath. "So when your dad and I moved from California to Baltimore, Linda and I severed our therapist/client relationship and had no communication."

"She was your therapist?" Kenzie's eyes seemed to be processing all the files she'd stored on Nonnie and me. As the question sunk in, the inquisitive look turned into grin.

"Yes. The best. Next to your dad, Nonnie is the one person who knows me the best. She was there for my family and for me, even after all these years."

My eyes glossed over as I remembered. My heart began to fill with a tenderness that no one else in this world has ever replicated. Linda had taken me under her wing over twenty-five years earlier and had never let me down. Going from group therapy to individual therapy with Linda continued what I considered my triage therapy. Most importantly, it built a relationship that forever changed my life.

Chapter 22

RAINBOWS OF SAFETY

As I walked into Linda's office for the first time, I felt incredibly nervous yet excited. Having been around her in group therapy sessions over the past year, trust and safety had already been established, but something felt different—special—about going to her office alone. Unlike group, I didn't have to share her with anyone else. I wasn't accustomed to having the limelight, let alone someone's undivided attention—positive, healthy attention, that is.

During our time in group therapy, I had taken clinical stock of Linda. She had a presence about her like no one I had ever met. I knew she was someone I wanted to be around. Always meticulously dressed with a flair for a bohemian, hippie-style of fashion, she was adorned with matching accessories from the top of her head to the tips of her toes. Color-coordinated jewelry dangled from every appendage and makeup was always perfectly applied to her gently tanned, fair skin. Exquisitely manicured nails were painted to match her whimsical dress, and she had the most extensive collection of high-heeled shoes

I had ever seen. While her manner of dress was somewhat funky compared to what I was accustomed to, I found it very pleasing and inviting. Her short and curly dark brown hair was laced with delicate red hues, which reminded me of Cherry Coke. Being the only one in my family with curly hair, it was nice to see that someone else had found a way to tame her unruly manes. But ultimately Linda's electric blue eyes and enormous smile provided the safety and security I so desperately needed. Yes, Linda felt safe, and I was excited to finally step into her mysterious, private domain.

Our first appointment would begin ten minutes late, a characteristic that became the norm. As time passed, I came to understand that she would rather run late and allow her current patient to complete a thought process than stringently watch the clock. I sat patiently in the waiting room and took a mental inventory of my surroundings. Walls were adorned with eclectic pictures that drew your eye to their vivid colors—the exact opposite of the bland beige and brown hues I had grown up with. Chairs lined the walls along with a small refrigerator that housed a selection of beverages for the taking. Across the small room stood a five-gallon Ozarka water tank, which offered hot and cold dispensing. Hot cocoa I mixed myself soon became my comfort beverage of choice.

The door finally swung open and out walked Linda in a delicate flowing skirt. She looked as if she walked on air. "Lynnette, would you like to come in here with me?" Without uttering a word, I stood up and sheepishly proceeded to her private office. The small room felt like a serene sanctuary filled with every color from a springtime rainbow. The first thing that drew my attention was a beautiful cream-colored damask chaise lounge, so luxurious and inviting—the kind of chair only the rich and famous could afford. Opposite the chaise lounge stood a cushy midnight-black upholstered love seat with matching pillows. On the other wall stood a golden oak secretary desk littered with disorganized cubbyholes, scattered papers, and an extensive supply of pens, pencils, and markers, as well as colorful sticky notes attached to nearly everything. A glass fish bowl filled with various rocks and colorful crystals perched on one of the small side tables. I had never seen such a unique assortment of stones and found myself especially drawn to the beautiful pink crystal nestled against the bowl's edge.

For the first time in over seven years, I felt like I could truly breathe. I didn't know what to expect from my time with Linda, but I felt secure, protected, and genuinely cared for—unconditionally. Linda had a disarming way about her that made me feel incredibly safe. I knew she wouldn't hurt me or give me dirty looks for things I hoped I would have the courage to say someday. Intimate details regarding the abuse were never discussed in our group; rather, we focused on the aftermath and healing. So sharing specifics was unchartered territory. Nervousness aside, her office—which represented her care, attention, and wise counsel—felt like a place I desperately wanted and needed to be.

I saw Linda twice a week—once in group therapy and once in individual therapy. She never forced me to talk about anything I didn't want to. One of her many gifts was taking a subtle backdoor approach to therapy called distracted treatment therapy. Whether we sat on the floor and painted our nails or played a game or she allowed me to arrange the cubbyholes in her desk, our time together felt less like attending therapy and more like having a conversation. Sometimes I picked up the pink crystal from the glass bowl and a black pillow off the loveseat, plopped down on the elegant chaise lounge, and repeatedly dropped the crystal into the center of the pillow. Watching the crystal plunder into the black darkness reminded me that beauty could survive amidst the darkest of places.

Throughout the years of abuse, I'd been conditioned to deal with uncomfortable circumstances by avoidance and escape. Regardless of my emotional disconnect, Linda always managed to keep the conversation going in subliminal, therapeutic fashion. She never made me say icky words; instead, she always referred to body parts by their clinical names, which made them seem a little less disgusting.

Talking about details of the abuse was extremely difficult, but the most challenging hurdle was surrendering the responsibility and guilt I carried. *If only I had kept my mouth shut, none of us would be going through this.*

Every session, Linda continued to instill various truths in me, saying, "Lynnette, what happened to you is not your fault. It is not your responsibility. You have every right to be mad and express your feelings."

Unfortunately, I didn't buy into her assurances as quickly as she offered them. *If it's not my fault, why is everyone still mad at me? Why does Mom seem so broken? I can tell she's struggling. She's like a zombie, just going through the motions. Why does Mary still fight with me about everything? Why is Robert so determined to run away from the family?* No matter how many times Linda said those words, I couldn't get my mind around them.

Linda also worked to boost my self-esteem by telling me how pretty and smart I was. She desperately wanted me to break free from the innumerable, all-consuming insecurities I possessed, but her words made minimal impact, if any. When it came to what others thought of me, I remained shackled by self-doubt, fear, and disgust with everything I saw in the mirror.

No matter what Linda or anyone else said, my internal self-deprecation screamed louder; after all, I was responsible for the brokenness of my family. While I could relate to the girls in group therapy, that took up only ninety minutes of my weekly life. Aside from the guarded relationships I had with James and a couple of other classmates, I felt alone. My fear that someone would learn the truth prevented me from joining school groups or activities, which magnified the isolation.

Chapter 23

MOVING FORWARD BRINGS REALIZATION

*S*ummer flew by, and school set the daily schedule. The girls had been amazingly supportive after I told them about my childhood abuse. Unfortunately, Madison and I had become frustrated with my lack of writing progress. We both struggled to understand that, for every written page, I invested hours and hours to interview, remember, and endure pain and emotional exhaustion. Though I'd shared portions of my story before, neither he nor I anticipated the unrecognized and hidden pain writing in such detail would reveal. Regardless of our impatience and frustrations, though, he continued to encourage me along the way.

During my weekly therapy with Diane, she continued to use Eye Movement Desensitization and Reprocessing (EMDR) therapy to address the kinesthetic issues that writing brought up. She reminded me that using EMDR would allow me to move through the memories and reprocess the information with my now-adult understanding. During our session, EMDR revealed a surprising revelation.

During my abuse, I had tightly closed my eyes, turned my

head to the side, and said nothing. The full impact of what that meant hit me later in the evening as I lie in the fetal position, nearly paralyzed with pain and tears. Madison tried to understand what was wrong, but I couldn't come up with words to adequately explain the depth of my pain. Nightmares flooded my sleep, and my body shook throughout the night. It was all Madison could do to hold me and remind me that I was safe. "It's okay. I am here. You're safe," he lovingly reassured me.

Diane had explained the possible effects, but what I was experiencing was a combination of scary and exhilarating. I called Nonnie (Linda) the next day to talk over the revelations and the physical effects of the EMDR therapy.

Linda and I got to the purpose of my call after I gave her a brief rundown about how the girls, Madison, my parents, and I were doing. I then turned to how I had felt after the EMDR and what I was learning through writing and therapy.

"Emotionally, since that fateful day in September over twenty-five years ago, I felt my family, in a variety of ways, said that the had abuse stopped; the trauma was over. That I've been in therapy, and it's time to move on."

"Why do you think you feel that way?"

"I've felt that for years all of our lives had centered on the abuse. Maybe they felt that I'd gotten all the attention and they just got tired of dealing with it and me. 'We don't see anything wrong with you—you have no scars or marks. You look normal and talk normal, so let's just be normal already! Stop making such a big deal it. We're sick of hearing about it, and we don't want to talk about it anymore.'"

"I've heard you say this before, but has anyone ever said these things to you, Lynnette?"

"Not directly."

"I want you to know that while this trauma will never leave you, it doesn't have to hold you captive. I think what you're hearing from your family is they want to see you whole and happy. They, themselves, want the same for them. For a long time, your relationships with your family have had many ups and downs, but there seems to be a significant shift in the last few years. I also see how this time with Diane is allowing you to let go of the hurt, especially with your sisters and brother. I am amazed at the transformation I'm hearing with your relationship with your parents as well.

"It's time, Lynnette. Time to let go and release the pain you've held as your shield for so long. Try to really see who they are now, as adults."

I used my shirt to wipe away the tears as I listened to Linda. After I had explained all that had happened and how I had felt for so many years, I was able feel God's peace wash over me. Linda and I began to talk about who my parents and siblings are now and what kind of relationship I could have with them. Though I was physically sore from the muscle tension, emotionally I was free from the conscious and subconscious drain from guilt for destroying my family. I felt as if I might have found that elusive sense of normality and the family acceptance I'd longed for for decades.

Chapter 24

TRYING TO BE NORMAL

As my sixteenth birthday approached, our family entered the "be normal" phase, and their opinions toward me seemingly shifted. Though no one came right out and said it, I felt their message clearly: get over it.

It had been a year and a half since I had ripped my family apart. I take responsibility for it because that's how I perceived their behavior toward me. Oh, they *said* it was his fault. They *said* I wasn't to blame. But every glare, tight-lipped word, and crossed-arm stance told me otherwise. I went through therapy. I didn't tell anyone about the abuse I suffered from other people. I didn't talk about how alone I felt. And I didn't prolong my therapy with any other issues. In a sense, I hurried through my healing because I felt forced to. I believed my family failed to understand that I had emerged from the trauma with invisible Band-Aids all over me, yet no one could see the deep wounds that still existed. From the outside, I may have looked normal, but no one knew the depths of my emotional pain, and I felt powerless to make them understand.

Weary from the pressures of my family, I began to cancel appointments with Linda. Desperate to be free from therapy yet clueless about how to execute an exit plan, I was terribly afraid to cut ties with Linda, my one and only safety net. Linda recognized my mounting frustration and decided to begin working on my self-image by having me write a list of words describing how I saw myself. Following were the words that came to mind:

> I like helping people; Understanding; Lonely; Caring; Want to be a teacher; Sympathetic; Flexible; Harsh yet tender; Honest yet deceitful; Don't let others know who I really am; Hopeful; Clumsy, yearning to be graceful.

After reviewing my list, it became apparent that I was a chameleon. Depending on the circumstances, I had garnered the necessary skills to become what I needed to be—to survive. Therapy with Linda, my friendship with James, and budding independence had helped me find my voice, and I enjoyed the power I derived from using it. My day-to-day behaviors became passive-aggressive—I always did what people wanted but loathed them with obvious mannerisms. I employed several customary weapons, including making comments under my breath, rolling my eyes, and giving looks of utter disdain. I targeted everyone, especially my parents. *They deserve it. They hurt me. They don't care. They just want me out. I can't wait to leave.* Followed by *Can't they see I'm still hurting? Can't they see all I want is for them to love me? Why don't they fight for me? Why don't they love me? I will forever be alone.*

Weeks after my parents bought me a car, I got my first job at a fast food restaurant. Transportation and money brought a kind of freedom I'd never experienced, and for the first time in my life, I felt truly liberated. Though my mom and dad established boundaries regarding curfew and places I could and couldn't drive, it didn't take me long to learn the art of manipulation.

Newfound freedom also brought levels of experimentation. I tried smoking cigarettes, but I decided it wasn't for me after nearly turning green. Desperate to be desired by someone other than my father, I dated lots of guys, which ushered in my search for self-worth through others. While I never initiated intimacy, it seemed the only way to garner their affection. I had no boundary skills, so when I told boys about going to therapy, they either expressed disgust for my family or viewed me as used and therefore easy prey. Both scenarios merely fueled my lack of self-worth and loneliness.

A couple of months before my seventeenth birthday, I mistook conquest for love. It was the first time I consciously instigated intimacy with anyone. Within days of the encounter, I felt used and discarded, which left me devastated. Following the rejection, my emotions plummeted down the "I'm worthless" mentality I had fought so hard to overcome. *Is sex all guys want? Is that all any man will ever want from me?*

When I returned home after work one evening, I retrieved a straight blade from Dad's toolbox, went into my bedroom, and proceeded to slit my wrists like I had seen in the movies. Blood immediately began to trickle down my hands, but the pain kept me from going too deep. Inside I was dying, and it seemed I finally had an external representation of my internal trauma. I sat on my bed and stared at the mangled skin of my left wrist for a while, wondering what to do next. I eventually put large bandages on both wrists and wore a long-sleeved shirt to hide the wounds from my family. I had become a master at hiding my wounds. Part of me wanted everyone to know, but fear, once again, silenced me. At work the next day, I intentionally pulled up my shirtsleeves so everyone could see the bandages. My feeble attempt to garner sympathy and attention went unnoticed, which merely fueled the self-loathing.

From that point forward, I manipulated men to get what I

wanted—using them, if you will—and then I cast them aside before they had the chance to reject me. Cycling through boyfriends represented power. Unfortunately, I lacked the maturity to understand the lasting damage I would cause myself by recklessly and ruthlessly trading my body.

Feelings of isolation and loneliness always followed sex. I had so many questions about sex, questions I didn't dare ask anyone. I knew only one person to turn to for truth: Linda. She didn't chastise my reckless behavior; instead, she always explained things to me and cautioned me about the choices I made. Linda tried to explain the fear of abandonment I was experiencing and how to cope with it. Yet no matter the knowledge she shared, I couldn't help but feed the emotional leeches of abuse and the rebellion of adolescence.

FOR THEM, ALWAYS FOR THEM

In late August, not long after school started, someone broke into our home. Thankfully, no one was home when it happened, but everyone was shaken by the violation. Fearful for our safety, Mom asked me if it would be okay for Dad to move back home. *Are you kidding me? He's just going to start molesting me again. Why won't you choose me, Mom? But I miss Dad too—just like everyone else. Why am I so weak? Why can't I just hate him enough to keep him away?*

Wrought with mixed emotions of wanting Mom's love and approval and Mary's acceptance, I agreed to the request. But before he was allowed to return, Dad's parole officer wanted a letter from Linda stating the family was ready. Following a long therapy session with me, Linda wrote the letter of recommendation. Because her main concern was Mom being emotionally equipped to protect us, Linda stipulated that Dad was not allowed access to any of the kids without Mom's presence. By mid-October, we were prepared for his return.

I hoped that life at home would be like old times—only

without the abuse. Because Dad assumed predatory behavior only when he was drunk, and given that he had been sober since his arrest, I felt almost confident he wouldn't touch me. With truth on my side, I felt empowered and no longer feared him. If it had been up to me, I don't know if would have ever wanted him to come back, but our family's life was about more than just me. If that meant that Dad needed to move home, I was willing to do my part to try to be normal. I loved my family.

Chapter 25

MOVING FORWARD AND LETTING GO

It was hard to believe that September was nearly over. The daily routine continued—girls up and off to school, morning Zumba class, home, clean, work on the book, and therapy with Diane, where Ernie became the latest topic.

Nearly every other week I had talked to him about his moving to Texas. He said he wanted to escape the drama of his past and begin anew. Between medical issues, disability, rejection from family members and long-time friends, traffic violations, repetitive drug abuse, drug charges, jail, rehab, and turning sixty-three, he wanted a fresh start. He said he wanted to be near the daughter who, after all these years, still desired a relationship with him. I was the only one of his three children who had offered words of love and devotion throughout the years. I had yearned for him for so long.

"When is he coming?" Madison walked into the bedroom just as I hung up the phone.

"He's not sure. He said he as a few more things to handle, but hopefully next month."

"I'm sure that will make you happy." Madison bent down to kiss my head full of curls. He was right. I was happy and excited. The dad I had yearned for was finally coming to be with *me*.

Chapter 26

A FATHER FOUND

No one in my family understood the depths of my struggles and loneliness. Some days I believed their lack of understanding was one of the most difficult challenges I faced. Desperate to connect with someone outside the circle of abuse, I decided to use some of my newfound power to contact my biological father, Ernie. Wanting to meet him wasn't a one-time thing; rather, I never lost the desire to know my father. Over the years, my mother sparingly shared information about him and his family. Given everything that had happened, I felt I had the necessary leverage to convince Mom to let me see him. Basically, I tried a this-dad-wasn't-good-so-let's-try-the-first-one approach.

My father, Ernie, was the eldest of ten children; six siblings were from his parents' marriage and the last four were from his mother's second marriage. His parents divorced when Ernie was nine years old, and his mother quickly married. I'd heard stories of abuse targeted at Ernie and his siblings. He was often bullied in school for his lazy eye and dark skin. Based on appearances, people expected Ernie to conduct himself as a typical no-good, wetback Mexican.

All Ernie ever wanted was to be loved and accepted, but he had issues—major undiagnosed issues. He told me that doctors had diagnosed him with bipolar disorder and depression later in life, along with abandonment issues and emotional abuse. Sufferers typically mask mental illnesses of this nature with drugs and alcohol, and Ernie was no different. He hid his drug and alcohol use well. However, after they married, my mom became abundantly aware of his issues. He used drugs and drank to excess, which spawned unpredictable behavior. Mom explained his Jekyll and Hyde nature to me. Sober Ernie was loyal, loving, kind, generous, and romantic toward my mom. He doted on us kids and worked hard to provide. Mom fell in love with his complimentary and affirming personality. But when inebriated, he changed completely. He became physically and verbally abusive and demanding (borderline obsessive compulsive). He humiliated everyone around him through his words and deeds.

Nearly a lifetime had passed before I understood the complicated events that had transpired when I was young, but regardless of his flaws, I still yearned for my father's love and attention. Plus, I knew I had several aunts, uncles, and cousins I'd never met. When my biological parents divorced, Ernie's entire family seemed to divorce us as well. Presented with the opportunity to show my mother that she might've been wrong about Ernie, I took it. I desperately hoped someone would rescue me from my miserable, anxiety-ridden life, just like Cathy's mom had rescued her. Ernie seemed the only logical choice. But before approaching Mom about it, I decided to talk to Linda first. We discussed various reasons why I should and should not meet Ernie. After making a list of said items, it seemed that the pros outweighed the cons.

Armed with my due diligence, I pitched the idea to Mom. To my surprise, she agreed. Maybe her overwhelming guilt influenced her decision. It didn't take long for her to locate Ernie after she got in touch with his extended family.

Within days, Ernie called the house. I don't remember much of the conversation other than setting up a meeting at Denny's the following Saturday. Mom had no desire to see her ex-husband, but she didn't want me going alone either. So she made Mary and Robert accompany me.

On Saturday morning, Robert reluctantly drove us to the Denny's in Chino. Walking through the double doors, we scanned the diner. Though we'd seen a few old pictures, we didn't really know what Ernie looked like. It had been more than ten years since we had seen him. To our left, a man stood alone between the door and vending machine. We suspected it might be Ernie, but we hurriedly walked past him and stood across the waiting area next to an elderly woman.

Nervous giggles escaped our lips as we talked about the man near the door.

"Did you see him?" I asked.

"You talking about the man by the door?" Mary tilted her head in that direction.

I nodded.

"Yeah, I saw him."

Robert stood there, mouth agape. "Our dad is Mexican!"

With that admission, any attempt to contain our giggles proved futile. While we knew the origin of our father's heritage, we were taken aback by his appearance. Granted, we had only a handful of formal dance pictures in Mom's collection of photos to give us any clue as to what he looked like, but I'm sure we didn't hide well our surprise at discovering our own ethnicity.

The man, who was indeed Ernie, walked toward us, put his arms around the older woman sitting next to us, and said, "Hello. I'd like for you to meet your grandmother, Dorothy."

Shocked by his unforeseen introduction, I quickly replayed everything we had just said about our father in front of her. But it was too late now to do anything differently.

After we exchanged awkward greetings, the hostess ushered us to a semi-circle corner booth where Ernie and Grandmother Dorothy sat on one side and Robert, Mary, and I remained knitted together on the opposite side. Everything seemed so surreal. A million things rushed through my mind. For years and years I had dreamed of this day, but now that it had arrived, I didn't know how to act or what to think.

Our lunch tended to be less conversation and more Q and A—nothing specific or memorable per se, just general inquiries as to how we were and what we had been doing. While Ernie and Dorothy directed questions at all of us, Mary and Robert answered most of them. I don't know if I felt starstruck by Ernie's presence or struggled to find the right words that would entice him to love me, but nothing with any impact seemed to escape my lips.

Ernie looked directly at me from across the table. "You talked so much on the phone, but you seem awfully quiet now."

"Well, it's easier to talk on the phone." I bit my lip and glanced down at my hands, twisting my napkin in my lap.

With that, he redirected his conversation primarily to Robert with an occasional nod to Mary. I sat in silence, as if watching a movie. I left the meeting feeling somewhat high. My heart raced from the sheer excitement of finally meeting my real dad and being welcomed into his family. I hoped that, with Dorothy's influence, my enormous family would embrace me. I longed for them all to save me and love me.

Robert and Mary were less enthusiastic. "I already have a dad and don't need another," Robert said. Being the eldest, Robert had memories of Ernie that Mary and I didn't share. He never spoke fondly of him or had any desire to see him. Mary, on the other hand, had been an infant when Ernie left, so she had absolutely no memories of him. Bob had always been her dad, leaving no hole for Ernie to fill. But I was riddled with potholes and scars, covered in emotional bandages. For a million and one reasons, I desperately craved Ernie's love and attention.

I began phoning Ernie every chance I got. I also started calling him Dad instead of Ernie. I initiated all contact and made every call. After all, I wanted him to know that I was *his* daughter, not Bob's, and I loved him and would remain loyal to him. His lack of initiative never bothered me; rather, it fueled the steadfast desire I held to know him and for him to know me. *I just know it's only a matter of time before he learns to love me and be proud of me. And when he does, I'll finally be invited to all the family functions. After all, he's my dad. Of course he'll want to spend time with me now.*

WEARY LIFE

Dad's moving back home did little, if anything, to change the dysfunction in our household. Mom still seemed distant and, at times, angry with me. Mary continued to be mad at everyone. By the end of the year, Robert had moved out to live with a girlfriend. He always isolated himself when he didn't feel well, so I saw him even less than I saw Mom. Our family officially became part of the Victims of Crime Program, enabling us to continue therapy at no cost. Linda and I met once a month, and the entire family together saw her monthly as well. My wounds were as deep as ever, but I managed to mask them in front of the family to appear normal. Only one word describes our life during those months—*weary*. We collectively and individually remained isolated from one another. We merely went through the obligatory motions of being a family.

Linda diagnosed me with PTSD, post-traumatic stress disorder. I didn't really understand what that meant, but she encouraged me to continue our therapy sessions and work through discovery issues. Given that she was still my touchstone to reality and truth, I agreed.

Chameleon characteristics served me well during this time

in life. I felt the most powerful at work, where I was outgoing, jovial, authoritative, self-assertive, and confident. I saved as much money as possible and planned to move out immediately following graduation, in hopes that I could eliminate the negativity that home and school brought. At school I was guarded and insecure, an academic wallflower who never fit in. At home I was passive-aggressive, isolated, dissociative, and confused. I didn't fit in there either.

Over time, my anger and frustration swelled like a river overflowing its banks. My cries for help went unanswered. Either those around me didn't recognize my needs or didn't care. Didn't matter. The result was the same. I was an outcast. Following my unsuccessful suicide attempt, I couldn't find a way to expunge my pain. Frantic and with nowhere to turn, I felt desperate to find some release. One afternoon, I grabbed a large butcher knife from the kitchen, returned to my room, and began stabbing my bed pillow over and over until I couldn't stab anymore. Every stab symbolized how much I hated them, whoever "them" was. Physically and emotionally exhausted, I stared with tremendous relief at the mangled pillow. Emancipating the pain I had carried for so long in such a violent way brought a sense of peace and comfort to an otherwise troubled soul. Before going to sleep that night, I slipped a cover over the battered pillow, methodically placed my hand inside the pillowcase, and began stroking the innumerable holes. Every time I saw, touched, or slept with the pillow, I felt a sense of security and comfort wash over me.

That pillow took the brunt of my wrath. And from that moment on, I consciously implemented my life "Not's."

- I was NOT going to get pregnant like my mother did.
- I was NOT going to drop out of school like my parents.
- I was NOT going to smoke like my parents.
- I was NOT going to drink excessively like my parents.

- I was NOT going to be used by another man.
- I was going to be good, NOT bad.

With newfound boundaries, I felt more empowered than ever. James and I continued to grow closer and closer, despite the fact that my mother adamantly disapproved of our friendship. James helped build confidence in me, and with that confidence, I became more and more disobedient. Though we dated off and on, James and I were best friends more than anything. He was safe and affirming, and he held me accountable for my actions. I'd finally shared with him the whole truth about what had happened, but he never judged me or made me feel immoral for what I had been through. I could confide in him and never fear a negative response. We weren't physically intimate—just kisses and hand holding—which promoted complete trust and assurance. James didn't want from me what other boys did. The love we shared was pure yet unfulfilling in a romantic sense. While we lacked physical chemistry, our undeniable emotional chemistry grew stronger every day. Simply put, James understood me and I cherished him.

At times, I held onto James's strength so tightly that he felt overwhelmed and would push away, but we always seemed to come back together and begin "dating" again. His influence in my life allowed me to see the possibilities outside the dysfunction of my family. My life had been tainted by years of lies and deceit, but James helped me realize that the words people spoke could be generally true and sincere. In time, I found myself believing that someday I might find love—pure, true, and satisfying love.

Mom seemed to blame my newfound opinions and rebellion on James's influence. She told me she found his assertiveness to be controlling. Regardless of her disdain for James, he and I remained inseparable throughout my senior year. Between finishing school, working part-time, spending time with James, and dating other people, I found it relatively easy to maintain a safe distance from my family.

As 1990 drew near, things at home began to improve. My relationship with Mary got better, to the point of her being nice to me at times. Robert struggled with his relationship and living situation, oftentimes bouncing back and forth between their apartment and our home, but overall he supported my growing independence.

I generally dated older men but always seemed to end up back with James in the interim. Tensions between my mom and him continued to escalate to the point that he hated coming over to my house, but I resolved to not let my parents' views come between us. From time to time, James went to therapy sessions with me. Though he never had much to say, I liked having him there. Somehow his presence fueled my strength and confidence.

James faithfully asked me to the senior prom, and I wholeheartedly accepted. Mom was disgusted with my rebellion and boycotted my pre-prom preparations by leaving the house and refusing to help me get ready. Her anger was so intense that she rejected the notion of taking even one picture.

Graduation loomed on the not-so-distant horizon. Graduation meant freedom—freedom from the hurt and pain I felt I had been living in my entire life.

First Love

Immediately after graduation, I enrolled in community college where I met my first true love. Scott was three years older than me and served active duty in the military. His tall, muscular physique, messy hairstyle, and stunning blue eyes captured my attention from first glance. The military uniform was a double bonus. Sitting and talking for hours seemed like only minutes. I fell hard for him. Instantly.

With James away at college, having this new love in my life

minimized the loneliness and helped me to realize James's love had been more of a constant, unconditional, brotherly love. This new relationship was my first romantic love where I actually saw a future. We were together almost every day.

During one of our nights out together Scott surprised me. "I need to talk to you about something." He took my hands in his.

My heart pounded in my ears, but I focused on the deep blue of his eyes and refused to give in to fear. "What is it?"

"I'd like to move back to the east coast. I miss my family."

"But—"

"I can't wait for you to meet them. They'll love you!" He stroked my cheek lightly with his index finger.

"I-I don't know what to say. I need to think about it."

Over the next few days, my mind just began to swarm with anxiety and fear. Despite the dysfunctional nature of my parents and siblings, they were still my family. They were all I'd ever known. Fear ripped my heart, and the thought of moving away nearly paralyzed me. I didn't want to be so far removed from everything and everyone I knew. Flashes of my mother's life entered my mind—pregnant and dropping out of school. What if he dumps me? I will be stuck in Baltimore, alone. Alone scared me more than anything. I had felt abandoned all my life, but this would include physically alone too. Everything in my mind screamed no. As much as I loved Scott, I just couldn't do it. Without warning, I ended the relationship. I can still recall the look of intense shock on his face when I told him.

I was crushed, but I stayed steadfast in not seeing him. As difficult as it was, I knew I'd made the right decision. I heard from a mutual friend that Scott had gone ahead with his plans and moved back to Maryland. I thought I'd never see him again.

Two months later, Scott appeared on my parents' doorstep, unannounced. He professed his love and heart's desires and begged me to reconsider. *He drove all the way across the country for me—just me. It must be true love!* He even promised he would stay in California so I could be near my family and continue my education. How could I say no?

We got along well, and our relationship seemed to be moving in a positive direction. We moved into a house with roommates, and he enrolled in trade school. I continued working part-time and going to school. After nine months, he graduated and secured a job in another city. We decided that I would finish the semester of school while Scott worked on getting us an apartment near his new job.

At first, we talked daily, but as time went on, his calls became less frequent. Near the end of the summer, he called and ended the relationship. This time I was the one who was blindsided.

"I need time to myself," I remember him saying.

"Then why did you come back for me?" I wailed through tears.

"I loved you."

Loved … that was all I heard from the rest of his explanation. Loved, past tense. *What did I do wrong? Why was this happening to me? Why doesn't anyone love me? God, why am I so alone? Why do you hate me too? Everyone will leave me. Everyone. No matter what I do.* "Everyone *will* leave me" imprinted on my heart that day, and the internal negative dialogue continued for hours, days, and weeks.

My heart shattered into a million pieces like a dropped antique china doll. Even worse was the condition of my pride. I had failed at love. The last thing I wanted to do was go back home, but I had limited choices. The few friends I had were in college or married, so I knew I'd have to return to the very place I had worked so diligently to escape.

I resigned myself to the difficult task of calling Mom to ask if I could move back home. I took a deep breath. We exchanged greetings, and then I jumped right into it. "Mom, Scott dumped me. I had no clue it was coming."

"I'm sorry to hear that."

"Can I move back home?"

"I'm sorry, Lynnette, but we've decided to move to Santa Maria to live near Dad's brother and sister-in-law."

"Why?"

"We want a fresh start. It's a smaller town and simpler way of life."

Reeling from her announcement, I paused for a moment. "Will you please take me with you?"

"Yes, of course you can come, but you have to go to school and get a job."

"Okay, I understand." I paused and swallowed the lump in my throat. "Mom, thank you." I hung up and sobbed at how pathetic my life had become. *That was humiliating, simply humiliating. But still, she loves me. I should be thankful for that. And she took me back.* I packed up what little I had, returned home, and prepared for the move to Santa Maria.

SAME THING, DIFFERENT TOWN

I had few concerns about being alone with Dad in Santa Maria because Mom had to finish her job. Now sober, he seemed to have stayed on track since he had gotten out of jail. Also, Mary would be there. And unlike before, I felt empowered to handle situations that might arise. Linda had helped me find my voice, and I wasn't afraid to use it. I confided in Linda via letters and phone calls when I began seeing signs that Dad was drinking again. He had been spending a lot of time with his brother who was a heavy drinker, and I believed wholeheartedly that Dad had joined right in. I called Linda first and then my mom. Mom wasted no time confronting Dad, but he denied everything. Without seeing it firsthand, I couldn't prove my suspicions. The accusations I lodged made me appear paranoid and unstable, thus labeling me a troublemaker. Soon afterward, Mom moved to Santa Maria. Though Dad didn't drink, I felt a large degree of animosity present in the house, just like old times.

I enrolled in the basics at Allan Hancock Community College and secured a hostess position at a Marie Callender's in a local strip mall. I liked my new job and easily morphed into the work chameleon—greeting customers and working the counter from time to time. Inside the strip mall was a coffee shop. There I met Steve, the forty-something coffee shop owner and a daily customer at Marie Callender's. Everyone liked him.

Steve's genuine smile every day always cheered me up. While I wore a smile for those around me to see, it was purely from the neck up. Nothing in my heart radiated happiness. Still nursing the emotional wounds from Scott, my days consisted of school, work, and home. My parents, finally fed up with my lack of a social life, said, "You need to get a life. From today forward, don't come home until 6:00 p.m. Find somewhere to go, something to do." Miffed by their latest conditions, I went to the only place I could think of ... the library.

Every afternoon, I sat amid the quietness of the college library and watched seconds tick by until it was time to go home. Though I strived to be a good student and worked hard, reading was my least favorite thing to do, so the library did little to fuel my spirit. *You want to be a teacher, but you don't like to read, right? That makes no sense.*

Finally, I met a boy and started to date. We maintained a proper courtship, meaning we never had sex. I liked him, but we had zero chemistry. Regardless, I continued to date him since going out with him beat sitting in the library night after night.

School had always been such a challenge for me. It seemed I had to work five times harder than everyone else just to get a passing grade. Math and English were the worst. After graduating high school and completing a full year of college, I still struggled to pass my remedial math course. *Remedial math! Ugh! You're so stupid. You're never going to amount to anything.* Little did I know that God would use that English class to change my life in two very dramatic ways.

The professor gave us an assignment to find various grammatical errors in several sentences. I took home the assignment, but I became frustrated trying to complete it. No matter how many times I reviewed the paper, I still couldn't identify any errors. The following day, I went back to the teacher and tearfully explained that I couldn't find them.

"Lynnette, based on what I've seen in your previous work, I believe it's possible you may have a learning disability. If you're willing, I'd like to refer you to the student center for further testing."

Though baffled, I agreed to her recommendation. A four-hour block of testing determined I was dyslexic. *How can I be dyslexic? I see all the words from left to right. I can read them. If I can do that, how can I be dyslexic?* Dumbfounded by the results, I sat back to assess my new reality. I knew my spelling and grammar were horrible. I knew reading was an extremely slow and labored process, so it made sense that my comprehension would suffer. In a moment of clarity, I decided to learn more about my affliction and how to overcome it.

Diving into the world of dyslexia, I learned I had a glitch in my mental processing. Things I heard or thought somehow got lost in what I would say or spell. Looking back over the challenging years of primary school, everything began to make sense. I decided to drop English Composition and focus on other areas of study I could master. More than ever, I was determined to succeed.

Chapter 27

BEYOND "WHY ME?"

*D*oubts. They consumed me sometimes. I had no doubt that these insidious thoughts plagued others; but at times, I seemed to waste hours thinking through each doubt. Each mistake. Each fear. On the outside, people saw the cheerful spitfire, the bold, sassy woman I am. But sometimes I just want to cry. I felt the insecurities well up within me and consume days and weeks of my life.

"Mom? Can I come in?" Alexandra was outside my door. She was going to want something. Ugh. I straightened to sitting in bed, where I had retreated after picking up the girls from school.

"Sure," I said as my emotions got stuffed down so she wouldn't see me sad/depressed yet again. "What's up?" I tried my fake smile.

"Nothing. I just wanted to hang with you." She climbed into bed beside me and leaned her head on my arm.

It was like this a lot. I think Alexandra and Kenzie just knew when I needed a hug. My selfish depression screamed, "Go away!" But my heart melted with gratitude.

Over the years I had turned to people pleasing, food, or television to escape the capture of depression, but recently

I'd taken my tears to the Lord. I seemed to talk to Him almost everywhere. Driving to visit friends, off to the grocery store, or while I was folding laundry. I felt that I was not alone. I felt His presence, yet just when I didn't feel Him, He sent someone to hug me, usually the girls or Madison.

As this journey of writing continued, I had asked Him many times if I was doing this for the right reasons. Was this book hurting my family? Would anyone benefit from the book? Would I just embarrass my family and myself? Time and time again, He led me to those who supported me, to those who saw value in my story.

"Hey, how is your book coming along?" my friend Crystal asked.

"You almost done with your book?" my friend Donna asked.

"Where are you in your book?" Marcy asked.

"Need anything?" Moina asked.

"I haven't heard from you in a while," Laurie said.

Even the ladies I had befriend in Texas started to filter in with words of encouragement. God was sending in His army again.

I don't have any special wisdom to share or any special techniques for healing, but I trust Jesus more than I trust myself, so I kept moving forward. Trusting Him has brought me so much joy. He had brought me so many people in my life. People who truly love and understand me and go the extra mile to support me. He even orchestrated my meeting Madison. As I looked back, His fingerprints were all over our meeting.

Chapter 28

MADISON

While at work one afternoon, Steve walked in with a very familiar face by his side. *That guy was in my English class. I wonder how Steve knows him?* Once I scanned past his tall, strong body clad in a polo shirt and khaki shorts, his piercing blue eyes and gentle smile mesmerized me. I couldn't wipe the smile off my face.

I leaned to whisper to one of my coworkers, "Hey, who's that with Steve?"

"That's his son, Madison."

"Really? I know him. He was in my English class."

I felt sure he wouldn't recognize me. Why would he? After all, I was merely a wallflower in a sea of beautiful people.

"Good morning, Steve." I hoped my grin wasn't too big.

"Good morning, Lynnette. How is your day going?"

"Pretty good. Kind of a busy breakfast rush, but lunch is a bit slow."

I grabbed two menus and led them to their table. After they were seated, I handed them menus. I returned to my station, but I kept darting my eyes their way while trying to appear busy. *He's cute, but there's no way he would be attracted to me.*

I had never cared much for coffee, but after I learned that Madison was Steve's son, I soon discovered a fascination for its delightful aroma. As often as possible, my coworkers and I began walking down to the coffee shop, smelling the various blends just so I could see Madison. Still, no matter how hard I tried, I simply couldn't acquire a taste for coffee. Fortunately, Steve introduced me to cinnamon-orange tea. Soon, a mug of steeping tea offered the perfect disguise for my continued visits.

On most days that I worked, I also visited the coffee shop. Madison rarely said a word to me, but his gorgeous eyes and gentle smile fed my soul. I had no doubt that Steve was aware of my infatuation.

One day, Steve asked, "How's school going?"

"It's okay, I guess. I'm having trouble with math, but everything else is fine."

"Really? You know, Madison's good at math. He could tutor you, if you like."

I couldn't believe what I was hearing. Steve had offered up Madison's one-on-one attention on a silver platter, mine for the taking.

"I'd really appreciate that."

"He'd be happy to help. Come on by the coffee shop when you get off work tomorrow."

Beaming with excitement, I blazed out the front door and ran back to Marie Callender's. *Madison is going to tutor me— alone! What should I wear? What will I say? Oh no, he's cute and smart. But he's barely said a word to me … ever. Who am I kidding? He doesn't even acknowledge me, so he obviously doesn't like me.*

The following day, I took extra care putting on makeup and inspected every stitch of clothing and strand of curly hair before going to the coffee shop. Madison and I sat down at a small round table and began reviewing my notes. As with our previous encounters, I did all the talking. Madison's verbal contributions were limited to short, to-the-point answers. Nothing came out of his mouth that wasn't related to math.

In a desperate attempt to connect about something— anything—else, I asked, "What other classes are you taking?"

"I'm only eighteen. I just finished high school. I went to college for English, computer programming, and calculus last term." I hoped my speechless surprise didn't show on my face, but his grin and smiling eyes let me know it did.

Madison's integrity never allowed me to cheat, and he wouldn't provide the answers. Rather, he always made me work the problem until I understood the concept. I struggled at first because I was so distracted, but his instruction proved immensely beneficial in the long run.

We met regularly for quite some time, but he never hinted at any sort of attraction to me. On Friday, July 17, 1992, I walked down to the coffee shop after work. The school semester had ended, so I had no *real* reason to go. Steve, Madison, and I were the only people there. Madison's incredibly shy demeanor remained untethered to my ridiculously obvious infatuation.

Exhausted after a seven-hour shift at the restaurant, I told them I should really head home. Before I walked away, Steve gave Madison a note. He unfolded the paper, quickly looked at it, and immediately blushed beet red.

"Don't you know it's rude to pass notes in front of other people?" I asked and quickly grabbed the slip of paper from Madison's hand. On it I read the words Steve had written. "Why don't you ask her out to Hudson's Grille?"

I'm certain I felt as awkward as they looked as all three of us turned deep red with embarrassment. I knew Madison would never ask me out now that I had read the note, so I stood up and announced, "Umm, I've got to go." I walked out slowly in hopes that Madison would run after me to ask me out. Sadly, he didn't. I got into my car. On the way home, I had time to think about what had transpired. It was all I could do to process my embarrassment and dread. Once home, I decided to call the coffee shop and speak to Steve. I was glad when he answered the phone and not Madison.

"Hi Steve, this is Lynnette. It's obvious your son does not like me. Please don't do anything like that again. You embarrassed Madison and me."

"No, no, hold on a second."

Madison got on the phone and wasted no time saying, "Lynnette, would you like to go to Hudson's Grille with me tonight?"

"Yes."

We made arrangements to meet. As I hung up, I had fleeting thoughts of the library guy I had been dating. Every single ounce of chemistry missing with him was ever-present when I was in Madison's presence. Nervous (in a good way), I decided to follow my heart. After showering and changing into my cutest outfit, I drove to the coffee shop to meet Madison. Just as his father had suggested, he took me to Hudson's Grille, where I met some of his friends. Though slightly awkward, I felt thankful to finally be on an official date with Madison. From there we went to a movie before he drove us back to the parking lot and we said our good-byes.

At work the next day, I felt light as air and absolutely smitten. Not long after I arrived at the restaurant, Madison walked through the door and handed me a note—the first of many to come. Day after day, on note after note, we passed our feelings and thoughts back and forth. The sweet and tender sentiments he wrote often left me speechless. All I wanted was to be with Madison.

I ended the relationship with the other guy over the phone, but he showed up at my doorstep, unannounced. When Mom answered the door, she told him I was working, but he insisted on waiting for me. When I arrived home, I was shocked to see him there. Mom cast me a familiar frown before she left the two of us alone. We had a short conversation. I knew I didn't want to date him, and he finally accepted it.

As I walked into the house, Mom promptly bawled me out.

"I don't want your drama going on around here. Don't bring another boy home unless there's a ring on your finger. Do you understand?" After my many on-again/off-again relationships back in Chino and the drama with Scott, Mom had had enough.

"Yes." I rolled my eyes as I walked to my room. *Whatever! You don't care if I go out with an ax murder. God, I hate you. Why can't you just be supportive? Why do you help everyone else but me?* Given the new requirements, I didn't bring Madison home to meet my family.

Madison was so sweet and smart, and he always conducted himself like a gentleman. Whenever I talked, he genuinely listened. Still, in the back of my mind, I worried about how he would respond when he learned about all the dirty little secrets about my family. *Is he going to be like all the other boys and leave me or try to take advantage of me? Probably. From what I've seen, all men are the same.*

I had lived a lifetime worth of secrets and lies and had grown sick of it. I decided to tell him everything, and I mean everything. *I'm not going to string this out and get my heart broken yet again. All my life I've been invisible. I want someone to know me—really know me.* James had known me, but Madison was different. We had a physical attraction. This relationship had potential. But I felt so broken and lost at this point in my life. Most days I just barely hung on. I knew Madison would abandon me if I told him about my past, but I just had to put the truth out there and let go. Either he would stay and fight alongside me or the shock would scare the bejeebers out of him and he'd take flight.

On our third official date, we went to dinner. After, we headed to the car, where we sat and talked.

I adjusted myself sideways in the seat, swallowed, and took

a deep breath. "Madison, before we go any further, I want to tell you some things about me."

"Okay, shoot."

For the next two hours, I explained everything to him—my parents' divorce, Mom's second marriage, my stepsister, brother, and sister, the adoption, and how I had been physically, emotionally, and sexually abused. I paused briefly. When Madison said nothing, I continued. I told him how I had forgiven my parents and was living with them again. Throughout the entire confession, Madison never uttered a word. He allowed me to pour out my heart, while he listened with empathy, not sympathy. When I finished, I looked him straight in the eye, "Now that you know everything about my past, if you don't want to see me anymore, I'll understand."

He didn't say anything to the contrary. In fact, the next day at work, Madison gave me a note that read, "I'm in 100%."

I don't think he knew what he was getting himself into, but later, when we discussed my past in more detail, he got very angry with my parents. He didn't understand why I continued to live with them and still seemed to love them. I thought this would be a deal breaker, as it had in the past, but he was willing to accept the fact that I wasn't going to just leave my family. I explained that Ernie had left, and they were all I had. He tried to understand but made it known that he thought the sexual abuse and the way they'd treated me were egregious and unforgivable. *On one hand, I agree. But on the other, they're all I have. If I don't pretend to forgive them, they'll leave and I'll be alone. I can't risk that. Just pretend with me. Please.*

MEETING DANIELLE STEEL

Our courtship immediately took off. We saw each other nearly every day, but one day in particular changed the course of my life. As usual, Madison had planned our evening date. After dinner, we decided to walk the strip mall. We strolled along, chatting endlessly as new couples do, when we wandered upon a bookstore's window display. Madison stopped and pointed out a few books he liked, sharing intricate details about various authors and literary genres. I looked at him in awe, mesmerized by his obvious confidence. Madison knew I had dropped the English course where we first had seen each other, but he never knew why. Enamored by his intelligence, I didn't have the confidence to tell him about my dyslexia. Instead, as I had done so often, I feigned interest in a green book with a beautiful jewel on the cover. "I like that author." As it turned out, it was a Danielle Steele book.

At the end of our incredible summer together, Madison prepared to leave Santa Maria to attend college at the University of California San Diego. Experiencing his unconditional love and support over the past two months felt very natural, so his departure left me feeling alone again. Madison called often, but between long distance charges and his incredibly shy nature, we rarely talked for any length of time. To stay connected, Madison lovingly wrote to me every day—and I mean every single day! Sometimes the letters would lag behind and two or three of them would get bunched up in my mailbox. Receiving several letters at once was better than Christmas morning.

I took painstaking effort to write him back. Thankfully, a pencil allowed for corrections, and the dictionary was never far from my side. In addition to letters, Madison sent the Danielle Steel book we spotted in the bookstore window. Confident he would want to have some sort of literary discussion about it, I began reading the book. After a full two weeks and thorough use of the trusty dictionary, I finished the first book I had ever read cover to cover—a feat I'd never completed in high school or college. During one of our phone conversations, I proudly said, "I finished the Danielle Steel book you sent me."

"Cool."

"Well, don't you want to discuss the plot or the characters?"

He stifled a chuckle. "Danielle Steel is a romance writer. I don't read that stuff."

Floored and a bit deflated, I finally explained my dyslexia. I poured out how long it had taken me to finish the book, the difficulty I had had with the words, and how I just knew he'd want talk about it. He told me he was proud of me and asked me if I liked the book. Regardless of the time and effort invested, I did. From that point on, Madison bought me *every* Danielle Steel book, and I've read them all.

I slowly realized that Madison and I were sharing our deepest fears and dreams and were falling in love—real love. *This is never going to last. Madison will leave like they all have. Eventually he'll see the real me and bolt.*

The week of Thanksgiving, Madison came home for an extended visit. I couldn't wait to see him. Throughout our letter exchanges and phone conversations, we mutually agreed that we wanted to live closer to each other. Over break, we formulated a plan for me to move to San Diego. Since Madison lived with his grandparents, I would have to support myself, so finding roommates seemed the only viable option. What happened next would bring the first major test of our relationship and pour fuel on my burning sense of inadequacy.

THANKSGIVING 1992

Madison and I discovered we had many polar opposite characteristics. Our first Thanksgiving together would prove to be no different, especially in the ways our families approached the festive occasion.

We joined my family for Thanksgiving lunch—an uncomfortable situation given it was Madison's first holiday with us. Our impending announcement increased the tension and added to our anxiety. We sat there, waiting, as Mom, Mary, and Grandma Mary made last-minute preparations in the small kitchen. I could have counted the seconds on the clock as they slowly ticked by. Once the food was arranged, my mom announced in typical fashion, "Come on, let's eat." Like a band of emaciated soldiers just coming home from war, the entire family jumped up, hurried to the table, and the feeding frenzy began. We all heaped mounds of food on top of the paper plates supported by cheap wicker plate liners. We crisscrossed one another's arms as we reached for the next serving spoon. The volume of the family chatter increased as the food piled on our flimsy plates grew. Madison's eyes were as big as silver dollars as he watched the animalistic ritual unfold. *Yep, my family eats like a pack of homeless dogs.* I wanted to crawl under the floorboards to escape the embarrassment. Since we had plans to eat again later with his family, Madison and I agreed to eat small portions to appease my family.

Once everyone got their food and found a seat on the living room floor, Madison and I looked at each another, our signal that it was time to tell them about our plans.

"Mom and Dad, there's something I—we—want to tell you." They just stared at me, waiting for what they knew I was going to say. "Madison and I want to be closer to each other. Well, we love each other, and it's really hard for us to spend time together with him off at school, so I've decided to move to San Diego."

Mom spoke first. "Are you sure that's what you want to do, honeybun?" Using her term of endearment for us kids softened my heart. Still, I knew I had to get out of this house.

"Yes, Mom. I'll continue to go to school down there, and … and I will have roommates." My voice shook nervously as I explained the plans Madison and I had made.

Though my parents had just met Madison, they knew we were "hot and heavy" for one another. Naturally, they raised a few questions of concern, which I answered dutifully but firmly. From what I could gather, they knew I was an adult, Madison seemed to make me happy, and I wasn't happy living with them. Without much discussion, they give me their best wishes. *Wow, that was easy! I guess they don't want me here any more that I want to be here. Maybe Madison's announcement to his family will be just as easy.*

Arriving at Madison's parents' house for dinner, I walked into an entirely different look and feel to the holiday. The dining room table was dressed with a tablecloth and real plates with glasses and silverware neatly set. His mom had tidied the house by neatly tucking away small stacks of belongings. Delicious aromas filled the air, not the cigarette smoke I was accustomed to. Madison's parents, Steve and Sandie, his brother, Morgan, Madison, and I would presumably dine on delectable Thanksgiving favorites. The formality of their holiday compared to the casual gatherings I grew up in made me uncomfortable, but I resolved to do my best to impress them.

We sat down at the table where we were served very different foods compared to the turkey, German potatoes, green beans, and rolls I had grown accustomed to. The spicy potatoes were seasoned unlike anything I had ever tasted. "Sandie, your potatoes are really different. What did you use to season them?"

"Those are turnips, dear," she responded smiling.

"Oh."

Growing up, we were accustomed to sitting on the living room floor when we ate and then getting up and leaving the room when we were finished eating. We never waited for everyone to finish or paid any attention to one another, unless it was to run to get seconds before the food was gone. Not so at Madison's house. The entire clan stayed seated at the dining room table until everyone finished and then furthered their roosting by tacking on a lengthy conversation. I couldn't have been more uncomfortable, but I was determined to follow protocol.

When the opportunity presented itself, Madison finally broached the subject. "Mom and Dad, we would like to tell you some things. Lynnette and I are in love. We would like to live closer to each other, so we've decided that she is going to move to San Diego." I heard the heater click on. My stomach churned, as the shocking silence filled the room.

"I'm going to continue to live with Grandma and Grandpa and go to school, and Lynnette is going to get an apartment with roommates near the community college."

As Madison continued to deliver the announcement, I watched their faces go from red-hot shock to pale with worry. They sat patiently and waited for him to finish before uttering a word. I hoped they would share my parents' same passive response.

Sandie began first. "Madison, there are a number of reasons why this is a bad idea. First of all, you've only known each other for a short time. What's the rush? Trying to maintain a relationship will detract from your studies. In addition, you are both so young, and trying to find an affordable place to live there will be difficult. We simply don't understand what the hurry is. You both have plenty of time to make this decision at a later time when you've completed your education."

The conversation escalated as our explanations didn't seem to satisfy Madison's parents. At some point, Steve began yelling at us. I can only assume that our announcement was contrary to the plans he had in mind for Madison's life, and he left no doubt I was never part of that equation. "This is unacceptable, totally unacceptable!" he yelled.

As Steve's composure spiraled out of control, I could feel tears beginning to well in my eyes. *This isn't the way this was supposed to go! What's wrong with me? Why don't they like me?*

Sandie did everything she could to diffuse the situation amid Steve's yelling. "Okay, listen. Have you considered waiting awhile or possibly taking more time to get to know each other? What about setting goals to better prepare yourselves?" But nothing she said or did affected the downward spiral of the situation.

After what seemed like several minutes of Steve's tirade,

Madison finally spoke. "Mom, Dad, I'm sorry you both feel this way, but we love each other and want to be together. We can do this." There was nothing more any of us could say.

I glanced from Madison to Steve and Sandie. The looks on their faces told me they realized our minds were made up. I further understood that no matter what we said, they would not agree with our decision.

When we left, I couldn't have felt worse or more scared. Growing up, I was always taught not to buck the system. If Mom and Dad said no, that was the end of the conversation—no questions asked and no rebuttal accepted. I feared the backlash Madison would receive from his family. I worried that they would always hate me. If his family abandoned him, I would feel 100 percent responsible.

Following our departure, we discussed their reaction as well as my concerns. No matter what I brought to the table, Madison stayed cool and totally prepared to take on the world for the sake of our relationship. *If he's willing to go against his family's wishes, he must really, really like me.*

The following Sunday, Madison returned to San Diego and I resumed my usual routine at work and school. My anxiety had reached an all-time high with anticipation of Steve's daily visit to Marie Callender's. Not long after I arrived at work, Steve walked in as jovial as ever, but he didn't so much as look my direction. His dismissive, passive-aggressive behavior toward me continued for the next several weeks. It was as if I no longer existed in his eyes. *What? I'm good enough for a summer fling with your son but nothing more than that? You honestly believe I'm going to damage his future, negatively affect the rest of his life?*

Frequent phone conversations with Madison provided me with a safe and somewhat comforting sounding board. "Madison, he won't even look at me, let alone speak to me. What did I do that was so wrong?"

"It's no big deal, and I don't care what he thinks. We know what we're doing. He's just going to have to get over it."

No matter what he said, I couldn't help but feel as though Madison was choosing to give up his family for me. At times the guilt felt so overwhelming it brought me to tears.

I knew I had to contact the one person who had never steered me wrong: Linda. We chatted about my relationship with Madison, our parents' different reactions, and what I wanted to do. By the end of the two-hour phone call, I knew I had to do something. With Christmas fast approaching and Madison scheduled to return home, I decided to humble myself.

With what little guts I could muster and a rehearsed script running through my mind, I walked over to Coffee & Company to face the situation head-on. But as I waited patiently for Steve to finish with a customer, fear and intimidation multiplied. I felt certain he could see me shaking on the very ground I stood. The moment he was free, I walked up to the counter, appearing braver than I felt.

"You can't go on being mad at me. I know this may all be happening too fast, but I believe in Madison. I love your son, and he loves me. I'm not moving down there to ruin his life. He's going to school, and I'm going to go to school. We're going to support each other. We just want to be closer to each other. The drive back and forth has become too much for him, and you know … well, we just want to see where this goes. I don't know what's going to happen. If I get down there and we end up not liking each other, I may have to move back. I just don't know. But you can't hate him, and you can't ignore me because I'm not going anywhere."

I stood there, waiting for his rebuttal, thoughts swirling in my head. *Did you think I was just a passing fling for him? I'm sure that's all you thought of me when you all but offered me up to your son. I thought you liked me and believed I was good for your son. Your charm lifted my spirits, and when you intervened to get us together, I thought it was because you saw something in me—something good, pretty, worthy. But I was wrong. You know I'm not smart or worthy. I'm just poor white trash as far as you were concerned. I'm sure he told you about my past, so I'm also tarnished goods. I guess I was nothing more than a call girl for your son. Well, forget it! I'm grabbing this opportunity and running.*

But what if Steve and Sandie are right? What if I'm not worthy? Deep down, I know I'm not, but Madison thinks I am. He's so confident about us, and I want so much to believe everything he says about me. He says I have potential, but is this love or just an escape from my life, my family? Madison seems to be more in love than I am. Do I even know what love is? I'm scared, confused, and worried.

I don't remember what, if anything, Steve said to me in response to my standing my ground, but our conversation lessened the tension. Unfortunately, though, whatever truce had been created would be immediately desecrated the day after Christmas.

Our Christmas traditions proved as strangely different as Thanksgiving had been. My family opened presents like a pack of hyenas ripping through a carcass all at the same time whereas Madison's family opened one present at a time while everyone watched. It took forever! After seeing our families, Madison and I went to Pismo Beach to exchange the gifts we had gotten for each other. Pismo Beach is a very romantic location with a small cliff that hosts a steep stairway to the bluff below where a white sand beach lies. Madison and I walked down to the bluff and took a seat just as the sun was beginning to set.

Since every bit of extra money went toward my dream of joining Madison in San Diego, my gift to him consisted of a couple of CDs and a book. After he opened his gifts, he reached into his bag and handed me a few wrapped packages. I opened the modest lot while we exchanged short, uncertain glances. Then with a near-perfect poker face, Madison handed me a wrapped package about the size of a shoebox. Tearing through the paper and opening the box, I was surprised to find another box inside, and then another, and then another. As the packages got smaller and smaller, I imagined he had gotten me jewelry—perhaps a pair of earrings, a necklace, or maybe a promise ring. I finally reached the end when what remained in my hands was a small jewelry box. I slowly cracked open the hinged lid. When I spied the contents, my mouth dropped open like a gaping largemouth bass. An engagement ring! I was utterly speechless.

Madison took my hand in his. "I've been thinking about this, and I want you to know that I love you. I take our relationship very seriously. I want you to know how important you are to me. Will you marry me?"

Before I could answer, he continued. "On one condition …"

Oh no, here we go. The other shoe is finally going to drop.

"Will you marry me on February 29, 1996, after I finish college?"

I gazed at the beautiful one-carat diamond solitaire, found my voice, and fairly shouted my answer without hesitation. "Yes!"

Wow, he does love me! But how can he love me so much so fast? Is this real love? Do I really love him that much? Are we going too fast? Well, at least we have four years to figure it out. Like Madison always says, "Let's wing it."

We arrived back at Steve and Sandie's and shared the news with them. They were anything but pleased. I felt grateful, however, that we avoided confrontation like the Thanksgiving fiasco. I believed Madison's condition to getting married after he graduated was primarily a compromise to appease his parents' concerns. Maybe that's why they didn't jump on the emotional bandwagon. They stood firm in their position that we were making a mistake, which felt like they were saying our relationship was a mistake and that we were rushing into things. Regardless, as legal adults, we weren't swayed by their intolerance.

Madison returned to San Diego, and I immediately began packing my things for my move in just five days. Lying in bed at night, I couldn't help but think about Madison. *He knows everything about me—all my insecurities—yet he still proclaims to love me. He's actually willing to take me away from this mess. I think I love him, but I'm not really sure. I mean, how does a person really know that? I guess if I end up not loving him, at least I'll get to wear this beautiful ring for a while. It'll be an adventure! I just have to see where this is going to go. Anything is better than being here.*

I was scared beyond reason, but Madison possessed a sense of maturity well beyond his years. He had such a reassuring way about him that I knew everything would be okay. I gave my notice at work, and on December 31, 1992, Madison drove his grandfather's truck to Santa Maria. We loaded up my things, said our obligatory good-byes, and began the five-hour journey back to San Diego. *What a great way to ring in the New Year—just Madison and me. It's going to be a great night!*

Given that I had not secured an apartment yet, Madison told me he had gotten a room at the Lucky Eight Motel and a small storage unit to house what little furniture I had. We stopped at the storage facility to unload the truck before we headed to the motel. It wasn't a very nice place to stay, but it was all he could afford. While Madison was inside getting the room key, the proverbial to-do list raced through my mind. *I've got to find an affordable apartment with roommates, enroll in school, and get a job as soon as possible. I don't want us to stay here any longer than we have to.*

Within minutes, Madison returned. He drove around the side of the building to the designated room. Thoughts of our first night together—alone—felt like a dream come true after the past weeks battling our families. Then, just as we finished unloading my immediate belongings, Madison broke the news. "Lynnette, I can't stay with you. My grandfather is waiting for me and expects me to return the truck to him tonight." Devastated, I could do nothing but choke back the tears and kiss him goodnight.

As the door latch closed, I found myself alone in the big city on New Year's Eve without a soul nearby to turn to. *This is not how I pictured my first night in San Diego—alone in a dingy hotel room with a nasty cheap metallic bedspread. What was I thinking? What have I done? Here I am, flying by the seat of my pants, and all I have to show for it is a diamond ring. Maybe it's not even a real diamond.* I lay down on the bed and, amid constant tears, began praying. "Lord, please help me know this is the right thing to do. Help keep me safe in this neighborhood. I have no idea where Madison is, but please let him be the person you want me to be with. Just protect me."

Looking back, I had no idea who God was. I prayed only when I needed something or when Dad abused me. *God never answered my prayers before, so why should He now?*

Prior to being abused, I had attended church for about two years. While I believed in God and had been baptized, I possessed only a baseline level of belief with absolutely no depth. I had minimal conviction or remorse for the majority of my juvenile sin or any level of gratitude for God's sovereignty. Faith and a relationship with God were not taught in those days; rather, instruction was more or less based on reading and memorizing the Bible. I had no understanding of God's overall plan. My life lacked meaningful spiritual assurances, but my prayers for provision and safety continued throughout the night. As the New Year rang in, I had exhausted every request I could muster to God and eventually cried myself to sleep atop the cheap bedspread.

The following morning, Madison returned to pick me up, and we began the quest to secure suitable living arrangements. His bright, cheery face was dramatically different than my puffy eyes and tear-stained cheeks. I couldn't have been happier to wrap myself in his loving, safe arms. During breakfast, we scanned room-for-rent ads in the local newspaper. Within minutes, we located a low-income condo not far from the community college and about twenty-five minutes from Madison. The place seemed perfect. By the end of the day, we had met with the two female tenants, garnered their joint approval, and began moving my things into the new residence. While my heart longed to be with Madison, the condo was far better than staying another night in that disgusting hotel.

My next two priorities were enrolling in college and securing a job. Within the week, I accepted a hostess position at Jolly Roger Restaurant and enrolled part-time at Mesa Community College. To say that times were lean would be an understatement, but my blue-collar survival skills definitely worked to my advantage. Work provided the means for rent but left little for food and other necessities. Many times, I bought a potato and a can of cream of mushroom soup, which I could spread out over two meals, or a package of tortillas, a can of refried beans, and a small package of cheese to make burritos. Madison introduced me to tuna melts—an inexpensive, quick, toaster oven meal that immediately became a dinnertime staple.

In March, Grandma Mary came for a visit and bought me an early birthday gift of pots and pans. Between school, work, bills, and Madison's grandparents, I remained in a constant state of anxiety. Still, I clung to the love and strength Madison continued to provide. For my twenty-first birthday, Madison took me to dinner and gave me a VCR and blank tapes to record my favorite soap operas—a habit I picked up from my mother and James. *I'm absolutely amazed at how generous he is to me, how much he looks out for me, even against his own family. He seems too good for me. This won't last. I know it.*

Madison helped financially as much as he could. His resources were limited as well, especially after purchasing my engagement ring. He told me he'd ventured to downtown San Diego to find a wholesaler to save money. After researching all the diamond qualities, he got a great deal. Though he was a savvy consumer, a college student's income is exceptionally limited. We spent our evenings together with Madison tutoring me through various courses and editing papers. On occasion, we visited his grandparents, Betty and Clark, for dinner, but no matter what I did, I always felt out of place in their company.

Chapter 29

THE OTHER WRITER

It was amazing that after all those years I still got nervous talking to her. Betty Simm was the matriarch of the Simm family. For years, I calculated everything I said or did around her, but now we chatted freely and lovingly.

"I'm trying to get through this big house and box up what I'm planning on taking to my new place. So many memories and not enough room for them all, which is why I'm calling," she said.

Rich treasures. That's what went through my mind. Madison's mom turned over such rich treasure when she and Steve moved from Colorado back to California a few years back. Madison and I opened the box and enjoyed the binder filled with pictures and awards that Madison had earned throughout his school years. We thrilled over seeing his Boy Scout badges, baby blanket, favorite teddy bear, and all of his baby teeth. Rich treasures. I can only imagine what Betty wanted to impart to us.

"I have unearthed several tablecloths and napkin sets. I thought you might want them."

"I'd love them. I love collecting rich treasures for the girls from their favorite great-grandma." I smiled sheepishly as her laughter filled the phone.

"I don't know about rich treasures, but I like knowing some of these things will be passed on. One of these my grandmother gave to my mother. Oh, the time goes by so fast."

Her voice softened, as I was sure she was thinking of the past. It was hard to believe Clark had been gone for nearly seven years.

"By the way, how are your memoirs coming along?"

"Good. Every day I sit and write. Every time I begin a story, one memory leads to the next, and I have pages and pages. I haven't met you yet. I'm in the seventies now." Betty laughed that tender grandmother laugh I had heard for years now. "How is your writing going, dear?"

"It's coming along. I'm not as committed as you are, though. It's been hard, but I'm at the time where I meet Madison, and you. Remember, Betty? So much has changed since then."

"I remember. Just write the truth as you remember it. That's what I'm doing. People may cringe, but they are your memories. I'm so proud of you and Madison. You a doctor and Madison a banker, and you've done such a great job with the girls. Just keep writing."

Years earlier, I never would have thought this conversation would have been possible. Years earlier, I knew she hated me.

"And Lynnette ... make sure you write about how therapy isn't a bad thing, and about how the Lord can change us all."

"I will, and I won't forget to look for those boxes of rich treasures. I love you."

"I love you too."

Over twenty-two years knowing that lady, and she still surprised me.

Chapter 30

KNOWING MY PLACE

In their early seventies, Betty and Clark were well-versed, educated people. They lived on an expansive piece of property in an affluent area in Encinitas, California. From the start, Madison made it clear that they were wealthy. Whether they worked for their fortune or inherited it was never divulged to me. Clark held a doctorate degree in geology and ran several businesses while Betty focused her time and energy on various charity leagues and her daughter's budding horse farm.

My initial impression of Clark was a relaxed approachability, but I found Betty's cultured, well-read mannerisms rather intimidating and somewhat snobbish. Desperate for their approval, I displayed good manners by always addressing them as Mr. or Mrs. Simm, being incredibly polite and respectful toward them, and attempting to use proper vocabulary whenever I spoke with them. The last thing I wanted to do was embarrass Madison, but it seemed like nothing I did would ever garner their approval—especially Betty's. Her passive-aggressive comments made it clear I could never be good enough for her grandson. She constantly chastised Madison, both in my presence and when she was alone with him, harping on the quantity of time he spent with me. No matter what, he always came to my defense and stood his ground. When the situation got exceptionally volatile, Madison would phone his parents and ask them to advocate on his behalf. No matter the defense, it seemed nothing would curtail the disdain she held for me. Thankfully, every negative comment from Betty's lips was met with more than double the love and reassurance from Madison.

The first day of the fall semester at UCSD arrived, and Madison stayed home sick with the flu. According to college rules, failure to appear for the first day of class would result in an automatic drop by the administration. Being in the pre-med program, dropping a class would have taken Madison out of his cycle.

He called me early that morning. "I can't possibly make it to class with this flu. Would you go to the campus today and stand up for me when they call my name? If I don't show up, they'll drop me."

"Won't they know when you go back the next time and you're a guy instead of a girl?"

The illness softened his laughter. "I'm one of one hundred-plus students in a lecture hall. They'll never remember."

"Okay. Fine. I'll come by and get your schedule."

When I arrived at the house, he gave me the instructions I would need—which classes to attend and where they were located on the campus. Being the ever-faithful girlfriend, I attended each of his classes and stood up when his name was called. Oddly enough, it would be the first of many times I would claim his identity.

After completing my task, I returned to Betty and Clark's house and gave Madison the various syllabi I had acquired that day. Seeing his flu-ravished body broke my heart. "I'm gonna head out. You're obviously sick."

"Please don't go," he pleaded. "Stay here with me."

"But you need to rest and get better."

"I don't want you to leave. There's a TV in here, or we could play some cards. Please just stay and keep me company."

"Okay, but only for a little while."

Not long into our time together, Betty returned home and entered Madison's room. With her polite but icy tone, she acknowledged me. "Thank you for helping Madison, but it's time for you to go."

"Madison just wants me to hang out here with him and play cards."

She immediately frowned. "No, honey, you don't understand. You're dismissed."

My eyes darted toward Madison, whose face instantly flushed red with embarrassment. He cut his eyes toward his grandmother's. "Really? You're *dismissing* her? She's not a servant, you know. I want her to stay."

Within seconds, an argument ensued, and I quickly decided to leave on my own accord. In no way did I want to add more stress and tension to Madison or his living situation. Later that evening, unbeknownst to me, Madison pleaded his case to his grandfather and then called his parents to summon any willing advocates on his behalf. He explained how I'd helped him with school and stated once more that I was his girlfriend. He told his family he wasn't a child, and they couldn't tell him what to do. While his parents understood Madison was an adult, he was living in his grandparents' home, and they didn't approve of our relationship or me. Madison fought a losing battle and ran the risk of isolating his family—all because of me.

From that point on, Betty and Clark began tightening the reigns. Betty, more so than Clark, acted more like a controlling parent than a grandparent. She gave Madison a curfew and told him when he could go and study with me. Invitations to have dinner at their home lessened over time, which sent a very clear message my way: "You don't belong here. You need to go back on the other side of the tracks where you came from. You're not now, nor will you ever be, of our class. Madison is above you."

In my eyes, it seemed my curly hair and olive skin meant I was no better than the Mexicans who worked their ranch. While these words never directly came from their mouths, their behavior said it all. Aside from "dismissing" me that fateful day, Betty was never overtly rude to me, but I always felt her eyes pierce me with judgment, as though she were just biding her time until Madison realized I wasn't worthy of him.

The tensions between the Simm family in Santa Maria and the Simm family in San Diego escalated. Steve and Sandie did everything they could to stand up for Madison—to no avail. By the end of the semester, Madison had had enough. When my lease ended, Madison decided we should move in together. I couldn't have been happier. After a year of struggling to see each other, I would finally have him all to myself!

When news of our impending cohabitation broke, the reactions we received from our families were as polar opposite as the previous holidays we had spent together. The Simm clan, both San Diego and Santa Maria, were anything but happy. Betty's church-going mentality immediately spoke about living in sin while Steve and Sandie feared living together would compromise Madison's long-term goals. *I hadn't even given thought to the fact we would be living in sin. What do I care? God never helps me. My whole life I've been surrounded in sin. Madison and I are in love, and we can make it.* My parents, on the other hand, were relatively complacent about it. If I was going to school and paying my own way, they didn't seem to care. Objections aside, we had made up our minds. Support or no support, we were going to be together.

Just when I thought I knew what I was doing ... he showed up.

Scott called, saying he wanted to see me. He said he would drive down to San Diego. Can he come?

I was shocked. I thought he was gone forever. Thoughts race through my head. I could leave Madison. His family would be happy, but he would be devastated. Against my better judgment, I agreed to meet Scott, but in a public place.

We met at a park near the beach. People walked along the concrete pathway; it was a beautiful Southern California day. We found a bench just off the path, close to the parking lot where we had met.

"I've missed you." His blue eye captured my heartstrings again. "How have you been?"

"Good. I'm still going to school and working. I'm dating a really nice guy." I added that to put in a weak boundary, as I was already meeting Scott without having told Madison.

"I just had to see you. To see if ... to see if we have a chance."

What I would have given to hear that a year earlier. What I felt next had to be the Holy Spirit; I can't explain it any other way. I loved Scott, but what I had with Madison was real, and it was being tested.

"Scott, I may love you for the rest of my life. You were my first love, but you left me. I can't explain it, but what I have with Madison is something different. He loves me and keeps putting me first. Over everything and everyone. I can't leave him to gamble on what might be with you."

His head lowered just a bit. I took his hand. "Should my relationship with Madison end, I will try to find you. But for now, I just can't. I won't hurt him."

"He a lucky man. I hope he knows that." His half smile brought back memories.

"I'm the lucky one. I need to get back." I stood up and gave him a hug and a light kiss on the cheek as we said good-bye. We both hesitated in our cars, but finally, I pulled out and headed back to my roommate-filled apartment. I didn't tell Madison about my visit.

TRYING

By year's end, Madison and I had moved in together and started making a home. We purchased a bed, set of dishes, pots and pans, clothes, and the ever-important apartment futon. We combined income from our individual restaurant jobs to pay our bills. Life as starving students was pretty normal—work, attend school, and live primarily on love.

Madison's major contribution to setting up house was a desktop computer and dot matrix printer. I didn't have much experience with this relatively new technology, so Madison willingly typed and edited all my English papers. We argued over very little, except schoolwork and housekeeping. Neither of us was exceptionally messy. Instead, like millions of other couples before us, we had to settle the menial annoyances of growing accustomed to each other—Madison leaving his shoes in the middle of the floor or my hanging a wet towel to dry across the top of a wooden door. When not at work or school, we spent every waking moment together, cooking, cleaning, paying bills, doing laundry, and shopping.

Sadly, Madison's abrupt departure from his grandparents' home left a rift in their relationship. Fed up with their controlling ways, he had little desire to be around them. I felt it was my responsibility to encourage and foster the relationship as often as possible.

"I know you're angry with them, but they're your grandparents. You need to see them."

"Why?"

"They're not going to be around forever, Madison. They have rich knowledge of who you are and where you came from. Besides, they're family. My family always said that friends come and go, but family is always there."

"But they're mean. They only like me when they like what I'm doing."

"You know what? They're just looking out for you. We need to go see them."

Eventually, he gave in to my insistence and called them. Over time, they began to see the positive impact I had made in fostering a continued relationship with them, and their discontent toward me began to subside. Though the relationship with Betty and Clark was improving, I still felt like I was auditioning for a part, which generally left me feeling like a failure.

Even alone with Madison I felt like I was constantly *on*. *If I keep doing what he wants, he won't abandon me.* This mind-set applied to everything. How to pay bills, where and what to eat, when to move, what to do at school, how to clean—everything.

Emotionally, I was *in* the relationship and feeling connected. True intimacy— holding hands, cuddling, kissing, and whispering words of encouragement—were wonderful, but I always sensed my inadequacy when it came to sexual intimacy. Because I wanted so desperately to please him, I always had sex when he wanted to, but it was never anything I particularly cared about. Though I fulfilled his physical needs, Madison became keenly aware of my emotional absence.

Endless discussions took place regarding his intimate desires. He wanted me to be present when we had sex—and by present I mean truly connected, emotionally, verbally, and physically. I was, for lack of a better analogy, a dead fish merely going through the motions. My lack of emotional connection truly bothered him because it left him feeling undesirable. While our intimate life was good—meaning I never felt scared—the underlying problem was, I never really felt anything at all. My body went through the motions and responded accordingly, but my heart just wasn't in it.

All my life, I'd been programmed to remain quiet during sex and let my abuser do what he wanted. My job was to lie there and basically disappear. The last thing I wanted was for Madison to pay the price for things other people had done to me. While my dad was the primary perpetrator, others had abused me too. After witnessing what had happened to Dad and the effect it had on my family, I never talked about the other abusers with Linda. I wasn't going to cause any more pain than I already had. But holding in pain and memories from the additional abuse prompted the nightmares to return. And all of it began to weigh heavily on my relationship with Madison.

In the midst of an argument, Madison's anger flared to heights I hadn't seen before. "I'm not them. I've never hurt you, have I? No, I've only loved you. I would never make you do anything you didn't want to do. I'm here for you, and you're safe with me. Don't you love me?"

"Of course I love you!"

"And don't you love being with me?"

"Yes, I love being with you!"

"Then why don't you want to have sex with me?"

Crumbled by the validity of his words, I longed to engage in complete intimacy. I also longed for the right words to help him understand. "I *do* want to have sex with you, but what you're asking me to do is hard. You want me to be animated and *enjoy* sex. But unfortunately, my mind doesn't like it and my body doesn't like it. I'm not like you, Madison. You of all people should understand that men and women are not the same. Men have a higher sex drive than women. I love you, but I don't need sex to love you. I could live without it." *Disappear to your pink palace, Lynnette. Just let them finish doing what they want with you and deal with the aftermath later.*

Madison wanted all of me, but I had no idea what that looked or felt like. I had no understanding of how to get there. He wanted to have sex in certain positions, the thought of which made me physically ill. He didn't hold any deviant desires. In fact, what he suggested was what any normal, healthy husband would want. But the mere idea disgusted me. Initially, I faked intimacy and enjoyment, but as the relationship progressed, Madison cued in and wanted more. What he wanted was less sex and more lovemaking. No matter how hard I tried, I was clueless how to fulfill his desires, which fueled my feelings of inadequacy.

Madison's eyes deepened with anguish. "I can't live without it, Lynnette. It's part of our relationship and very important to me. Making love connects us, and it's more than just sex to me."

My eyes filled with tears. "But you knew this going in. I told you when we first met all the things that had happened to me. And you're trying to make me behave in a way that you know is the hardest thing for me to do!"

"But I'm not them! Why do I have to continue paying for what *they* did to you?"

"You're not paying for what they did. I do love you, and I *have* sex with you!"

"But it's not … There's no passion in it. It's not like you need me or want me. You never initiate sex. You're not excited about it. It's like you're just lying there."

"I don't know what you want from me. I don't know how to do this. I'm having sex with you, and that's all I can do right now. But I'll try. I promise I *will* try!"

At the end of every argument, I cried uncontrollably. So much so, it seemed my tears would have no end. And each time, Madison would hug me and say, "Everything's gonna be okay. We'll work it through."

This sort of argument occurred every three to four months, and the dialogue was nearly identical every time. Inevitably, Madison would succumb to my brokenness by stepping back and apologizing and then telling me everything would be okay. Sometimes I would call Linda in hopes of garnering some level of insight. Though we never concretely resolved my issue, I found great comfort in her affirming wisdom.

"Lynnette, you're okay. You're not a horrible person. This level of disconnect is perfectly normal for someone with your past. You have to keep in mind that Madison never had abusers, so he has a difficult time understanding the depth of your pain. It's impossible for him to grasp the lasting effect it has had on you. As you work through things, your relationship with Madison will improve, I promise."

Our relationship continued to grow, as did the love I felt for him, despite the many issues stemming from the childhood abuse that we hadn't yet addressed. Issues I didn't even know about, issues that carried extensive and potentially deadly tentacles.

Chapter 31

TRYING TO HIDE
THE WOUNDS

*A*fter I finished writing the child abuse section of this book, I thought the rest of the story would just fly off the pages. Unfortunately, I never imagined that as hard as it was to talk about being abused, it was even harder to talk about how I had hurt others in the wake of my abuse. I felt compelled to share about that particular struggle during a therapy session with Diane.

She sat in her brown leather chair and listened intently. She took minimal notes and instead focused primarily on my tears.

I took several deep, ragged breaths before I shared with her. "I'm still so ashamed of what I did. How am I going to tell my girls, let alone write it down for the whole world to read? Madison said I can't write about the abuse and not explain how it affected me— the depths of anguish I underwent. But I don't want to embarrass him or the girls with my sins." Tears streaked my cheeks, and I reached for yet another tissue from Diane's side table.

"It sounds like Madison is fully aware of your sins and forgives you. What makes you think your daughters won't forgive you?" Her eyes contained understanding and sincerity.

"I can't know for sure, but I imagine it will taint how they see me. Over the years I felt lost and wounded, so I hurt everyone around me. I pretended I had forgiven everyone and that everything was wonderful."

"It seems to me like you can't forgive yourself. Why do you think you're unforgivable?" She paused, waiting patiently for my response.

For a couple of minutes, I remained silent and stared at the diploma on the wall behind her. "For years, friends who heard my story of childhood abuse showered me with accolades for my ability to forgive. When I told them how Madison's family didn't like me at first, they reacted with awe at how I had encouraged him to stay connected to his family with calls and visits. I thought I had them all fooled, but I was merely fooling myself. I hadn't forgiven them, any of them, but my fear of being abandoned remained so strong I pretended to forgive. Madison's family could tell I wasn't being authentic, and my family knew my so-called forgiveness paved the way for me to continue playing the victim—a role I had embraced for so long that it seemed permanent and eerily comfortable."

Regardless of how much therapy I had already done, I realized a tremendous amount of work lay ahead.

Chapter 32

NOT GOOD ENOUGH

My feelings of inadequacy never diminished. I continued to believe I was nothing but damaged goods and would never measure up. No matter how much love and tenderness Madison poured into me, I viewed myself as nothing more than broken and pathetic. No matter how much effort he put forth, I never felt like I deserved his wholesomeness. Because I believed such negative things about myself, it was easy to see how Madison loved me more than I loved him. In the back of my mind, I kept waiting for him to see things clearly, to realize I would never be good enough.

Everyone in my family had been divorced, so it was just a matter of time before Madison abandoned me as well. *Talk the talk and walk the walk, but don't fully invest your heart. Don't fall in love because you'll only end up with a broken heart.* But Madison continued to demonstrate unconditional love. Always present, he encouraged me by recognizing my accomplishments. He constantly defended me against anyone who spoke negatively about me, and he remained faithful in his love. But his countless, consistent efforts had little effect on my self-loathing. *Just get it over with. He's going to leave you; they always do.* One evening, I finally worked up the nerve to have a long overdue conversation with Madison.

"I need to tell you something. I don't think things are working out. It seems like I mess up everything. Your parents don't like me. Your grandparents don't like me. You spend so much time helping me with school, but I still struggle. I just feel like you could do so much better. You need to find somebody who can be what you need them to be because I'm never going to be good enough."

He listened to the words pour out of my heart. Then with tender eyes that seemed to search the deepest parts of me, he lovingly responded, "Lynnette, I love you. You are so important to me and are such an important part of my life."

I focused through my tears and saw the deep love he held for me in his piercing baby-blue eyes. I knew I could never hurt him. I may have been broken and pathetic, I may have been the worst person in the world, but I could never hurt someone who loved me so much.

After that conversation, I realized for the first time that I wanted to spend my life with Madison. After all, no one had ever loved me to that extent, unconditionally. To have a relationship where I could reveal anything about myself and still be loved suddenly seemed invaluable to me. He knew about the abuse and the other boys in my life, and yet he still loved me.

Oh, silly girl, you're stupid and disgusting. You'll never have love. You're not worthy of it. Just wait. It will all be taken away. Just wait.

ONE STEP FORWARD

The following years provided a time of growth and trust in our relationship, and our long engagement provided a strength and fortitude that otherwise would not have been present. At various times, I told Madison, "If you have any doubt at all, don't marry me. I am not going to be like my family and get divorced. I mean it. Divorce is not an option for me. So tell me now if you think it is." *Give him the out, Lynnette. Make sure he remembers you gave him an out.*

Fears aside, Madison was never short on words when it came to affirming his love and commitment to me. These years also proved to the Simm family that I planned to stay.

One memorable day during a visit to Madison's grandparents' home, I was walking with Mr. Simm around the property as he told me about all the work being done. "What do you think of our plans?" he asked.

"Well Mr. Simm—"

"From now on, I'm Clark and she's Betty, okay?" He smiled and gently put his arm around my shoulder.

This bittersweet moment offered subtle acknowledgment that said, "You're in." While they may have never liked our living arrangement, they respected our commitment to each other and the fact that we had followed through with achieving our collegiate goals, as promised.

Madison was in the last year of his bachelor's degree, and I would be graduating with my associate's degree. As per our agreement when he proposed, we began to prepare for our February 29, 1996, wedding date. I could hardly contain my excitement and anticipation.

Realizing neither of our parents would bankroll the wedding, we began to scrimp and save where we could and utilize what resources we had to make it a wonderful event. To our surprise, Betty and Clark agreed to have the reception at their home and help with the catering expenses. Wedding invitations were created and copied at Kinko's for sixteen dollars. From his days working at the coffee shop, Madison was quite proficient at making bows, so we bought inexpensive ribbon and he made bows for all the floral arrangements. Madison and his sister baked and decorated the wedding cake at Betty and Clark's the night before the wedding. My mother drove down to shop for an off-the-rack wedding gown that Grandma Mary helped pay for. The greatest surprise was having Mary, my sister, attend; she flew in from Japan for the wedding. Initially, she didn't think she'd be able to make it, so I was quite surprised when she arrived!

Our wedding marked the first time I truly felt like an adult. Madison felt the same way. In the eyes of our families, we had matured. Fears that had plagued Steve and Sandie regarding Madison's education never came to fruition. But many positive things did. Our relationship had thrived over a period of four years. We were graduating college. We had lived on our own without any financial assistance. We accomplished everything we said we were going to and had proved we were intelligent, responsible adults. So when the wedding finally took place, the attendees celebrated us with sincerely grateful hearts. It was the first time I could recall being surrounded by loved ones who came with the sole purpose of offering love and support.

When our wedding day arrived, excitement overflowed as both families came together from near and far. Over the past four years, Madison and I had been able to rebuild relationships with our parents. I thought about inviting Ernie, but my mother made it clear that she would boycott the ceremony if I did. The thought of Ernie giving me away crossed my mind, but in the end I wanted to have my parents with me. While we may not have been getting along, Mom and Dad were the people I wanted love from the most and to heal varying levels of brokenness that still existed in our relationship. *I want your love, your unconditional love. I want you to like me. I'm still mad, and the hurt is still raw at times, but I'm trying. Please be there for me. Please see me as worthy. Please love me.* After thinking everything through and talking with Madison, I decided that Dad would give me away. That gesture would provide a major, yet bittersweet, step toward healing our relationship. No matter what he had done, he was the only dad I had ever truly known.

Mom helped me get ready for the most important day of my life. She lovingly held my hand and told me how much she loved me, leaving me washed with joy. Right before the ceremony began, Dad and I took our positions at the back of the church, posed for a few pictures, and waited for our cue. Mary walked over to give me the necessary bridal elements—something old, something new, something borrowed, and something blue. Witnessing the exchange between his daughters, Dad's eyes pooled with tears and his lips began to quiver. He didn't have to say a word. I knew where the emotion was coming from. *I have allowed you to stay in my life because I love you, Dad. Yes, I could have kicked you out of my life, but you took ownership of what you did. You were willing to take whatever punishment to keep me from having to experience the pain of testifying— even if that meant spending thirty years in prison. You did your best to love me through hurting and betraying me. No matter how much anger, pain, and bitterness I lobbed your way, you took it. You never made me feel that the abuse was anyone's fault but yours. You even understood and allowed me to search out Ernie and never made me feel guilty for doing it. You know I may never forgive you, but for every wrong action, you've tried hundreds of ways to make it right, even while I say I forgive you and don't. How could I not love you?*

Dad was bursting with gratitude for the opportunity to be in my life. Though he didn't know Madison very well, he recognized the love I had for him. He believed Madison and I were good for each other and vowed to do everything in his power to provide for me. As we reached the edge of the aisle, our fingers tightly intertwined, Dad looked into my eyes and gently whispered, "I love you." While I hadn't forgiven him completely, a surge of genuine love and tenderness flooded the space between us. For the first time in years, I truly felt like Daddy's little girl.

MR. AND MRS. MADISON SIMM

Immediately after marrying Madison, I set out to prove I could be a good wife. Determined to be nothing like my mother, I planned to finish my education before having children. Because Mom divorced early on and had children to provide for, she had limited choices and had to settle for whatever life brought her. In some regard, my mother's life had become my example of what *not* to do. I resolved to not to become the aloof and disconnected individual I believed her to be. Dad continued to keep his distance, only talking to me if I initiated it. After Madison and I married, my parents never called to check on me. I felt as if they had washed their hands of me and were saying, "We're done. You're on your own." This lack of connection merely fueled the abandonment issues already in play from the lingering wounds left by my biological father and confirmed why I couldn't forgive them. They talked about loving me, but their actions demonstrated otherwise.

Though poor, Madison and I had our degrees and were working diligently toward our next goals. We didn't use drugs or alcohol, and we resolved to manage our money responsibly. Like any newly married couple, we had issues, but they rarely centered on big stuff. I consciously decided to take a partnership role in our marriage and initiated discussions (and sometimes arguments) about moving, purchasing a new car, managing our finances, or pursuing further academic studies. I refused to let a man control me—a natural response given my history. I was quick to argue my point about everything. Unlike my mother, I resolved to be a strong woman who stood her ground. But deep down, I was merely naïve and scared. Madison seemed so confident and strong that most times I fought just to fight but, eventually, submitted to his advice. Secretly, my *modus operandi* was "just tell me what you want, and I'll do it." Fueled by mounting insecurity, I became the ultimate people-pleaser who fought the urge to incessantly satisfy Madison. *Don't let him ruin you, but don't lose him.* I spent a great deal of time and energy fighting to be heard and then falling apart because I felt weak. One minute I was strong and demanding; the next I was an emotional child completely unable to handle life's challenges.

As strong as he was, Madison had his own baggage from childhood. Insecurity and the desire to be wanted were his driving forces. While most people labeled him as cold or shy, his reserved nature made him appear distant and unapproachable. At work he was the ultimate task manager with professional goals to make more money, climb the corporate ladder, and provide a secure life for his family.

PERFECT ON THE OUTSIDE

I adopted a fear-based approach to marriage. I understood that knowledge is power. And because I never wanted to provide my family with information that could be used to speak negatively about Madison, our marriage, or me, I avoided confiding in any of them. I wanted everyone to think I was strong and had everything together. Linda served as my primary source for counsel when the challenges became more than I could bear. Distance prevented me from seeing her on a regular basis, but she remained dedicated to my continued success through countless phone consultations. From the outside looking in, Madison and I had a fairytale marriage, but a firestorm was brewing under the surface—an emotional battle that nearly destroyed our marriage, particularly because we never saw it coming.

Having an education and being married helped boost my external self-worth, but self-deprecating forces remained hard at work. Internal battles raged like the violent swells of white-water river rapids. Regardless of the amount of therapy I had completed after Dad's arrest, I was far from healed from the abandonment issues, sexual abuse, and disregarded feelings that continued to plague me. The devastating emotional wounds of abandonment and abuse deposited negative internal messages that inundated every thought, regularly annihilated my defenses, and left me powerless to keep things under control. It took everything within me to take two steps forward, but the onslaught of negative thoughts inevitably shoved me three steps back.

I'm a failure. The only reason I graduated college was because of Madison's help and encouragement. I hadn't achieved my educational accomplishments—at least not alone. Without Madison, I would have failed. He is a genius—literally— yet I felt too intimidated to even attempt taking an IQ test. Everything he touched turned to gold, and I knew he would always be better than me. I had a potty mouth that rivaled that of a medieval sailor. I threw or broke things when arguments erupted. In contrast, Madison remained completely calm and relatively disengaged. His stoic demeanor fueled my anger because I thought he didn't care. After allowing me adequate time to release my juvenile tantrums, he was always quick to apologize, even when he wasn't to blame.

You're a fake. If anyone knew the real me, the emotional turmoil that swirled in my head on a daily basis, no one would like me. I didn't belong or feel embraced by any member of our extended families. Both my parents knew I hadn't forgiven them. I tried, but the hurt I carried just festered after every visit or phone call. While Steve and Sandie were more welcoming, I continued to feel like an outsider—and never quite good enough. Even my relationship with Ernie wasn't authentic. I wanted him in my life so much that I never dealt with all the hurt he had caused by leaving or breaking his promises.

Please others until it hurts. I'd spent my life as a chameleon, adapting to whatever circumstances dictated. *Just tell me what we're doing, where we're going, what to wear, and I'll be that person. I'll morph into whoever you want me to be.* I had no true understanding of who I was, and I found self-validation only through the perceived acceptance of others. I became the consummate people-pleaser with no boundaries.

Nobody wants me. Day after day was bathed with loneliness. While I loved Madison, I needed more than just him. I was born the consummate extrovert, but the abuse had left me guarded; however, the company and pursuit of others fueled my aching soul. If no one called, then no one cared. The only friends we had were family—and it seemed I was always the one doing the reaching out and calling. *If I died, who would come to my funeral? Who would miss me? Anyone? Oh, Madison would miss me, but he would eventually find someone better and be happier than he ever was with me.*

You're ugly and fat. The snowballing pain in my heart had become paralyzing. Without a female confidante or a local therapist in my life, I never addressed my deep emotions. Over time, food became my primary coping mechanism. Every two or three days, I binged on a wide variety of carbs and sugars— chips, ice cream, crackers, candies, sliced bread with butter, cookies, you name it. In secret, I stealthily grazed in such a way that the quantity of my consumption would go unnoticed. Like a child, I made sure to hide the wrappers under layers of trash so Madison wouldn't find them. School vending machines filled with Hostess pies, chips, and cakes became a mainstay and served to further my self-destructive path outside of home. It didn't take long for the added weight to become bothersome and quite noticeable. Yet no matter how much weight I gained, Madison never failed to love enough for the two of us. Every morning, I'd wake up with the best of intentions but was never able to follow through. By day's end, I was cramming something into my mouth, trying to compensate for the pain in my heart. Even more troubling was coming to the realization that I saw my authentic self only when I was bingeing alone—a very private chameleon I refused to expose to anyone but to myself. While in the company of others, I had meticulously perfected the emotional skills needed to appear that all was well, but inside I was dying. Never a day passed that I didn't see myself as unworthy, damaged goods. Emotionally, I began to feel more and more disjointed from my body, mind, and soul. I realized I had become merely a spectator of my life rather than participating in it.

Chapter 33

TALKING TO MY FAMILY

Talking to Madison and the girls about writing the book turned out to be wonderful and encouraging, and they continued to be my biggest supporters. But that was before I wrote a single word. As my writing progressed, I knew I'd have to tell my extended family about the project. After all, I needed their permission to write about them, but having those conversations proved to be challenging.

I called Mary first. As expected, my sister lovingly reassured me. We had a long conversation about what I wanted readers to get from the book. "Hope. I want them to see that there is hope." We talked about our childhood and all that we had learned. Our conversation gave me the strength to call my other siblings.

The call to my brother started off a little rough. His thoughts leapt to concerned about and for his immediate family. When he asked what I planned to say, I explained it wasn't going to be a tell-all book. The focus was to convey how and why my life had changed and give readers hope in the midst of their own struggles. Eventually, he, too, gave me his blessing to write what I needed. I was a little surprised by his support, yet I know he loves me. Over the years, we have healed a lot of old wounds from our childhood and now reap many of the blessings that come from forgiveness.

The call I feared most was to my stepsister. I hadn't talked to her in a few years. Over the decades she and I had tried to connect, but something always seemed to cause a rift. Even after all these years, losing my relationship with her still brings tears to my eyes. The passage of time had turned us into strangers, much like the people you remember from school. Back then they were the most important people in your life, but now you know nothing about them or what they have experienced. With butterflies raging and a heavy feeling in the pit of my stomach, I dialed her number. I held my breath and prayed she wouldn't answer and I could just leave a message. Since I fully expected her machine, I sat in stunned silence when she answered.

The conversation yielded a begrudging acceptance of the fact that I planned to write the book. I tried to reassure her I didn't have any hurt feelings about our relationship and wouldn't paint her in a bad light. I heard the pain in her voice. I think I surprised her by my understanding of how much she still hurt, and I tried to mend some old wounds I had caused. I asked for forgiveness and explained that I loved her then and still love her now. My transparency seemed to reconnect us in a small way. Yet the weight of too much time and too much hurt still felt like a vast chasm between us. In my heart I love my sister—not my *step*sister, but my sister. Unfortunately, I feel that I might never get to know her. Our relationship remains distant and strained, one of the biggest casualties of our childhood.

In the past, I had talked to my parents about possibly writing a book, but this time my intentions were real. The most challenging part would be retrieving some of the details from them. Things I didn't remember. Things I needed clarification about. Still, just thinking about my past caused me to revert into a little girl looking up to them in search of their pride and approval. I constantly had to remind myself that I'm a grown-up now, especially now that I have my two girls who look up to me. Me, a mom.

Chapter 34

ME A MOM?

We moved from San Diego to Baltimore when Madison got a job at Johns Hopkins University. Scared, yet excited, I ventured out of our Baltimore apartment to get a home pregnancy test. Thoughts rushed through my mind as drove to the nearest convenience store. *We've just moved from San Diego. How am I going to tell Madison I'm pregnant? I have no family nearby. I still have two years of school left. As hard as I've tried to avoid repeating the cycle, it looks like I'm turning into my mother after all. I know Madison will support me going to school and having a baby. But will I be a good mom?*

After I purchased the test, I returned to the empty apartment, where I contemplated whether or not to wait for Madison to return home from work. While my mind said to wait, the girlish excitement and desire for an answer was simply too great. I walked into the bathroom, ripped open the package, followed the instructions, and patiently stared at the stick. Within moments, the results window turned the most beautiful shade of blue I had ever seen, thus confirming my suspicions: officially pregnant. *I can't wait to tell Madison! I should wait and surprise him when he gets home. I could make a nice dinner and tell him over dessert, or maybe wait until bedtime and share the glorious news. I want it to be so special—romantic, tender, and filled with love. Just like in the movies!* But my romantic plans were once again squashed by my excitement. With Olympic speed, I dialed Madison's office.

The moment I heard his voice, I nearly shouted, "Madison! Madison! I'm pregnant! I mean, *we're* pregnant. Did you hear me? We're pregnant!"

"Yes. I heard you. Are you okay?"

"I'm fine, a little excited. I'm sorry I should have waited for you to take the test."

"Don't worry about that. I'll be home soon, and we'll talk then. Do you need anything before I get home?"

"No, honey. I'm good. Just come home."

I chuckled and smiled. We'd been married only eighteen months. The comedy of it all rested in a prediction Steve had made shortly after we married. "I give it two years and you'll be pregnant."

"Oh, no, we're going to wait awhile. I want to finish my degree first," I had said. So when Madison got home that evening, I had to eat a slice of humble pie when we called our families to share the exciting news. No doubt we were nervous about becoming first-time parents. We wondered how we could afford to raise a child and if we were ready for the responsibility. But there was never a doubt in our minds that we wanted this baby.

Madison immediately began making plans. Getting out of Baltimore topped our agenda. Though he liked his job at Johns Hopkins, neither of us liked Baltimore. Given the cost of living, California was out of the question. Then it dawned on us: Colorado. During our move to Baltimore, we had driven through there and stayed with Madison's aunt. The magnificent beauty of Colorado had captivated us, so we collectively decided to put down roots in Colorado Springs to be near his extended family.

By the end of December 1997, we had made the move to Colorado Springs—two unemployed, uninsured students with a child on the way. I immediately signed up for Medicaid and food stamp programs, a very humbling and somewhat embarrassing experience. As poor as they were, my parents never utilized social or government services of any kind. Simply put, when unable to afford it, we did without—a lesson that helped Madison and me later in life. But being pregnant, I was willing to do whatever it took to ensure my child was properly cared for. We knew it would be a temporary situation, that one or both of us would soon secure employment.

The week prior to our arrival, Colorado Springs had been blanketed by a blizzard. Unbeknownst to us, the woman who handled the accounting for Madison's uncle's print company had somehow been injured in the blizzard. Knowing we had no income, Madison's uncle asked if I would be interested in filling in during her absence. Though temporary, it would be enough to keep us afloat until we found something else. In addition to part-time employment, I enrolled at the University of Colorado in Colorado Springs to finish my bachelor's degree in psychology.

Being dyslexic, accounting certainly was not without its challenges. Yet the accounting software program confused me most. As with every other challenge I faced, I called Madison for help. After a few visits to the office, Madison's uncle recognized his skills and offered him a full-time position as company accountant. Relinquishing my position was delightful, especially knowing that Madison would complete the work I struggled to understand. Within weeks, I secured a position as group counselor for juvenile delinquent girls, undoubtedly a better fit for my professional goals. It was my dream to be just like Linda—and to counsel girls.

Colorado Springs offered breathtaking beauty, but loneliness was never far away. I had no family or friends to cling to. Though Madison's aunts, uncles, and cousins lived in surrounding cities, they each had their own lives and work, leaving little room for social interaction with us. As the loneliness escalated, so did my eating. With each pound of pregnancy weight, I managed to add a pound or two of carbohydrate-laden, comfort-food weight. Hormones and unhealed, festering emotional wounds began to turn my life upside down.

KENZIE

A midwife helped us prepare and deliver our daughter. My beloved little one had no plans to arrive early. In fact, the day my mother-in-law, Sandie, was scheduled to arrive, MacKenzie, whom we nicknamed Kenzie, made her glorious entrance into the world.

Kenzie was born slightly more than four hours following the onset of labor. Throughout the entire labor process, Madison barely said a word; rather, he was soaked in sweat and looked frightened as he helplessly watched me experience so much pain. The doctor announced our daughter's arrival. "Congratulations! It's a girl!" He then turned to Madison. "Mr. Simm, would you like to cut the umbilical cord?" With a look of shock and awe, Madison quietly whispered, "Yes." Later that day he told me, "It was like cutting an outside garden hose with dull scissors."

After the staff completed the requisite tests on our newborn, Madison returned to me carrying our swaddled infant and placed her on my chest. His faced beaming with pride. For the next several minutes, we collectively embraced our new daughter with amazement and adoration. The moment couldn't have been any more perfect, but the days and weeks to come and the realities of motherhood were nowhere near picturesque.

Once home from the hospital, I called my parents to let them know they had a new granddaughter. They were excited to hear all the glowing details surrounding the birth. With fall classes commencing in just seven days, the conversation turned to my future plans.

Mom said, "It's okay if you don't finish your college degree. Everyone knows that having a baby will take up too much of your time."

"Mom, I have Madison's full support. There's no doubt in my mind that I can finish." I didn't try very hard to keep the frustration out of my voice. Though plagued with doubt and fears, I resolved to finish if for no other reason than to prove my mother wrong. *Why does she want me to fail? Was her life so horrible with children that she felt she had to give up everything? I know she didn't finish high school because she got pregnant with my brother. I guess she's just being realistic and giving me an out so I don't feel like a failure. Why can't she just support what I want for a change?*

Riddled with more questions than answers, I opted to change the topic and inquire as to when she planned to come meet her first granddaughter. "Sorry, but we can't afford it." My heart cried out, *Sandie took time away from work, rearranged her schedule, and flew all the way to Colorado to help me with our new daughter, and my own mother won't? I realize finances are an issue, but she's had nine months to plan for it. "I can't afford it" is not a viable excuse to me. Besides, aren't mothers supposed to sacrifice for their children? Am I not worth it? I want my mom. I want my mom! But she's not coming.*

Sandie's presence during that first week blessed us immensely. Her maternal experience proved invaluable. She taught me how to swaddle, change diapers, breastfeed, and clean the umbilical cord. She also made sure I rested when the baby slept. Sandie took such wonderful care of Kenzie and me. I couldn't have felt more secure and loved. Madison stayed home for three days after Kenzie was born, but we couldn't afford to have him miss more work than he already had. Reluctantly, he returned to work.

At the end of the week, Sandie prepared to leave. In no way was I equipped for her to go. *How am I going to be a mom? I don't know how to do this!* The moment she left, I began feeling overwhelmed. I cried uncontrollably as she and Madison drove away. *This is my first child, and I have no one here with me. NO ONE! This isn't how it's supposed to be—Madison at work all day and me alone with a baby.* Fear gripped me, particularly because I had no one to turn to. Looking back, I realize this was the beginning of postpartum depression.

The first day of the fall semester began the very next day. Remembering what my mother had said, I refused to forgo my education. After getting dressed and then feeding and changing Kenzie, I drove to Madison's work to drop her off. Fortunately, his boss was very accommodating to our needs as new parents; he allowed Madison the flexibility of caring for our daughter at work while I was in class.

Toward the end of November, Linda came to visit. Her presence was most welcome, though this time she didn't come into my life as a therapist, she came as my beautiful friend. Two years had passed since I had last utilized her as a therapist, so now my *friend* Linda was coming to visit my beautiful daughter and me.

We settled on Nonnie as the name Kenzie would call Linda. With much emotion and tears, I sat down with Nonnie, looked her in the eye, and said, "You are my godmother, Nonnie. The woman God sent to help me." Her loving arms were so welcoming that I nearly fell into them. I desperately needed her love and support, especially in the absence of my own mother. *Why isn't my mom here? Why can't she help me? Is she still mad at me about Dad? I just don't understand her!*

After conversing with Nonnie about the challenges I faced, she lovingly explained that I was probably in a bit of a depression. Between schoolwork, a new baby, and out-of-control hormones, it was all I could do to keep it together. I wanted Nonnie to be proud of me. While I felt strong in her presence, I knew she detected underlying pain in my heart. When the day arrived for her to leave, my incessant tears flowed once more. Feelings of isolation and loneliness returned with a fury; I felt their crushing weight upon me. Yet somehow I managed to physically keep going. *Kenzie needs me.*

Madison and I had worked out a schedule for Kenzie, but the loneliness I felt fueled tensions between us. *I know he has to work, but I'm drowning here!* As the Christmas season arrived, things began to calm down. I was on break from school for a few weeks and initially enjoyed being at home with Kenzie, but the cold weather and lack of friends and family began to take its toll. Postpartum depression mixed with holiday blues crashed in with a vengeance. *I can do this. I can do this. Madison is with me. Kenzie is healthy and a good baby. Why do I feel so sad all the time? Why do I feel so alone?*

No matter what I did or said to myself, I was overwrought with negativity. I felt sad, lonely, depressed, and worthless, like a total failure. That's all I saw in myself. That sense of helplessness and hopelessness would prove to be only the first indication of greater complications still to come. But nothing could have prepared me for what January would bring. Nothing.

Chapter 35

BOWEN

Have you ever felt the absence of someone so great that your heart and eyes tear up at the mere thought of that person? We've all lost people we love and will continue to lose loved ones until we are the ones leaving. Now imagine not being able to talk about that loved one. The hurt is magnified. Now add onto that the cold, hard fact that you're the reason that person is gone. The pain is nearly unbearable. Finally, add to that hurt that the person you're missing, the one's whose death you're responsible for, is your child. That pain is without words. It is simply all-consuming. It feels like your whole heart has had been ripped from your body and no one is sympathetic because, after all, IT IS YOUR FAULT.

That's the kind of debilitating pain I have carried since January 1999. Fifteen years of shame, guilt, pain, and fear. Yes, fear. Fear of judgment is a wicked tool the enemy uses to crush his victims, and he compounds that judgment with the fear of rejection for a near- fatal concoction. Shame and guilt is sometimes the final blow from this deadly, painful secret. Yet with the soothing balm of truth, light, and love, healing begins. And there is no deeper healing than the love from your child.

It was time to tell the girls about my abortion. Once I decided to tell them, I had to do it quick or I would lose my nerve. As the August evening sun fell below the skyline, the girls and I were all reading in the living room. I had just gotten a text from Michelle to discuss our next writing appointment. I took a deep breath.

"Girls, I need to talk to you."

Kenzie lowered her tablet, and Alex lowered her book. "Dinner?" Kenzie assumed the topic.

"No, not about dinner. It's about my book. I need to tell you about the next section coming in the book." My heart was coming out of my chest, yet it felt so tight I almost couldn't breathe. Looking at Kenzie, I said, "You know how I've always said you're my first baby, and, Alex, I've said you're my last baby? Well, I've always wanted to make sure I never lied to you either of you, yet I've held a secret. I had a baby between you two."

The nervous smiles disappeared and both girls just looked at me. Nervously, I continued to talk to avoid the deafening silence. "I was pregnant soon after I had you, Kenzie. It had only been four months, and I was in a horrible place emotionally. The best way I can explain it to you is to mix abandonment with postpartum depression, add insecurity, and with that I believed I was messing up being mom to you."

The tears slowly slid down my cheeks, but I kept on. "I let insecurity coupled with fear and anger decide that I wasn't a good mom to you; therefore, I couldn't be a good mom to Bowen. I told Dad I was pregnant, and we decided to have an abortion. I'm so sorry."

"Who is Bowen?" Kenzie surprised me with the question.

"He was your baby brother. I was only pregnant six weeks, but I felt the pregnancy was different from the two of you, so I believe the baby was a boy. I named him Bowen; it was the name we had for you if you had been a boy. Losing Bowen was the worst mistake I have ever made, but I wasn't strong enough then."

"But, Mom, you were strong enough. You're the strongest

mom I know." Alexandra got up and hugged me, and Kenzie quickly followed. They mended a hole in my heart in that moment. The scar will forever be there, but their love was the final piece. God's love was the first, followed by Madison, Mary, my parents, Nonnie, and myself, but the love from my two gifts from heaven has sealed His love.

The girls pulled back, and I saw tears in their eyes. Then Kenzie was openly crying. She looked like I had given her a gift and then ripped it away. Yet instead of hating me, she loved me even more. "Mom, I'm so sorry you had to go through that. Alex is right, though. You're an amazing mom. I know you would have loved him."

"I do love him. I love him every day. I miss him too."

I lost my son to fear, insecurity, depression, and to every dark corner of my mind that said I couldn't do it. I lost my son to evil. Pure evil. Yet my daughters saw strength in me I never recognized, and His love poured out from them and covered me.

As the days and nights continued to pass and I thought of my sweet son, Alex and Kenzie's words continued to echo in my head and heart. Those girls spoke truth, a truth I didn't believe or understand the day I made that horrible decision to kill my son.

Alex made an extra effort to be sweet since she learned about Bowen. She loved me with her cuddles every morning. One morning I nestled her close and asked, "How are you feeling with all these revelations about your mom's life?"

She showed the depth of her faith in her answer. "If God forgave Grandpa for what he did to you, I do too. And if God forgave you for what you did, I do too. I'm sorry you hurt, Mommy, and I'm sorry I didn't get to meet my brother."

Since I had told them, I feel that the news of Bowen had brought the girls closer. They bring up his name from time to time, saying things like "Think Bowen would like that? Bowen would be in this grade or that old." Just for a moment in their lives they believe their brother is missing. Each time, I answer, "Yes, he would."

Chapter 36

ME OR IT?

December had been wrought with a firestorm of emotions, so when the New Year arrived, I felt somewhat optimistic that 1999 would bring some sense of normalcy. Despite my sunny outlook, something felt wrong. I had an inkling as to the cause, but I was too afraid to do what I needed to do. But near the end of January, I couldn't avoid the issue any longer. I loaded Kenzie into the car, drove to the drug store, and purchased a pregnancy test. Within moments of arriving home, a pink line confirmed my suspicions. Pregnant. Again. Too soon. I immediately crawled into bed. Hormones took over, and I sobbed until I could barely breathe. *I can't do this. I CANNOT do this! I'm going to be just like my mother having back-to-back kids. I'm not strong enough. I don't want to resent my children. I need to finish my bachelor's degree. No, no … NO!*

No amount of tears soothed my anguished heart. When Madison came home from work, one look at me told him something was terribly wrong.

"What is it? Are you okay?"

Sobbing. "I'm pregnant."

"It'll be okay."

"Wh-what are we going to do?"

"Well, you don't have to keep it. It's hasn't even been five months since you had Kenzie, and your body's not strong enough."

In typical fashion, he wrapped his arms around me. Quick to place his concern for my well-being in front of his own feelings, he spoke in soothing tones. I leaned into his strength like never before as the wide range of emotions threatened to overwhelm me. He held me at arm's length and stared into my eyes. The moment I heard those words, I knew Madison's focus was solely on me. At no time did he voice his wishes or perspectives regarding another child. Rather, he instantaneously shifted into protector mode. He pulled me to his chest and held me tightly.

"It's okay. I'm with you."

"Can I talk to Mary about this?"

"If feel you need to, yes."

Despite the fact that my relationship with Mary had been strained for many years, she was the only one I thought to call. After all, I couldn't admit to Mom or Nonnie how I had failed. Though I desperately needed the love and support of my sister, in reality I probably sought some level of empathy and approval. Like me, Mary was also a new mother, and I believed she, above anyone else, would understand my situation. After hearing my news and the desperation in my voice, Mary selflessly agreed to help us. I was having abortion.

Within days, we scheduled an appointment to terminate the pregnancy. Intellectually, I felt a sense of relief, but emotionally I experienced a deep sense of loss, pain, and confusion knowing what I was about to do.

I won't be like my mom. I won't resent my children. I am so selfish. Kenzie needs my attention. I don't have enough to give. Madison is working so hard and long. He is beyond stressed. I'm so stupid. Why didn't I protect myself? Every time I looked in the mirror, I hated myself more. Disgust and anguish washed over me.

The day of the abortion arrived, and it was all I could do to keep from throwing up. My heart raced, and my breath shortened. *I can't do this. This is wrong. I don't want to do this. I have to do this. I owe Madison. I owe Kenzie. I hate you. I hate you. Leave.*

With wet cheeks, I felt as if I were in a fog, completely disconnected from any and all reality going on around me. We arrived at the facility, and a nurse gave me a stack of paperwork to complete. With every pen stroke, my stomach churned and I inched ever closer to collapse. I was numb; running wasn't an option.

In the back of the room, a glassless, sterile white door opened.

"Lynnette."

Like a deer in the headlights, I looked up and was met with an expressionless stare. With his hand in mine, Madison and I stood up together.

"Sir, you'll have to wait here. Only patients are allowed in the procedure room."

Procedure? Is that what this is? If it's just a simple procedure, why am I so distraught? This is way more than a simple procedure. Killing is a procedure.

My mouth opened and tears poured down my face. *No! No! I can't. I can't.* Madison turned his tender, loving eyes toward mine and kissed my wet cheek. "I'll be right here." He gently guided me toward the door. My feet weighed a thousand pounds as they thumped down the hall and the door closed behind me. I quickly looked back.

I entered the procedure room awash with the same feelings I had when I succumbed to the rape test. I felt utterly alone. I had no one to hold my hand, no one to reassure me or love me through this. I was there, but yet I wasn't. It was like a foggy dream. Everything was in silent slow motion.

The medical assistant asked me a series of short questions that I answered but don't remember. She handed me the paper gown and a paper sheet to drape across my midsection. Then she left. No long waiting; no time to think. Within moments, the assistant returned with the physician. They wasted no time getting down to the business at hand.

"Place your feet in the stirrups." The doctor guided one foot and then the other. I didn't utter a word, as I began to shake inside and out as one foot then the other touched the ice-cold metal. Every muscle in my body began to tense, and then I was gone. No time for thoughts.

Within seconds, a horrible sucking sound gurgled from the machine. I was back. *Oh, God, help me. This is wrong. No! No! I don't want to! NO! God, NO!* The suctioning sound drowned out my internal screaming. Then the room went dark as I closed my eyes. I soaked the small paper-wrapped pillow as tears ran into my ears and down.

My eyes flew open as my stomach began to cramp. I felt as though the pain would tear me in half as my heart was ripped out of my body. I gripped the sides of the bed until my knuckles whitened. Mere inches from my right foot, the sucking tube met the reciprocal canister where the contents of my uterus were being expunged. Seeing blood, I turned my head. The procedure had taken only a few moments, yet it seemed like an eternity.

"We're done." The doctor pressed his lips together in a grim half-smile and then exited the room as quickly and professionally as he had entered.

"You can get dressed now." His assistant patted my arm before she, too, left the procedure room.

I sat on the table—alone—reeling with a range of emotions. No matter how I tried to justify my actions, my heart was inconsolable.

I dressed quickly in my effort to escape the horrible place. Madison listened to the discharge instructions as I stood unresponsive at his side. He tried to hold me, and I tried to return to the safety of his arms, but I was torn between two worlds—nowhere, yet in the real world. Tightly clutched in his embrace, I felt the huge weight of empty vacancy, clueless how to fill the hole that now remained. Lying thoughts began to bring me back.

There. I did it. It's over. I did it for us. I did it for Kenzie so I could be a better and stronger mom for her. I can't be a failure. It's not that big a deal, and I can go back to life the way it was before. I mean, it's just a procedure, right?

Initially, life returned to normal. We went about our days—working, going to school, caring for Kenzie. Madison and I avoided the topic, except when we occasionally discussed how I felt physically. We told no one what had happened. Regardless of our efforts to try and bury what happened, though, the emotional pain and trauma I carried was far from over.

Weeks later, in the midst of our first intimate encounter, my body and mind began violently rejecting the very notion of lovemaking, but I did it anyway. Immediately after, I backed away from Madison and curled into the fetal position as I cried out in near hysteria, "I can't do it again. No, no! It's going to happen again. I can do *that* again. I can't. I can't. I can't do it again!" My suffocating sobs and uncontrollable screams frightened not only Madison and Kenzie but also me. Again, it seemed as if I were outside my body watching this crazy lady rage on and on. "Don't ever touch me again!" I screamed and kept screaming uncontrollably.

After I exhausted myself, I laid there almost catatonic, my mind going a thousand different directions. *I want to die. Please, oh please, don't let me get pregnant again. I can't go through another abortion. God take me. Take me now.* My entire body hurt from head to toe, inside and out.

Madison's face contorted as though he questioned my sanity. Clearly shocked by my statement, he inched away and gave me the space I demanded.

I feel like I'm going crazy. Just make it stop. Make it all go away. Physically and emotionally exhausted, I succumbed to the need for sleep.

Madison and I never talked about the abortion or the incident that followed. In an act of desperation and to avoid exploding, I confided in a friend. After I explained what we'd done, she shared her personal experience with abortion. She lovingly and wisely advised me to name the baby and then allow myself to grieve the loss of my child. Though I never knew the sex of my unborn child, in my heart I believed it was a boy. Only one name that came to mind: Bowen.

Grieving Bowen has been a long process—one I still actively do to this day. In truth, I'll probably never be completely healed from killing my child; healing will be an ongoing process. At times I became very emotional when trying to talk about it.

Madison did his best to calm me down with logic and reasoning. He often said, "It was too soon after MacKenzie's birth. We made the best choice." He never seemed to regret it. In fact, on several occasions he stated he would do it again given the same circumstances.

His attitude made me believe that he didn't have any guilt or remorse. But in his mind, he had stepped in to save his wife and family. When we had one of our infrequent conversations about it, I viewed myself as being entirely too emotional. So I tried to approach the experience with logic and reason. *Madison knows what he's doing. He's so smart. He has a great plan to guide this family the best he knows how. And here I am, doing nothing but whining about a baby that wasn't even a baby yet. I was only six weeks pregnant. Get over it already. It's no big deal, so just move on.* But no matter how many times I repeated those words in my head, the grief never waned.

Chapter 37

PAST LOVES

I'm surprised by how I have connected with so many people I knew while growing up. Facebook had connected me with friends I knew from grade school, middle school, and high school. While I was still living in Colorado, James found me through his brother on Facebook. It was amazing to hear about his life and accomplishments. It also gave me the opportunity to thank him for his love and friendship all those years ago. We've kept in contact over the years, as I have with others who knew me when. It's occurred to me, though, that only James really knew me. Knew what I had been going through back then. Other friends only knew the Lynnette I showed them at school. The girl who just wanted to fit in, be accepted, be loved.

Eventually, he found me: Scott. How amazing is my Lord. Scott, now married and with a beautiful little girl, lives in middle America. His life went from the airlines to the sea. I guess he loved the navy too much. We talked briefly via Messaging and with the full consent and knowledge of our spouses. Gone were the feelings I once held onto as I waited for Madison to leave me. Surprisingly, our lives mimicked each other's in our journey toward Jesus. We laughed (lol) as we chatted about our lives and about how God knew the plans He had for us. We were both happy.

I thought to myself, *I never had to call him. Madison never left me. Not once. Not for one minute did he abandon me.* But still, as Madison and I continued to walk through life together, we had so much to work through.

Chapter 38

FOCUSING ON SCHOOL

*L*ater that year, I received my bachelor's degree in psychology, a seemingly hollow triumph given what I'd done to get there. Since only Madison and Kenzie could attend the ceremony, I decided not to walk the stage. Still, I had completed my goal. I chose psychology out of a desire to follow in Linda's footsteps. I wanted to become a counselor. My dream was to give to others in the way she had given to me. Unfortunately, terminating Bowen triggered extreme depression that left me feeling inferior, guilty, and ashamed. I found myself ill equipped to provide any level of help to others. *If I can't even manage to help myself, how can I possibly help anyone else? But if not counseling, what?*

Being dyslexic made school challenging. But no matter the obstacles, I always loved school. As a little girl, I played school in my room and assigned my stuffed animals homework. During class, I often took notes about different teachers, listing things I would and wouldn't do when I became a teacher. So when a deep sense of inadequacy filled me, I decided to return to my first love—teaching. In the fall of 1999, I began taking classes at Regis University to work toward my MBA in education.

Between a new home, college, and a one-year-old, Madison and I barely made ends meet, but he worked harder and harder, doing whatever he needed to do to provide. By the end of 1999, he made a decision to return to college for his MBA as well. Not only was he on the fast track to getting his MBA, he also held down a full-time job, helped around the house and with Kenzie, and assisted me with my schoolwork on a daily basis. Throughout most of 2000, our lives consisted of trying to develop a good schedule with Kenzie while we juggled work, school, homework, and our day-to-day responsibilities. Work, school, and Kenzie—that was our life.

Regardless of the all-is-well front I tried to put forth, I felt emotionally, physically, and mentally exhausted. Madison never made demands on my time or me, but I wanted to be the perfect wife, to the point where the expectations I put on myself became more and more overwhelming. I longed to be as together and balanced as he was, but no matter how hard I tried, I failed time and again. I obsessed over my inadequacies. *If I could just get it together and be the perfect wife, mother, student, and homemaker, maybe I'll finally deserve him.* When life became too overwhelming, emotional breakdowns fed the pit of depression. Worse, I beat myself up for my shortcomings. *I'm stupid and unworthy. I don't know what I'm doing. Everything is out of control and a total mess. Bottom line, I'll never be good enough.*

Being a perfect wife meant I was responsible for keeping the house clean at all times, preparing all the meals, and being the primary caregiver for Kenzie. I also required myself to exude happiness and stability rather than the emotional wreck I had become. In addition, I needed to give my husband sex whenever he wanted it. Now and then we experienced moments of true intimacy, but generally speaking, sex was an obligatory chore.

The way I saw it, Madison viewed sex as the essential element to our marriage and wanted our intimate encounters to be laden with romance and emotional connection. But no matter what I tried, I simply couldn't get there. Many times I tried to rationalize my lack. I explained the differences between men and women to him, but my words always fueled feelings of inadequacy and never amounted to any level of resolution.

Every three months or so, the same argument about sex ensued. His words, though truth-based, stung and inevitably resulted in a flood of emotion and tears. Every problem between us seemed to begin and end with me. *It's not that I'm not sexual. I simply never initiate it. Could that be the problem—that I'm not initiating it? I don't know why I feel this way. I don't know why my body won't react. I don't know what's wrong, but I'm trying. I really am. I want to be better. I want to be all you want me to be, but I just don't know how. I guess I'll never be good enough.* The conclusion of every argument resulted in a sexual encounter. Not that Madison demanded it, but I knew he desired emotional and physical intimacy, and I was willing to succumb to his desires.

Over time, Madison recognized my enormous disconnect surrounding intimacy whereas I denied it and harbored tremendous anger toward him for wanting it. My stance was to present myself as "I'm fine. Everything's fine!" Having spent so much of my life afflicted with wounded-person syndrome, problems always seemed to surround me. For once, just once, I wanted it to be someone else's fault.

Between mounting emotional turmoil and physical demands, my attempts at conflict resolution consisted of either a meltdown or aggressive behavior. Without warning, I would throw things or spew vulgar profanity at Madison. Each choice exacerbated my self-hatred and loathing.

To Madison's credit, he apologized for things that were his fault, but I rarely accepted his apology at face value. In addition to owning his mistakes, he attempted to diffuse situations by apologizing for things that were not his fault—adopting an apologetic nature that often angered me. I never realized that wanting to be a good, caring, and involved husband was his own agenda. Years later, it's easy to see how our individual insecurities aggravated the other's, but—thankfully—our love and devotion kept us together.

PRAYING FOR A CHILD

Midway through my master's degree, Madison and I began talking about having another child. Madison was concerned about my ability to handle another child, and rightfully so. On the other hand, I worried that God wouldn't allow me to get pregnant again. For weeks I prayed—prayed for forgiveness, prayed for another baby—and offered promises to God if He would bless me with another child. But thoughts of Bowen were never far from my heart. *Why would God give me a child when I just threw away the last one? I promise to work harder, be a good mom, and love my children. I'll make you proud, God. Really I will.*

By December 2000, we learned we were expecting another baby after only a month of trying. We couldn't have been more elated.

The following month, Mary, her two-year-old son, Taylor, and Madison's younger brother, Morgan, came to live with us. Always having someone around to play with and help care for Kenzie made the pregnancy very easy and provided me with a tremendous amount of free time to rest or focus on my studies.

Eight days away from my due date, I was resting on the couch when I received a phone call from my cousin. Without so much as a hello, she asked, "Have you seen the news?"

"No, I haven't even turned the TV on yet. Why?"

"Turn it on, now!"

Within moments of tuning to the local news, I sat and watched in horror as the second plane crashed into the south tower of the World Trade Center. Glued to the television, the shock and horror of what I witnessed rendered me barely able to breathe. I cradled my bulging belly and prayed my baby daughter wouldn't come soon. "Please don't come. Please don't come. Not today, baby girl, just not today." The uncertainty in our nation and the looming threat of further attacks weighed heavily on my mind. Living in Colorado where NORAD and several military bases were located merely added to my concern. Fortunately, I managed to get my emotions under control, and the baby continued to nestle in the safety of my womb.

The following week, I had my final appointment with the obstetrician before the September 19 due date. Having decided to induce, the rush of excitement we experienced with the birth of Kenzie became more of a controlled anticipation. The birth was a real family affair. Sandie, already in Colorado for a visit, partnered with Madison to act as birthing coaches. Morgan would take care of Kenzie, and Mary would be our camera girl, an assignment Morgan was more than happy to relinquish. I smiled as I thought about the well-oiled machine we had assembled.

We arrived to the hospital at 7:00 a.m. on September 20, 2001, and my OB induced labor shortly thereafter. By 2:00 p.m., labor pains were rapidly increasing. Mary's eyes filled with tears as she watched me labor through the pain.

"Breathe, breathe," she repeated as she stroked my hair away from my sweaty face.

Seeing her so emotional brought about a greater strength and determination. *I'm the older sister here, and she's crying just watching me cycle through this pain. Come on, now. Be tough!*

At 2:28 p.m., the nurse stood to read information on the monitors. Suddenly, I felt an overwhelming sensation. I screamed, "I have to push! I have to push!"

"Hold on, Mrs. Simm. Let me get the doctor." She quickly exited the room.

I hollered after her, "Don't you understand? I need to push!"

Twenty seconds later, the doctor rushed in and immediately began pulling on her rubber gloves. "Hold on, Lynnette. Stop pushing!"

I did the best I could given the circumstances. Then, with one final push, Alexandra was born. Joyful tears flowed freely. The nurse cleaned blood and mucus off of Alex, swaddled her, and then gently handed her to Madison. He appeared a much calmer husband and father compared to Kenzie's birth.

Madison and Sandie stayed with Alex while Mary never left my side.

"How are you feeling?" Mary squeezed my hand and smiled gently. "I'm here for you," she added.

I couldn't have felt more blessed to share this moment with my sister.

Later that day, Kenzie walked into my hospital room, took one look at her baby sister, and lit up like the Times Square Christmas tree. "Mommy, can I hold her too? Can I? Peeeze, can I hold her?" she asked in her tender, sweet, three-year-old voice. The excitement of Alex's arrival was incredibly special, but the most precious thing of all was watching Kenzie immediately nurture her baby sister. Madison helped Kenzie nestle to the back of the vinyl armchair in my hospital room, and then he gently placed Alex in her arms. "She's all mine, Mommy." It was one of the most precious moments in my life.

CREATING A HOME

Settling into a new routine with another baby proved to be challenging, but Sandie stayed with us, once again, to help with the transition. Her presence calmed and comforted me, just as it had when Kenzie was born. Madison and I felt blessed to have her there.

Throughout my pregnancy, Mary worked diligently to establish herself in Colorado, and shortly after Alex's birth, she secured an apartment for her and Taylor. Our relationship had truly come full circle over the past couple of years, making her departure from our home bittersweet, but I was incredibly proud of all she had accomplished. We felt blessed to experience such healing.

Madison and I spent the majority of the year finding our new groove and working toward completing our MBAs. Regardless of the daunting tasks and responsibilities before us, we both resolved to finish strong. His ability to successfully multitask and breeze through school continued to feed my festering insecurities. *I'm never going to be as smart as Madison. He's working full-time while helping me with homework, housework, and the children, all while getting his MBA. Yet he never seems to struggle like I do. I'm so stupid. I'll never be good enough.*

Three months after Mary's departure, Steve and Sandie decided to move to Colorado. They arranged to live with us until they found a home for them and Morgan, but their plan never came to fruition. With seven of us living under one roof, it wasn't long before Madison expressed a desire for more land and privacy. I wasn't sure we could afford more land, but I conceded to Madison after many heated discussions. Within weeks, we secured six acres in Black Forest, a quaint, countryside town thirty minutes northeast of Colorado Springs, and we began designing a custom home. Black Forest was just far enough away that the few casual relationships I had made would eventually fade, forcing me to begin anew for the fifth time in our married life.

Every time I turned around, another family member moved to Colorado. By the end of the year, my parents, one of my cousins, my brother, an aunt, and Grandma Mary had all moved to there. While I loved my family, being surrounded by them on a regular basis was like having the past catapulted into the present. *As if there isn't enough stress, now everyone will be here to judge my competency as a mother. I thought I had left all the insanity behind, but it's back.* No matter what I said or did, everyone seemed to have an opinion, and having them in our business merely added to the repertoire of arguments between Madison and me. *Will it ever end?*

By the end of December, all of my (and Madison's) hard work paid off when I was awarded my MBA in education. As grueling as it was to accomplish, several underlying factors motivated me: proving my parents wrong and striving to achieve more than anyone else. With most of my family in attendance, walking the stage this time held a special meaning and brought a sincere level of pride. *They said I couldn't do this once I became a mother. Everyone doubted my ability to achieve an education. Guess I proved them wrong!*

Following graduation, peers and college professors encouraged me to go for my doctorate. *Me? A doctorate degree? There's no way. I'd never even be accepted to a doctoral program let alone be smart and disciplined enough to accomplish it.* I succumbed to insecurity and pushed the notion of a doctorate to the back of my mind.

New home construction in Black Forest was well under way, and in March, I accepted a job at Remington College as a general education teacher. Truth be told, I felt completely incompetent and out of my element. However, I disguised the insecurities by dressing for success, slathering on a bold shade of lipstick, and emulating what I observed from my peers. *These people think I can teach. But I've never done it before, and I have no idea what I'm doing. Pretty soon, someone is going to realize the truth and they'll fire me.* I returned to the familiar role of a chameleon and did whatever the circumstances dictated.

One would think that with dyslexia a school would be the last place I'd want to be. Oddly enough, it was the place I felt most comfortable. In an enormous leap of faith and a bit of insanity, I decided to apply for a doctoral program, but this time, I resolved to do it on my own. I refused Madison's help with the application and didn't even allow him to proofread the required essay. Going it alone, I felt certain a rejection letter would follow. Four weeks later, I was utterly shocked when the congratulatory acceptance letter arrived. *What have I done? Now I have to go through with it, if for no other reason than to prove myself.*

Madison had been doing very well at work. He was taking on more responsibilities, and they rewarded with him with a new title and a raise, vice president of finance. Financially we were doing better, yet we were still struggling internally.

After the doctoral orientation, Madison and I performed the final walk-through of our new home. With a separate in-law residence, the custom home boasted an array of unimaginable luxuries I never dreamed would belong to Madison and me. *How did I get here? This doesn't feel like my home, let alone my life. I don't deserve these luxuries. It won't last. In my childhood we had the nice house and nice things, and then we lost it all and ended up in the bus. This is just one step closer to losing it all.* I just couldn't get the negative thoughts to stop. They ruined every joy, every accomplishment.

Moving in was definitely a family affair. Sandie and Steve took the in-law residence, and Morgan stayed in the finished basement on their side. With a house full of in-laws, Kenzie nearing five, and Alex approaching two, the expectations I put on myself far outweighed those assigned by others. *I have to make this huge house a home, take care of the girls, and be a good wife, daughter-in-law, and sister-in-law. And if that weren't enough already, now I've gone and signed up for a long, tedious academic program and a part-time job. I must have lost my mind.*

Madison's frequent words of reassurance had little impact on my stress, doubt, and lack of self-worth. *All eyes are on me. I just know it. No matter what I do, I'll never measure up.* Desperate to be Super Mom, Super Wife, and Super Daughter, I felt ill-equipped to conquer normalcy, let alone succeed at being super anything. I just tried to keep from drowning in my own life.

In July, my grandmother unexpectedly passed away, a loss I never took the time to grieve. *You've got to be the strong one. There's no time to mourn. Everyone is counting on you, the successful one who "has it all."* The sudden sadness of her death served as another unprocessed emotion I pushed to the back of my mind.

The turbulent year ended with Steve and Sandie separating.

After over thirty-three years of marriage, and several fights about moving, life, and everything, Steve moved back to California. With Sandie and Morgan living with us, Madison felt an enormous amount of responsibility to provide for his abandoned mother and brother. Underlying tensions in the house left me feeling like I had to do my best to help everyone. Being the consummate people-pleaser, I always questioned what I should or shouldn't say out of fear that I would upset someone. Everything I did or said was an attempt to appease everyone else. This furthered the emotional stuffing I had grown accustomed to.

Sandie's contribution to our lives was invaluable. She began teaching phonics to the girls and babysat them while I taught classes. Having someone I wholeheartedly trusted to care for them enabled me to escape and feel free from whatever demands were placed on me to be wife, mother, homemaker, student, and daughter/sister in-law. It was a freedom that over time I desperately craved and at times manipulated to obtain.

Teaching at Remington brought tremendous levels of anxiety. In the midst of the spring semester, my supervisor asked me to take on the role of general education coordinator. Part of my responsibility would be engaging with the faculty and getting to know them and their needs or desires for the various departments. As unworthy as I felt, the people-pleaser in me knew only one answer: "Yes."

I began by interviewing each of the faculty members one by one and identifying their passions, strengths, and vision. While I got to know my coworkers, I began making friends. At times, I felt so lonely at home and did everything in my power to win the approval of my peers. The more effort I put into work, the more I pulled away from my family. It became easier to live apart from my home life. Work offered the enjoyment of friendship as well as a level of contribution and success, especially compared to the loser I felt I was with Madison and my girls.

As relationships at work grew, I invested more time and emotion into sharing my intimate feelings with friends rather than with Madison. This weighed heavily on my marriage and created more stressors between us than ever before. I spent the majority of my evenings having phone conversations or chat sessions, which tried Madison's patience. Arguments regularly erupted and, of course, always included his discontent regarding lack of intimacy. *I'm so sick of arguing about sex. Ugh … I could just scream! I wish he'd just shut up and leave me alone.* Personal life and underlying fears overtook me. Every thought was full of negativity and left me feeling utterly defeated, bordering on suicidal. *So what if I died? I doubt anyone would miss me or bother coming to my funeral.* The reflection I saw in the mirror resembled nothing but fault, fear, and disgust. Self-loathing reached an all-time high. *If I keep this up, Madison will leave me. I just know it.*

Toward the end of the fall semester, I began interviewing for an adjunct faculty member to work in the General Ed department. Among the many interviewees, one in particular stood out. From the moment her five-six, medium-build frame entered the room there was no denying she arrived with a mind-set of walking away gainfully employed. Yes, Crystal was a take-charge kind of woman who readily shared her understanding of the job and how her experience would benefit the department. I listened intently as she spoke. Discernment and wisdom seemed to ooze from her and immediately drew me in with ease. Of her many obvious attributes, learning that she was newly pregnant resonated with me. Like me, Crystal had recently moved to the area and needed a job but had been turned away by several potential employers because they feared she would quit once the baby arrived. Her revelation brought back memories of trying to secure employment when I was pregnant with Kenzie.

Over the coming weeks, Crystal and I worked closely with each other. Her Virginian drawl made me laugh and became a source of playful teasing, especially when she said, "I'm going to get some woodder" (water). But Crystal radiated confidence, and though I found it to be somewhat intimidating, I was also drawn to her strength. Though not a very girlie girl, she had her own brand of femininity amid a barely painted face and conservative yet elegantly accessorized clothing.

Little by little, I began to talk to Crystal on a personal level. She had a way of sharing her life hurts while drawing me into sharing mine as well. But I was careful to keep her at a safe distance. From the beginning, Crystal made her love of Christ "crystal" clear, and I made my "I don't subscribe to that religious stuff" abundantly clear in return. Regardless, she never judged or made me feel less as a woman; rather, she continued sharing her faith with me when opportunities presented themselves. *She wants me to be like her. If she only knew that was impossible. I'm not good. I'm damaged. I'm not smart, organized, dedicated, or passionate like she is. Boy, is she passionate about Jesus!* Given Crystal's level of discernment, it didn't take long for her to see the person behind the façade. She recognized my needs even before I voiced them and spoke to me from a place of love and knowledge. *I've never had a female friend like this before. She worries about me as if she really truly cares.* The closer we became, the more I came to rely on her as a source of strength, comfort, and truth.

Through many conversations with Crystal, I began to see and understand the huge disconnect between life at home and life at work. No matter what hat I wore at the moment, I sported a fake persona. The result? I was losing sight of reality. I was trying to be all things to all people, yet never being true to myself. I alternated between exhaustion from manipulating all the masks I hid behind and exhilaration as I began to see myself outside of my home. But most of the time, I felt confused about my life and love, sad about the hurt I had caused, and overwhelmed by shame, fear, and depression.

Madison and I fought constantly about big things, little

things, basically everything. The array of emotional baggage from the past and present left me feeling like a failure. I muddled my way through the doctorate program feeling completely burned out. Even Madison felt I should be further along than I was. In reality, I wanted to quit. *What's the purpose in doing all this anyhow? It's not like I'm a good teacher. Besides, I'd never be able to get a job at a "real" university.*

As always, sex remained a problem in our marriage. I didn't even want to think about sex. It had always been an issue, but after kids it became more of a concern. *I can't get those horrible images out of my mind from the abuse. Why won't they just go away?* Madison desired the passion and youthfulness that he remembered, but I was unable to produce the girl he fell in love with. My love for him was very real, and he was always a very mindful and compassionate lover, but I hated sex. My heart longed to be there for him and enjoy sex, but he never enjoyed true, intimate lovemaking; rather, he got a woman with no voice, no desire, and no passion. Though none of it was his fault, I could tell he'd grown tired of paying for what others had done. *Where's the woman he fell in love with? Did she ever even exist? The problem is me. It's always me. If it weren't for me, Madison would be happy. It's all my fault that he's not happy. What if he wants out of the marriage? He deserves better. The girls deserve better. Madison works so hard, but I'm still not happy. I don't think I've ever experienced true, deep happiness.*

Every attempt to avoid dealing with my home life yielded more time spent with my peers. Over time, conversations with them began crossing appropriate boundary lines to include problems at home and with family, especially problems with Madison. He didn't have to say it, but I knew Madison didn't trust me. The truth of the matter is I didn't even trust myself, and I knew why. I didn't engage in deep, emotional, and very personal conversations with Madison, and the mounting tensions took their toll. *Something is going to break. It always does.*

Family history dictates that it will. On the brink of an emotional meltdown, I knew I had to talk to Madison.

"I think I need to get back into therapy." I lay on my side in bed facing him.

"Really? What brought this on?" He sat up and leaned against the headboard.

I offered only a few scant half-truths. "I don't know how to explain it, but something's not right. I'm depressed. I have a ton of anxiety. You and I are fighting all the time, especially about sex. All the issues I have with my family and Dad. I'm just not in a good place, and I don't know what's wrong." But I did know. I knew all the lies I'd told, the sins I'd committed, and the overwhelming guilt and shame that threatened to envelop me. I knew my marriage threatened to implode—all because of me.

"If that's what you feel like you need to do, do it."

"Crystal says it should be a Christian therapist."

"Crystal is controlling and should mind her own business. We don't need religion to fix what's broken."

"Um, well ... okay. I was just sharing with you what she said. I'm going to start looking for a therapist."

After Madison and I talked, I knew getting back into therapy was the right decision. It had been over ten years since I had worked with Linda. The once-strong girl had morphed into a woman full of open, seeping, and infected wounds that were ruining her life. *I need help or I'm going to lose everything.*

Chapter 39

OMITTING

We'd been in Texas over a year, and while I still missed my life in Colorado, I was beginning to make a new life here. Madison worked long hours, but he provided faithfully for us. The girls and I had gotten back into the school routine. Michelle and I were spending more time writing, and I could see the book coming into focus. Yet I read scenes I wanted to omit—things I was too ashamed to tell others.

What would they do once I revealed the last secret?

I knew I had to talk to Madison about it. I waited for the girls to go to bed and for Madison and me to perform our nightly check on them before we settled in for a heart-to-heart conversation. He rested on our bed clad in a white T-shirt and pulled the quilted blanket over him.

I waited till we finished our normal exchange about the day's events before taking a deep breath and looking toward the ceiling. "Madison, I don't want to write about the hurt I caused you. I don't think it's fair to you." Holding his gaze felt uncomfortable, so I looked away.

"Why? You've shared so much thus far. Don't you think the

reader needs to see just how far you fell so they can see how far you've come?" His body stiffened.

His questions surprised me. I thought he'd be relieved to learn that I didn't want to write about everything. I bolted upright and sat cross-legged, my usual position for one of our long late-night chats. "This isn't a tell-all book. I don't see how possibly humiliating you is necessary. I think the reader can see how badly I was hurt and how badly I hurt others, especially you, without having to reveal it all. And the girls. Haven't they had enough revelations about their mother? I'm so scared, but I'm mostly embarrassed that I hurt you."

Madison's tired blue eyes softened. He must have realized that this was going to be one of those nights. He's familiar with my *modus operandi*—beginning a deep topic at 10:00 p.m. and refusing to go to sleep until we've exhausted the discussion. He breathed a deep sigh as he gave in to what he knew would be very late night. "Leaving out this part would be hiding something. It's best if you share it all. Be authentic."

He went on to talk about how much he and the girls love me. He reiterated all the words of encouragement I've learned to lean on. I continued to bring up my anxieties and fears, but he wasn't swayed. As the evening discussion wrapped up just after midnight, I said, "I'll think about it and pray."

I turned off my bedside light. Madison turned on his side, placed his arm around my waist, pulled me closer, and whispered words of encouragement. His strong, masculine voice soothed me. My mind continued to play every sin, fear, consequence, and thing that was wrong with or about me. I barely slept.

The next day, I had lunch with my friend Kim, whom I met on a recent mission trip. Her natural curly hair was an immediate draw for me, but it was her openness about her family and her struggles that captured my heart. Tears flowed, and an immediate bond was formed. Over the months, we'd become close friends, sharing our joys and woes as mothers and wives, but also sharing our souls.

For months I'd shared my writing process with Kim. During this particular lunch, we talked about the usual kid stuff and the ongoing laundry battles with our husband's white T-shirts and kids' socks. We enjoyed a long chat over soup and sandwiches, and I left feeling okay but empty somehow. As I drove off to take Charlie, our yellow Labrador, to the groomer, I felt an overwhelming sense of fear. I decided to call Kim.

"Did you forget something?" she chuckled.

Near tears, I explained to her the conversation I had had with Madison the night before. I told her how I wanted the book to be authentic, but I didn't want to hit the girls with yet another painful part of my past. She lovingly listened and told me that I'd know when the time was right to share with my girls. She lifted my spirit with words of encouragement about how strong, loving, and understanding my girls are. She wrapped me with comforting words about how I'm a good mom and a good person. She ended with advice on just how to reveal this last piece of my sinful past.

In the twenty minutes it took me to get to the groomers, I felt stronger than I had in days. I also felt incredibly loved because God had sent yet another wonderful woman to walk beside me on this journey.

Chapter 40

ON THE PRECIPICE: LET THE HEALING BEGIN

The emotional decline I had experienced over the past several years had taken its toll on every aspect of my life. The slow torturous pining of guilt and shame had now become rapid-fire, leaving me powerless to gain control over anything. Overcome with emotion, I called Nonnie, the only person I truly trusted. During our conversation, fear and anxiety brought me to tears. As always, she was there to listen, comfort, and guide me. I shared with her my desire to return to therapy. Nonnie said, "Lynnette, you need to find a therapist who is certified in marriage and family counseling. I'd suggest doing an interview to make sure you're a good fit."

By late January 2006, I had scheduled an interview with the one counselor who agreed to a free initial consultation. Nervous yet full of excitement, I walked into her office armed with a plethora of questions to determine if she was the right therapist for me. Following customary introductions, Jenny and I settled into her cozy office.

"Would you tell me a little about yourself, your approach to patients, and therapy practices?"

"Well, I'm a Christian therapist."

Without allowing her to speak another word, I interrupted to inject an unyielding position. "I'm not looking for a Bible-thumping therapist—just someone to listen to my problems and help me figure out what's going wrong."

Jenny's body stiffened, and her mouth went slightly slack. My directness left her utterly shocked, but she needed to understand that I wasn't fooling around with all that religious stuff.

She regained her composure and out popped an enormous smile. "I promise to respect your wishes and not 'Bible-thump' you."

"Fair enough."

From the moment I met Jenny, something about her calm demeanor reminded me of Linda in a grandmotherly sort of way. Her clothes were matronly, conservative, and sensible. Her modest makeup and minimal accessories were opposite of Linda's bohemian fashion, but I found nothing to be afraid of or put off by; rather, I instantly felt welcomed. Bottom line: I felt safe, and feeling safe was critical to finding the right therapist.

"I use a combination of talk therapy and cognitive behavioral therapy. Do you know what those are, or have you experienced them before?"

"Yes, I've done talk therapy and am familiar with the concept of CBT."

Therapy with Linda was traditional talk therapy. I would explain a particular situation, and then she and I would talk through a variety of outcome possibilities and/or deal with the range of emotions. My psychology undergrad studies exposed me to the concept of CBT, though I'd never participated in that form of therapy. CBT focuses on a person's negative thoughts and the true origins of those thoughts. This method allows a person to incorporate positive behavior to effectively respond to and decrease the negative thought process. I knew it was a very helpful tool in treating anxiety and depression, but I also recognized this level of therapy required intensive action, accountability, and 100 percent honesty.

Over the course of thirty minutes, Jenny graciously answered all of my questions until I had only one left. "Would you take me on as a client?"

Without hesitation, she responded, "Yes."

Wanting to dive in as quickly as possible, we agreed to weekly meetings.

Following the first month of therapy, I worried that things were progressing too slowly. Regardless of the work I was doing, Madison and I seemed to be growing further apart. Desperate to be everything he saw in me and wanted from me, I clung to the hope of someday being the kind of wife, mother, and daughter my family deserved. *I can and will be smart, beautiful, talented, and capable. Someday.* But no matter how much CBT we weaved in and around my emotions, I still experienced times when I felt nothing at all and found myself buried by depression.

"You need to trust that we're making progress. These things take time," Jenny explained.

Her encouraging words helped me push forward. The mere fact that I continued in therapy was an enormous step in the right direction. I guess I expected miracles, but I needed to be reminded that I didn't arrive at the place I was overnight and I wasn't going to heal overnight. I had to commit to my restoration for the long haul. Still, ripping the bandages off the festering childhood wounds was difficult and seemed to cause more anguish than I ever expected.

When I was young, I experienced vivid nightmares. While I can't remember details for the majority of them, I do recall how real they felt. I remember being abruptly awakened by extreme fear. Major change, such as being newly married or just having a baby, triggered these nightmares. Since life changes seemed to be the catalyst, my recent return to therapy proved no different. This time, however, the nightmares were significantly more intimate and personal—things like my being grabbed in the dark, my girls being abducted, or Madison being killed. The crying, thrashing, eyes-wide-open, yet still-dreaming night terrors took their toll not only on me but also on Madison.

In time, he became adept at recognizing my symptoms. By gauging a noticeable change in my breathing, Madison was able to detect the onset of these nightmares, and he would attempt to awaken me before I was deeply entrenched in horror. Sometimes it worked, but the vivid images I did experience plagued me. Madison could see the toll the nightmares took on my emotional and psychological welfare.

A frazzled mess, I questioned everything I did and doubted everything I was. *Am I a good mother? Or am I damaging the girls with my burdens? I yell, cry, and fall silent for no reason; I'm obviously not in control of my emotions. Are the girls scared of me? Does Madison even like me anymore? I mean, why should he?*

At times I ran to Sandie seeking comfort and solace. Regardless of her response and its intended delivery, growing paranoia twisted her words into negatives and left me hating myself for allowing her to see such weakness. *I know Sandie thinks I'm crazy, but I'm so glad she lives with us. My daughters deserve someone kind and patient—a loving, consistent, and predictable female role model. And that's certainly not me.*

It seemed no amount of therapy could make a dent in my depression. In fact, my mood and outlook grew significantly worse. I hated myself. I hated my life. I hated my extended family. Yet at the same time, I loved them all so much it hurt. The devil seemed to whisper horrible thoughts into my mind: *"Sex is sex, and the heart is the heart; they don't have to align. They never will. You're broken and don't deserve your husband! You don't deserve your girls! You're nothing!"* No matter what I tried, I couldn't get life's puzzle straight in my mind, and the smoldering embers of fear, insecurity, and self-doubt began raging like wildfire.

A LOVING FRIENDSHIP

Outside of therapy, my friendship with Crystal continued to grow. Even as her pregnant body raged with hormones, she remained supportive by engaging in long conversations over lunches and just being, well, *normal.* Crystal never came with an agenda; she merely loved me for who I was, a completely new and exhilarating experience for me. I marveled at how well she understood me, but inside I feared she would pull away if the vulgar truth of my past ever came to the surface. Given the depth and strength of her faith, I kept waiting for her to Bible-thump me, but she never did. Though she didn't avoid her faith, she didn't ram it down my throat in a judgmental way either. Rather, she shared it in a loving, wholehearted, and unapologetic way. I had never known someone to have so much faith and not use his or her religious ideals to hurt or demean someone.

Growing up, my experience with religion consisted of bus rides to the Baptist church while my parents stayed home. Once there, I had to attend a different grade-appropriate Sunday school class than my siblings. I hated being separated from my brother and sister, and I felt less than worthy to be around the other church kids. Family gatherings, especially Christmas, were often religious warzones between Grandma Mary and another family member who didn't share her views. Vehemently torn by religious doctrine, Grandma intentionally undermined others' wishes surrounding their religious practices. Their conflict merely fueled my confusion about what it meant to be a Christian. When I met Madison, we talked about religion and agreed we wanted nothing to do the hypocritical environment that did nothing but make good people feel bad and bad people look good.

Given how confusing and phony religion seemed to me, I kept waiting for my religious cynicism to come between Crystal and me. But it never did. In fact, with each passing conversation or interaction, she became more loving and generous. No matter the question—whether work, personal, or a very rare religious inquiry—Crystal was readily equipped with resources to appease my curiosity. I'll admit her responses were at times a bit overwhelming, but it was easy to see that her actions were based on genuine love and concern.

In therapy, I purposefully steered clear of religion. I wanted to work on the issues that were killing my marriage and my relationship with my daughters. In my opinion, Jesus had nothing to do with any of that. After getting to know me and covering a bit of my past, Jenny and I created a priority list of issues that plagued my life—sex, marriage, depression, feelings of inadequacy, lack of true forgiveness, my daughters' needs, and my extended family issues. Looking at the list in its entirety felt daunting, but like before, I knew I had to start somewhere. We went right to the heart of marriage: sex. Ugh.

Jenny was aware of my father's abuse, as well as the others who had sexually abused me, yet I never went into the physical details of the abuse. As I detailed previous consensual sexual relationships and marital sex history, it seemed the abuse was always right in the middle of it all. "When I'm with Madison, I feel nothing. I close my eyes and just wait for it to be over. I've tried to convince him that I love and desire him, but he's not buying it. On the outside I'm trying to be one thing, but on the inside my body screams, *'Liar!'* Worst of all, Madison internalizes the lack of connection and believes it to be his fault, as if he's not good enough or hasn't loved me enough. His eyes reveal the depth of the ache in his heart, yet all I do is cry inside and vow to try and fake it better next time. I want to work things out. No, I *need* to work things out, but I don't know how or where to begin." I grabbed for Jenny's tissues throughout every session.

So as to not rehash the painful details of my past, I called Linda and asked her to speak candidly with Jenny about my history from a clinical perspective. Hesitant at first, eventually both therapists agreed. Afterward, I talked with Nonnie—not Linda the therapist but as someone who loved and cared for me. "I recently reviewed my books on cognitive behavioral therapy, and the reading sparked the love I had for psychology during my undergrad. I was curious to see if I had repressed memories, but that seems unlikely since I have so many vivid memories. I just need to know if there's a clinical reason for my sexual vacantness."

"What did you discover?"

"Well, some of the memories are mixed up or I have bits and pieces of them. I know I was abused. I knew the men who did it."

Men. This wasn't the first time I talked to Nonnie about the others who had hurt me. What a childhood! Sexually used by three people, before I was fifteen. Without family boundaries, boys had access to behave as their hormones dictated and they had witnessed. This type of rampant immoral behavior warped everyone around us.

"I remember some of the when, where, and how, but I can't remember specific details. It's like some of my recollections of abuse last only a fraction of a moment. I can see who abused me, but I have no account of the number of times it happened or exactly what took place. I have no account of the number of times it happened, and at times the abusers change places or faces."

Nonnie paused before answering. "Lynnette, when I began seeing you, I treated the trauma first. The most important thing was to make sure you were no longer in danger and get you stabilized and able to function in your day-to-day necessities."

"I understand. When I think back to the time we spent together, it was like you were the ER doctor. Your job was to try to stop major arteries from gushing, to keep me from bleeding out."

"Yes, and now you need to work on the long-term damage that was done. You need to explore the depth of the wounds and truly try to heal, not just put a Band-Aid on your wounds. You've finally admitted you didn't forgive and you didn't heal. I'm so proud of you and excited for your future."

"It's so much harder than I thought it would be. I'm hoping it will be worth the effort, the emotional turmoil. Yet I have to do something for my girls, for Madison, and for me. That's why I started researching on my own. In your opinion, could I have dissociative disorder?"

"I always suspected you did when we worked together, but you were so bent on not diving into the details. I was limited on what I could do to help you without you being willing to open up. Understandably, as a teenager, you were just trying to get to normal and didn't want to do the real, hard work of healing. What have you read about DD?"

"Well, it's a defense mechanism that trauma victims use to avoid or escape reality during traumatic events. People involuntarily leave their bodies and escape into their imagination or into nothingness to avoid living through what is happening to them. People who experience this unhealthy sense of disconnect can lose memories, thoughts, surroundings, actions, and sequence of events. In severe cases, trauma victims can develop a new and different identity. I've also read that people with dissociative disorder tend to develop symptoms, usually as a reaction to trauma, to help keep difficult memories at bay."

"When I began treating you, I realized you had missing memories and believed you possibly had some sort of dissociative disorder. It's not uncommon."

"Everything I read about it sounds as if they are describing me. I know I found new ways of coping after the abuse ended, but in reality, while I was attempting to live a normal life in the eyes of everyone else, I was barely surviving."

"I'm so proud that you're really working on this. You're a

smart girl. I suggest you let Jenny know what you've learned. It'll help you both as you work toward healing. I love you."

"I love you too. Thanks. I will talk to her about it during our next appointment."

Following the conclusion of our two-hour conversation, I finally felt like I was getting somewhere. I went to my next therapy session armed with a possible diagnosis. Jenny listened as I explained my conversation with Nonnie and the research I'd done. She agreed that I displayed all the parameters associated with dissociative disorder and discussed how it would affect my treatment and healing.

Leaving therapy that day, I felt almost exactly the same as I did when I was diagnosed with dyslexia. The label provided both a degree of relief and a crushing blow, knowing my life would never be truly free from it. It took me a long time to accept I was a dyslexic wife, mother, student, and teacher. Now I was going to be forever broken with a mind-body-soul separation. After delving into the specifics on dissociative disorder, I realized I didn't have split personalities; rather, I had a form of amnesia and depersonalization disorder. While my mind had managed to forget much of the trauma, it also lost many of my childhood memories along with it.

Dissociative disorder marked my life by creating the feeling of detachment and distance from my body and past experiences. With DD, feelings of depersonalization are recurrent at times, which makes the past feels as if it happened to someone else. All the emotions were lost, and I saw my life, past and present, from a place outside myself. These separations had caused underlying problems in my life, especially my marriage. As discouraging as it was, at least I understood what was happening to me. This allowed a small degree of hope to trickle in.

As previously stated, Linda served as a pseudo-ER doctor. She patched me up just enough to survive. But without a true understanding of the abuse and my efforts to forgive my abusers, the emotional wounds over time would become infected, fester, and hurt everyone around me. With my life, marriage, and family on the precipice of amputation, I felt driven to work on the healing therapy. With the use of cognitive behavioral therapy, Jenny and I plotted a course to not only manage my dissociative disorder but also to build a foundation of wholeness.

Understanding the crux of antidepressants and anti-anxiety medications, I felt confident in my abilities to work through the issues without the use of prescription drugs. While respecting my position, Nonnie and Jenny cautioned me to remain diligent in my commitment to therapy, always be honest with my feelings, and keep in mind that medications were an option, if needed.

The first step was to begin addressing the most critical issue of all: sex. To help me better understand Madison's needs, Jenny instructed me to have a conversation with him regarding his view of true intimacy. Over the years, Madison consistently said I wasn't engaged when it came to intimacy, so I wanted a clear understanding of what that looked like to him. With the girls asleep in their beds, Madison and I nestled back into the comforting softness of our living room sofa.

"What does engaged or true intimacy mean to you?" I asked.

He smiled, his tender blue eyes so soft. After a deep breath, he offered me an honest, detailed explanation. "I want you to initiate sex. That tells me that you want and desire me. For years I've been the one pursuing."

Knowing he was right, I simply responded, "Okay."

Madison flashed a boyish grin. "I want you to talk to me when we are together." "What do you mean?" Though not completely clueless, I needed specifics.

"I want you to become more vocal in your needs, wants, and desires. I want to know what pleases you and tell me that you're enjoying what I'm doing—or not. I never want to hurt you, so I need you to express yourself."

"That's going to be a hard one, but I understand." During

the years of abuse, I became conditioned by my abusers to keep quiet. They did what they wanted, but my thoughts, feelings, pain, or displeasure were irrelevant. Gathering strength from Madison's warm hand holding mine, I asked, "What else?"

"I want for sex to be something you genuinely desire. The way it is now, I feel like it's a chore or an obligation for you."

"Okay. Anything else?"

"No, that's all for now."

Our past discussions about sex always ended in tears, but this time he and I talked about what I was working on in therapy. "Madison, I love you with all my heart, and I promise to work hard so you'll know your love and grace were not wasted." I sensed my husband had given what he could give; now it was my turn. Change and healing were mandatory.

Armed with this information, I returned to therapy, shared what I had learned, and awaited my next homework assignment.

"This is where cognitive behavioral therapy is going to come into play. You have to begin to reprogram your brain. You do this by combatting what has been perceived as negative experiences with positive reinforcement ones," Jenny explained.

"Okay. How do I do that?"

"Going forward, I want you to begin changing the following things. First, you need to have your eyes open during intimacy. You need to literally see that you are in a safe place and that you're not being abused. You need to recognize that you're with your husband who loves you. You need to see the room, your room. Look at Madison. See your hands and body. Stay present from beginning to end."

"That's not going to be easy."

"But you can do it. Secondly, you need to smile when making love. By doing so, you're creating a positive, happy memory. Your mind is incredibly powerful."

I gave her a slight smile—no, more of a smirk, actually. "Really? That seems kind of silly. I can't imagine how Madison would to react to that."

"Third, try to begin making *sex noise*. Just as Madison said, this tells him you're engaged in the moment and enjoying the experience."

"Won't I sound stupid and fake? I've never done that. I've always been quiet."

Jenny nodded. "It might feel faked at first, but begin with a small sound or one word. The reason you were always quiet is because that was part of your escape and protection mechanism when you were abused. You're not being abused anymore; your husband cherishes you. And because he values every part of you, it's okay to be vocal during intimacy."

"It just seems so foreign and uncomfortable."

"I understand. All of these things I'm asking you to do are going to take time, consistent practice, and intentionality. Over time, responding this way will become more natural to you. Finally, I want you to begin planning and initiating sex. Did Madison mention how many times a week he would like to have sex?"

"No. He's never been that demanding."

"That's good. So what do you think is an adequate number for a healthy marriage?"

I simultaneously blushed and grinned. "Probably two to three times a week?"

"That sounds reasonable. You will need something to remind you—a posted note or something visual that you see daily."

"I can't make it obvious to Madison that I'm counting or tracking. I'll have to think of something he won't recognize. It would hurt him to think I had to have a reminder to love him."

"I'm sure you'll think of something. That's all for now."

I felt mentally and emotionally dazed. "It's a lot."

"Yes, but you can do it."

Returning home, I felt overwhelmed with the homework assignments, but I was determined to do my best to complete them. The first thing was to decide on a tracking system for initiating sex. Inside our closet was a bank of shelves that housed various baskets of personal items—socks, hair ribbons and clips, and nail care products. I decided to take three bottles of red nail polish and place them on one shelf. Every time I initiated sex that week, I would move one bottle to a new shelf. *Madison will never notice this.*

Weeks turned into months, and the struggles remained, but tracking progress became more natural. Some weeks, I moved only one bottle, other weeks all three. As the CBT techniques took hold, initiating sex became less intentional and more natural. *I didn't get to this place overnight, so it's not going to be resolved overnight.*

For the time being, therapy remained focused on my marriage, with sex always on the homework list. For once, Madison's birthday gift was just what he wanted: a wife who initiated physical intimacy. While it wasn't perfect, he could feel me trying. An incredibly intimate conversation followed our lovemaking, and for the first time in years, it felt as if we were talking, really talking.

As the therapy session came to an end, I knew I needed to find a healthy me, not the infected, wounded child I was. Madison deserved more. My beautiful daughters deserved more. And in time, I would come to realize that I, too, deserved more.

In later therapy sessions, Jenny and I discussed boundaries I never learned as a child and changes I would have to make to regain the trust I nearly destroyed. More surprising was the painful insecurity I exposed in Madison. Because everything had always been about me—my pain, my hurt, and my devastating past—I failed to recognize what my festering wounds had done to the one person who loved me unconditionally. Having his own childhood experiences to overcome, Madison was thrust into a life with a wounded child who had become a septic woman. Therefore, he was never afforded the opportunity to deal with his own insecurities.

Because I desperately wanted him to experience the life—and the wife—he so richly deserved, I knew it was time to mend all of me. I desperately wanted to meet that woman too. I knew what I had to do. Guilt, pain, and self-loathing needed to be cut off before it destroyed everything I loved.

Chapter 41

SHARING AND REPAIRING

I didn't want to do it. Yet again, shame, guilt, and fear nearly won. Nearly. I finally gave my book to my family. My parents, Madison, the girls, my brother, and sisters were all given opportunities to read the whole book. I asked each of them to provide feedback, but reminded them that the book was from my perspective. Their reactions were varied.

Madison began editing the book for grammar, but mostly he kept saying he didn't sound that way. I laughed.

"You sound that way in my head," I would tell him.

"I'm more matter-of-fact."

"I know, but I have a hard time writing like that."

Still smiling, he told me how proud he was of me. He gave me some suggestions, and in the end, I made some changes.

My parents read the book too. My mom wept through most of it. I was so worried about how much my view of her would hurt her.

"I've finished your book. She's a work of art. I just learned so much, and I'm so very proud of you honey bunny. I tried to read it as fiction, as if I didn't know the characters, but it didn't work."

"I'm sorry if I hurt you, Mom."

"You just told the truth from your perspective. I know this book will help others, if they get a chance to read it."

"Did I do as I promised? Did I tell the story in a way that honored you and Dad and God."

"Yes, I cried … a lot. It was the hardest thing I've ever read. Captivating isn't a strong enough word."

"I'm so happy, Mom. I want you to know just how much I love you and Dad. Thank you for giving me time to forgive and build this amazing relationship with you both and the opportunity to share this story with the world to glorify the Lord."

"I know God would tell us all, if we listen, thank you for putting your words and feelings on paper. It will help so many others get to where they want to be with Him."

Dad's reading the book was short of a miracle. He's not much of a reader, not even instructions or maps unless he has to. Really, it was hard for him to dive in yet again and be reminded of all he did wrong and all the hurt he had caused. But he said the end was best. I'm still amazed that he stuck around. He could have left so many times, but he didn't. Even when I wanted to kill him off … okay, just when I was really mad at him. Honestly, this book and my life now wouldn't have been possible if he had left.

Mary, well, she loved the book. Every single word. Okay, almost every word. She, too, understood that the book is from my perspective and gave me some feedback to incorporate into it.

"You did good, sis. It took me a bit to get through it all, but it was good."

"Thank you. I didn't think I'd ever get it done. And I was so scared to share it."

"God knows, and He is working it all in His timing."

She couldn't have been more right. The years have flown by as I wrote with Michelle for a year, edited for another year, and then sat on the book for almost another year. Fear, shame, and guilt didn't win. God knows the plans He has for us. He knew my brother and I would be ready to talk, really talk, about everything. God knew my brother and I would grow closer.

My brother called from an airport, waiting to catch another flight. He said he began reading the book on a flight from his home in South Carolina to California and was already a third into the book.

"Do you like it so far?"

"Yes. I couldn't put it down. It's captivating." My second captivating; I was soaring inside. "I don't know how you did it, Lynnette. I can't imagine what my life, our family's life, would have been like had you not chosen the path of forgiveness. I love you for that."

My heart was singing, and my hands were raised to God. It was all You, dear Lord. All You. Robert said he was proud of me, but he had to catch the next flight. He said he would read more and call me again once he landed. I began thinking to myself, *He hasn't even got to the good stuff, Lord. All that You have done. He is going to see how You saved me and our family so many times.* A part of me was not feeling vindicated per se but overwhelmed with love, gratitude, and finally acceptance. I had to dictate this conversation quickly, for I didn't want to lose one morsel of love. As I captured the conversation on my phone, I was looking up to the Lord, saying, "Thank You. Thank You for the strength. Thank You for the love." And then I waited for three very slow, long hours.

"Lynnette, I'm just blown away. My understanding of you and Mary is greatly deepened and yet ... there is so much I missed." Robert's voice tightened as he struggled with his emotions.

"I can't even explain how happy I am that my book is touching you. I had no idea about God's grand plan for our lives, but I know He watches over my family and me. We have been through so much, and now we get to enjoy the blessings of grace, love and forgiveness together, Robert. We all get the gift." The words were overflowing from my heart as tears ran down my face.

Robert was equally tearful. I could hear as he tried to cover up them, but he didn't have a chance. The emotions were so raw and real that he just tried to talk through them.

"I say this again, and it should stay with you forever, Lynnette. *None* of this would be possible without your courage and strength to commit this to part of the story. You forgave *and* you worked on healing. It's the twelfth step."

I got his reference to AA's Twelve-Step program, and I melted in the praise and love. Robert's comment meant that I had my spiritual awakening as a result of following the steps of recovery, recovery from years of hurt and trauma, and now I was trying to carry the message to others while I continued to practice the steps of forgiveness, mercy, grace, and love throughout my life. How amazing is my heavenly Father??

As high as I was from the reaction of my family is how low I felt after the reaction from my stepsister. Still hurting, she didn't give me any feedback about the book and refused to give her consent. Our family tried to talk to her, but her mind was made up. The fallout from her reaction can still be felt. It's a deep loss. I had so hoped that God and the miracle He had done in my life and the lives of my family members would touch her, but I won't know. She has chosen to back away from the family. We are all devastated and praying for His timing to capture her heart.

God and therapy are what saved my life. I know it can help others. Lots of both, mixed with a persevering, persistent husband and my willingness to be vulnerable and honest.

Chapter 42

THE PATH TO HEALING

For months, sex and intimacy continued to be the primary focus of therapy, though we periodically addressed life's daily stressors—annoying husbands who leave socks on the floor, never-ending laundry and household chores, parenting, lack of acknowledgment at work, etc. Though I had begun to see the light, some days I still felt blindsided by overwhelming darkness. Once I felt Madison's and my intimacy issues had improved, it was time to begin working on my depression.

"When you talk about the darkness, what does that look like to you?" Jenny asked.

"Well, it's not like I'm lying in bed all day crying or anything like that. It's just that I feel an ever-present sadness." I paused, closed my eyes, and took a deep a breath before I continued. "My happy never seems real. Like there's no true joy. It's like I wake up feeling fatigued and unable to motivate myself."

"What happens on those days?"

"It's a breeding ground for emotional binge eating."

"So you tend to eat your way through the feelings?"

Filled with disgust and embarrassment, I looked down and whispered, "Yes."

"Go on."

"Most days I can fake my way through it, but then there are those … those days I call 'blue days' that just overwhelm me."

"What do you do on those days?"

"Everyone who knows me asks, 'What's wrong?' Even they can see that I'm not right, and that really bothers me. It seems like those days have become more and more frequent. I generally isolate myself from the world, watch my soaps, nibble my way through hundreds of calories, and do the bare minimum to take care of my girls, the house, my husband, or myself."

"What's the worst part about those 'blue days'?"

"The look on my girls' faces when they ask, 'Mommy, why are you sad? What did we do?' There's nothing I can say to them to make them understand, so I just dig deeper and try to be there, try to mask it."

"How does Madison respond to you when you're having one of those days?"

"Oh, he tries to cover for me."

"By doing what?"

"He brings home dinner after working all day, or he entertains the girls so I can take a bath. He'll even do the dishes. The irony is that his efforts make me feel even guiltier." *What's my problem? My husband works all day and still comes home and takes care of* my *responsibilities.* "When the girls see that I'm having one of those days, they're angels. They sing to me, bring me books, play quietly, and tell me how much they love me. I see their efforts and try to muster a smile, but inside I feel like I'm dying."

"Is there any indication that a blue day is coming?"

"No, not at all. And they depart as quickly as they arrive. It's like I wake up the next morning and, presto change-o, the day is better. I bounce out of bed with energy and renewed determination. No one, not even me, knows what kind of day

I'm going to have. This has to stop." Tears escaped, and I grabbed a tissue.

We decided talk therapy would be the best approach to identify the root of my depression. I had buried so much pain, guilt, and shame that I was drowning in it all. I had no doubt things would get ugly when we finally untethered those shackles.

Thankfully, just as I was ready to dive deeper into my depression, the abuse of the past, and my personal mistakes, God, in His perfect timing, sent an army to rescue me from the darkness of my depression, and He started with the strongest, most influential person of all: MacKenzie.

FAITH OF A CHILD

Our daily commute down Black Forest Road afforded many familiar sites. The small strip center housed the local chiropractor, a Realtor's office, and a Subway sandwich shop. The winding road was laced with homes that could be seen through the tall pine trees. Along the way were three churches, the closest to our home being Black Forest Chapel. The simple building had no grass or flowerbeds around it or professional landscaping of any kind. Instead, nestled amid a bank of pine trees, thousands of fallen pinecones served as the exterior décor.

When we first moved to the area, Kenzie, then five years old, announced, "I want to go to *that* church!"

I played along. "When do you want to go?"

"When I'm seven!"

"Okay, when you're seven. You remember, and I will take you."

In August 2005, Kenzie's seventh birthday came and went, and she never said another word about church. Neither did I. Given we didn't subscribe to the church mentality, I had forgotten all about it.

Then in April 2006, she surprised me, saying, "I'm ready to go to church now."

Part of me hoped she had forgotten about it, but I had made a promise and intended to keep it. "Okay. I told you we would go when you were seven. When do you want to go?"

"On Easter."

I smiled. I knew she had seen the advertisements for the Easter egg hunt. "All right. I'll talk to Daddy."

Later that day, I shared the conversation with Madison.

"I'm not going to church."

"But Kenzie wants to go, and I promised her I'd take her."

"I'm not going."

"I want the girls to know Christ, and they have expressed a desire to go. I refuse to do it the way my parents did by making the girls go by themselves."

"You can go if you want to, but I'm not."

I saw no point in continuing the conversation. Madison had made his position abundantly clear, but this was something I needed to do. So a couple weeks before Easter, I loaded the girls in the car and headed to Black Forest Chapel. We thoroughly enjoyed the service. Something nudged my heart, something I couldn't ignore. I knew if my girls were going to attend on a regular basis I needed to meet with the pastor. For my daughters' sakes, I summoned every ounce of courage I had and approached the pastor after the service.

"Hello, Pastor James. My name is Lynnette Simm. We're new to Black Forest Chapel, and I wanted to take a moment to introduce myself."

"Welcome, Lynnette. I'm glad you've decided to join us."

"Well, Pastor, that's what I'd like to speak with you about. Before I join, I'd like to meet with you one-on-one. I have a few questions I'd like to ask."

"That would be fine."

"Would you be available next week?"

"Yes, I am. Just call the church to schedule a time that's convenient for you."

"Okay. I look forward to it. Thank you." My heart beat so fast, I was certain he feel the pulse in my hand as he shook it good-bye.

Clueless as to what I specifically wanted to ask him, I knew it was important for me to find a church that would acknowledge my girls and encourage them to be strong women. I didn't want them to grow up believing that their sole purpose was to be a man's servant. Anxious anticipation led the way as I walked into his office the following week. Pastor James also seemed nervous, but I did my best to alleviate the uneasiness by beginning with general questions about the church's doctrine.

"Well, here at Black Forest Chapel we study the Bible," he said.

"What denomination are you?"

"We are a Bible-centered church and are considered a nondenomination."

"Why are there no women in leadership here?"

He seemed a bit taken aback by the question. "Ah, well, we do have women in leadership roles here. They lead prayer groups, ministries, and Bible studies."

"Then why, when you call for the elders to come to the front of the church after your sermon to pray with the congregation, there are no women?"

"Well, according to Scripture, only men can be elders. We follow the Bible and hold true that there is no need for interpretation. Each person has his or her role, and the Bible makes that very clear."

He supported his position by reading Scripture that addressed how the church was to be structured. At no time did he talk down to me; rather, he was kind, patient, and very understanding.

"Can I be frank with you?" I asked.

He smiled. "Yes. Go ahead."

"Now that you've explained it to me, I understand that the Bible says women can't be elders. But honestly, there's no way a man can understand what it feels like to be a daughter, sister, wife, mother, or a girlfriend. The same could be said of a woman. I can't even begin to understand the stresses of a son, husband, father, or a male in society. How can I walk up to the front of the church and have someone pray for me when I don't feel they can understand me?"

He remained silent and thought before responding. "I understand what you're saying. Let me think about this and get back to you."

The very next Sunday I had my answer. At the end of his sermon, Pastor James stood before the congregation and said, "Could the elders and their wives please come forward?" He had a big smile on his face, and so did I. There was no doubt in my mind that I had found my church home. I felt like I belonged, that I was accepted. What an emotional high. I couldn't help but share the story with Crystal.

"And the next Sunday, the elders' wives were called too. I was completely shocked."

"Why? Did you think Jesus would get you in the door and have someone kick you out, silly? He has been orchestrating this all. He knew every day you'd have before you born. He loves you, and He wouldn't let you get so close and shut the door."

"Somehow I have always felt Him. Not always in a good way. I thought so many times He must hate me. But He doesn't. I thinking I'm getting this Christian stuff." I gave her an exaggerated wink. She just said, "Whatever," but smiled.

AN ANGEL FROM THE PAST

Two Sundays after Easter, I spotted a familiar person in one of the front pews. As I approached, the most beautiful, genuine smile graced her rosy cheeks and made me feel like I was home again. Carmen, the receptionist at the printing company owned by Madison's uncle, was one of the first people I had met when we moved to Colorado Springs. But not long after Kenzie's birth, Madison changed jobs, and I lost contact with Carmen.

Carmen always held a special place in my heart. Her authentic midwestern charm drew me in; she didn't have a pretentious bone in her body. Her manner of dress reminded me of Nonnie—always ladylike and meticulously put together. In no time at all, we reconnected and began spending time together outside of church.

Carmen's domestic experience inspired and welcomed me. Over time, she taught me the ins and outs of vegetable gardening, baking, and crafting. Watching her slender, graceful fingers soulfully plant the tender seedlings, masterfully handle dough for cinnamon rolls, or create a unique treasure from odds and ends was like listening to the symphony. I had no idea that God was going to use Carmen to speak to me in ways that would quench my unknown thirst. From her standpoint, she was merely spending time with and loving a friend.

Carmen was not aware of the extent of the abuse I had suffered as a child, but her astute discernment recognized how delicate I was. One day before Bible study, we stopped by the local coffee shop and I courageously shared some of the damaging messages that plagued me. "I don't know how to explain it. I have these negative pictures and thoughts that constantly run in my head. Even during good times. I can be hugging Madison and negative images come into my head that just make my skin crawl. No matter what I'm doing, it's constant."

Carmen gripped her cup in both hands. "I understand. It's common and happens to all of us, especially new Christians. The devil wants to pull you back and keep you trapped by those images and thoughts."

"But some of them are flashes from my past, and they're very real."

"The devil uses our past pain and insecurities to keep us locked in evil."

"But I just don't know what to do. It's overwhelming."

"Here's what I do. Say this out loud, in a whisper, or in your mind every single time it happens: 'Devil, get out of my head. I'm walking with Jesus. Jesus, please protect me and give me peace.'"

I couldn't help but chuckle. "Do you know how many times I'm going to have to say that? People will think I'm psychotic!"

"In the beginning you might say it every minute, then every ten minutes, then every hour. Then it'll be every few hours, then once a day. Eventually, it will become less and less."

There's no way this is going to work. My doubt showed my ignorance. I had no clue as to the power of Jesus's name. At first I didn't do it, but a week later, I awoke from a terrible nightmare and immediately remembered Carmen's advice. *Why not? At this point I've got nothing to lose by trying it.* I chanted those words over and over until I eventually fell back to sleep. The next morning I woke feeling refreshed and calm, not agitated in the least. Though I remembered having the nightmare, the intricate details escaped me. That experience provided all the proof I needed. From that day forward, anytime a negative thought came—while taking a shower, driving in the car, sitting on the toilet, shopping in the grocery store, no matter where—I recited the prayer as Carmen had suggested. When alone, I spoke the words aloud, but in public, it reverberated in my head. When Madison was present, I whispered it so he wouldn't think I had lost my marbles. *He has enough ammunition to believe I'm certifiably crazy, so why add to the mix?*

Over time, the negative images and thoughts began to dissipate, which made the depression and self-loathing somewhat manageable. I still had work to do, but for the first time in years, varying levels of hope began to take shape where darkness had previously reigned.

DISSOCIATIVE DISORDER

Just because I closed my eyes didn't mean I was invisible. My body still endured the humiliation, disgust, and pain of abuse. Always awake when it happened, I subconsciously escaped in whatever way necessary. In a conscious attempt to thwart my abusers, I slept fully wrapped and tightly tucked amid the covers. Anyone coming would rouse me because they had to tug at the covers to get to me. My hands were balled into fists and my arms protectively hugged my upper body. I always pressed my legs tightly together and allowed no body parts to reach the mattress edge. Regardless of the temperature, every part of me remained swaddled. The delicate breeze of a fan or cool night air seeping in the window made me shudder with fear, as it reminded me of his breath.

Sleeping was and continued to be my most vulnerable place. In my mind, both conscious and subconscious, I had yet to yield to the safety experienced during waking hours. The first fifteen years I was with Madison, the nightly rituals remained the same. No matter how often he emphasized security or pleaded with me to relax, I remained paralyzed by fear. Though at times I fell asleep on my back or allowed a toe to peek outside the covers, the moment negative thoughts or nightmares returned, I quickly resumed the cocooning effect. Carmen's prayer played a pivotal role during this time by chipping away at the endless insecurity.

Intellectually speaking, I understood the childhood dangers had long passed, but the lasting effects of the traumas remained firmly rooted. Dissociative disorder allowed my body not to feel—a form of coping with the years of abuse—but the tentacles of disconnect had seeped into adulthood and prevented me from enjoying what should have been healthy physical experiences. As before, it was Kenzie's innocent and forthcoming approach that brought the adult symptoms of DD to the surface.

"Mommy, why aren't you ticklish?"

"Because I lost my tickle." I prayed she wouldn't press the issue.

"How did you lose your tickle?"

Having vowed to never lie to my girls, I answered her in the most age-appropriate way I could. "Because it was taken away a long time ago."

She seemed fine with that response for the time being, but I knew eventually the day come when I would have to delve deeper into the reason.

During the next therapy session, Jenny decided it was time to tackle the dissociative disorder through the use of CBT. My homework was to ask Madison to tickle me, an exercise I was less than excited about. After explaining the objectives, we decided to start with my back. Rather than scratching my back, a healthy touch I had always enjoyed, Madison's stroke was to be whispery and gentle, the kind of contact that gives most people goose bumps. Moments into the encounter, I retreated to the safety of my emotional and physical cocoon, which rendered the assignment unsuccessful. It was obvious that conquering DD would take a very long time. *If ever …*

The therapy was paying off, and by the summer of 2006, Jenny and I were diving deeper into my history. Yet to successfully reconnect my mind, body, and soul meant I had to expose all my secrets. I had to lance every emotional wound in order to scrape out the infection. The following week I went to therapy expecting to continue discussing how CBT would help connect my mind, body, and soul. I wasn't expecting to have to reveal the secret that could destroy my family.

I began my session with Jenny with the usual "how are things going?" commentary. However, it didn't take long for me to dive in.

"Adultery is a vile word, but simply put, I committed adultery. I hurt Madison. It is the one way he said he would never forgive me for."

"And did it work? Did he leave you?" She already knew the answer.

"No. But that's because he doesn't know all the details." I crumbled into the sofa with more shame, guilt, and fear than I thought I could stand.

"Why don't your tell him all the details?"

"Well, first, I don't want to wreck other people's lives, but mainly because I don't want to lose Madison."

"Have you boldly told Madison that you have committed adultery?"

"Yes, but if he knew …"

"If he knew what? That you had sex with another person, and that you emotionally relied on another person? Then what? Doesn't he already know that?"

"Yes."

"Then what good will the details do? They will only deepen his wound. Is that your intent?"

There is never enough tissue. My tears feel like waterfalls down my face. Snot is overflowing, and my whole body is shaking.

"No," I barely let out. Little did Jenny know that she was saying the same things as Linda when I confessed to her. "But isn't it selfish or at least deceitful to not tell him the details?"

"No. Scripture says to confess our sins. It doesn't say we have to *detail* the sin. Scripture says to repent, to turn away from sin but also to apologize and ask for forgiveness. Have you done that? Have you said you're sorry and asked for his forgiveness?"

"Yes, so many times. It's just—"

"Are you going to cheat on him again, or are you going to learn to turn away from sin and work on your marriage and yourself to heal and grow?"

"Yes. I so desperately want Madison and me to heal and grow."

"Then leave it at the cross. Lay it down, Lynnette. Give it to

Him. He knows all you've done, and He still loves you. Madison knows all you've done, and he still loves you too."

"What about the people I've hurt because of my adultery?"

"Confess to them and ask for forgiveness. It's just that simple. Leave the old behind and become new."

"I know that is scripture. It's Second Corinthians 5:17. I memorized that verse when I was kid. Something about anyone who believes in Christ is new, the old has passed away. I don't remember the exact words, but I always loved that one."

Jenny smiled. She didn't have to Bible-thump me. It was already in there, and now I was realizing it too.

Amid the emotional sickness, I attempted to push Madison away with my brokenness and hide my emotions from him. In reality, I almost cut him out completely. Fortunately, he saw right through my self-sabotage. Though he made it clear that my past mistakes were to never happen again, he extended a level of grace I had never before experienced.

Chapter 43

BEING A PARENT

*I*n October, as the heat of the summer began to subside, my parents planned a visit to Texas. I had so much I wanted to talk to them about—questions I had and details I needed for the book. While they'd given me permission to write about my childhood, I feared how they would handle the specifics of my childhood from my perspective. We had talked over the years about the abuse but never as candidly as I was writing. I had no fear of abandonment, but I wanted to ensure them that I wrote the truth as best as I could remember and that I didn't hurt them in the process. I wanted to prepare them, protect them. Yet to my surprise, they did most of the preparing and protecting—and loving.

Just before their visit, I received a text from Ernie, whom I had been calling my dad for the last twenty-plus years. Since the previous December, Ernie had been promising to move to Texas and live near me, but his text informed me that he had met a woman and wanted to stay in California with her. He said, "I have to see where this goes. It may be my last chance at happiness." I felt crushed. Despite his track record, I believed him every time he promised to call, visit, send something, or repay Madison for helping him. I would have forgiven any debt, but he couldn't (or wouldn't) keep his promises to me, and the pain was ripping my heart apart again. Still, after all these years and all the therapy, I still just wanted my dad to be a dad to me.

When my mom called to confirm their arrival, I tried my best to keep the hurt out of my voice. I quickly got off the phone before I fell apart. I just couldn't bear to hear her say, "I told you so." But something moved me to text her about what had happened. What an amazing mother I have! Not one "I told you so," but rather, "I understand. I've been there." Her supportive and loving words filled me. She wiped away the shame I felt and replaced it with strength. She encouraged me to talk it through with Diane during our next therapy session. Before we signed off, she told me she knew I would be just fine because I strong.

I followed her advice and talked about Ernie during my next appointment. Diane used EMDR again to help me process the hurt I had tried to bury as an abandoned little girl. Then we discussed healthy boundaries for the strong woman I had become. I also had a profound revelation, one that freed Ernie and me.

I was a wreck when my parents showed up, and despite my efforts to mask my emotions, Mom and Dad saw right through me. At night's end, my mom and I nestled upstairs for a long conversation.

The day before they had arrived, I finally took a call from Ernie. He could hear the hurt in my voice, but what he heard clearly was that I wasn't calling him dad. I replied with Ernie this or Ernie that. I explained how hurt I was that he didn't visit me when I was in California two months earlier. Of course, he had excuses.

"But, Ernie, I still have every right to be upset with your decision to stay in California."

"So that's it."

"That's what?"

"I knew you were mad about something."

"What do you mean?" I kept my voice calm in spite of wanting to hurl the phone across the room.

"You're calling me Ernie. That's how I knew you were mad."

The thrust of the conversation opened the door for me to explain what I'd realized in therapy. "When I searched for you all those years ago, it was to find my dad, to find the one person who would care for me, look after me, put me first. All the things I believed at the time Bob wasn't doing. You stepped into your rightful role of dad and seemed interested in finding out what had happened to your children. But what had been missing all these years were all the responsibilities that come with being a dad. Out of anger, bitterness, and retribution, I gave you the title of dad, but you had done nothing to earn that title."

Ernie stayed quiet on the other end, so I went on. "What was even more unfortunate was that by giving you that title, I was demanding, expecting, assuming you would fulfill those responsibilities. I burdened you with my expectations without giving you the chance to be who you truly are, my biological father. A man who loves me but had never and could never be my dad. It wasn't in you to be more than that. And that wasn't fair to you. I'm sorry I put that on you. I apologize for expecting you to live up to what I wanted. Can you forgive me?"

Ernie sobbed on the other end of the line. "You have nothing to be sorry for, but you can forgive me for not being the dad you wanted and needed."

I told Mom that I had released Ernie of his title and role in my life. "While he will always be an important figure in who I am, he wasn't and isn't my dad."

Mom gently listened to me recount the breakthrough conversation. In the middle of my explanation, Dad walked upstairs and sat down to listen as well.

When I finished, Mom hugged me. "I understood the yearning to have a dad and putting those expectations on the wrong person."

I blew my nose. "I just wanted him to be my dad, to care about me enough to put me—and Robert and Mary—first."

Dad stood up abruptly. "I'll take that role. It's all I ever wanted."

I stared at him standing there. Suddenly a realization came over me. The person I saw before me *was* my real dad, the man who did, in fact, hurt me to my core but who always tried to put his children first. The man who raised us, taught us to take responsibility, love your family through the good and the bad, and stand up for ourselves. Though my legs felt weak with emotion, I stood and put my arms around him, and he tightly hugged me back. "Thank you. You are my dad. You always have been, haven't you?"

"And I always will be."

This conversation ushered in a beautiful beginning to our visit. Mom and Dad opened up about our lives before the abuse, the trauma of the truth being revealed, the pain of our family falling apart, and the long anguish they endured until their children could come to a place of healing. They shared their perspective of the events and revealed how they got through the very difficult time.

Dad shared stories of his abuse, and Mom shared about her feelings of inadequacy. Both revealed intimate stories about how God had reached out to them in their darkest moments. Their revelations strengthened me to continue to write about the anguish I had suffered and how I had worked to free myself with God's help.

Chapter 44

INADEQUACY BEGETS ANGER

*N*o matter how hard I worked, feelings of inadequacy remained ever-present. Madison had (and has) such high expectations of me and believed in my abilities to overcome the injustices done to me. He told me how beautiful and smart I was and called me a fantastic mother or a terrific student and teacher. Still, none of his affirming words made a dent in my feelings of inadequacy. The more affirmation he offered, the higher the pedestal went. Having someone believe in my abilities that much didn't soothe my soul; rather, it ignited the mounting fear.

Everyone in my family had been divorced, and I wholeheartedly believed my marriage would be no different. I kept waiting for Madison's patience to run out and his love to become conditional, but it never did. Regardless, I never felt I would be worthy of him. If I succeeded in taking care of our home, my care for the girls faltered. If I took care of the girls, the house was substandard. Going to therapy, yet again, was like admitting defeat and merely served to nullify the affirmations Madison offered.

"How can you love me? I'm such a basket case," I told him time after time.

"No, you're not. You just need to work things out."

"I don't know if I can."

"Yes, you can. I believe in you, Lynnette. Just stick with it and tackle the issues one at a time. You'll get there."

As Madison climbed the corporate ladder, it seemed my professional life remained stationary. My part-time work yielded menial pay, which fueled my insecurity. *What's so great or challenging about doing laundry or scrubbing toilets? Yeah, I can pick up the girls and cook dinner, but I'm never going to be supermom.* Even teaching seemed unskilled. *All the information is in the book, so if a student really wants to learn it, all they have to do is read the text. My students don't need me. I might as well be a bobblehead.* I never felt that anything I did could be deemed worthy. I was just an average housewife, pretending to be a teacher who really wasn't that special.

To work on my feelings of inadequacy, Jenny instructed me to make a list of everything I did—every duty no matter how big or small. The goal was for me to have a tangible reference for the abundant responsibilities. To actually see on a single list the number of hats I had to wear on a daily basis amazed me, and the exercise proved to be exceptionally beneficial.

"Lynnette, would you ever say the things you say to yourself to those you love?" Jenny asked during a session.

"No, of course not."

"Would you ever tell Madison he's not a good enough husband?"

"No, of course not. He's a wonderful husband."

"Would you ever tell the girls they're not pretty?"

"I would never say that! They're beautiful!"

"Would you ever tell them they're fat?"

"Absolutely not!"

"Then why is it okay for you to say those things to yourself? When you say them to yourself, you are in essence hurting your closest friend and your biggest ally."

"I guess I never thought about it that way."

"I want you to begin affirming yourself."

"What?"

"Every day, I want you to look in the mirror and talk to yourself as a friend—to begin seeing yourself as a friend. Tell that friend in the mirror all the things you like about her."

"Are you serious?"

"Absolutely."

"Ugh. Okay, I'll try it, but it sure sounds weird."

It had always been easy to see the good in others but never in myself. When I returned home, I went into the bathroom, stood in front of the mirror, and begrudgingly said, "Oh, you're so pretty." *This is so stupid. Who am I kidding? It's ludicrous.* Every affirming word felt like a ridiculous lie; regardless, I continued with the exercise as instructed. It marked the start of learning to love myself. While it would probably be an ongoing process, positive reinforcement is a critical component to fighting a negative self-image.

REPENT AND BELIEVE, BELOVED

Then it happened, the life-changing moment that saved me. As therapy continued, by the fall Jenny and I were still dealing with my feelings of inadequacy and self-loathing. I was justified in hating myself. I had broken every biblical commandment, and I had hurt so many people, especially my girls and Madison. How was I ever going to forgive myself for all the pain I'd caused? *God is never going to forgive me. I have done so much. I am not worthy.*

The girls and I had been attending Black Forest Chapel for almost eight months. Thanksgiving was just around the corner. Pastor James was finishing a series on forgiveness. I had heard about forgiveness, and I was trying to forgive. Yet forgiving myself proved impossible, until that day. *Could God forgive me? Really? With all that I have done, worse than my dad? I had broken every commandment. I killed. Even if others could forgive me, could I forgive myself?*

Like every other Sunday, Pastor James finished his message and called people to pray with the elders and their wives. I was sitting in my usual seat, near the back on an aisle seat. That's when I felt it. Something like I had never felt before was pulling me, gnawing away my resolve, the resolve I used to hold onto all the sin I was carrying. *My heart is being pulled. I can hear the calling to come. God, do You mean me? You want me to walk up there all by myself? Everyone will be looking at me. No, I will just stand. That all I can do now.*

I found myself standing as the musicians began to sing and the elders and their wives made their way to the front. Pastor James stepped down, and his wife joined him to welcome anyone who wanted to pray for his or her salvation.

I was saved. I did it when I was a kid. I was even baptized. But there was this pull, this yearning, that nearly knocked me down in the aisle as I slowly walked forward. *What are You doing? Why am I walking up there? What am I going to say? Will they judge me?* Alone. I took the steps toward Pastor James. He and his wife welcomed me, and I began to ask for a simple prayer. Then I couldn't continue. I began to cry. I wept in their arms and asked to be saved. I wanted to give my life to God again.

For what seemed like forever, I cried as Pastor James prayed for me. His wife hugged me as tears ran down her face too. Then I went to kneel at the cross. I went to my knees at the steps and began to pray for myself. The music continued as I whispered all my sins. I laid them all out—ignoring God, lying, sex before marriage, hatred for my parents, jealousy, worshipping others or things, adultery, and murder. *I am so sorry, Lord. Please forgive me.* I couldn't even say the words as my heart and mind rushed to get it all out. *Lord, love me. Forgive me. Redeem me. Hold me up during all this. Strengthen me. Lord Jesus, please. I can't do this alone any longer.*

I stood up, my knees aching and legs weak, yet I stood taller. An indescribable, unbearable weight had been lifted. I was lighter. I had hope. I was going to make it. My family and I were going to make it. A peace beyond my understanding had enveloped me, and I was no longer bitter, hurting, or fearful. I know it may sound like everyone else's experience, but this experience was all mine. I knew the work would be hard and time consuming, but I learned that day to repent meant that I had to change my life and follow God. And that day I began that journey. *Not* alone. I realized I had never been alone. Jesus, with the Holy Spirit and the Father, had always been with me. I am worthy. I am loved. And I added these phrases to my growing list of positive affirmations. Praise God.

Chapter 45

LOVE AND INTIMACY
AT LAST

I have shared so much about Madison and our intimate life. I want to make sure I reveal our progress.

It happened the weeks before Christmas. I didn't even realize the significance, but it had been almost twenty-three years on Christmas Day when Madison had asked me to marry him.

The days were now dark before dinnertime. The girls and I waited for Madison to come home before serving dinner. One night it was nothing fancy, just chicken and veggies. Madison came in like he usually did and kissed me hello before heading off to the bedroom to change out of his suit. Per our usual routine, I ask the girls to help set the table and get drinks for everyone.

Madison came out, and we ate dinner. Simple. We had our nightly chat and discussed school, work, and whatever else popped into the conversation. Madison asked his nightly questions: "Is your homework done? Do you need any help?" Both girls said yes, homework was done, and no, they didn't need any help. The cleanup went as usual.

After dinner, we all cuddled up on the sofa to watch whatever television program we had recorded. I think it was *Elementary* this time. We all like Sherlock and crime shows. By nine o'clock we sent the girls off to bed. They did their usual routine of brushing teeth, washing faces, and getting into pajamas.

Madison and I decided to head to bed too. We followed the same routine of bathroom time—brushing teeth, washing faces—getting into pajamas, and one of us checking on the girls. Just your average nightly ritual. As we both climbed into bed, we began to talk more intimately about our day, stress, struggles, and things we needed to do.

But then it began. The cuddling led to kissing, and kissing led to … well, you know. It was after our time together, while I was lying on Madison's bare chest listening to his heartbeat, that I noticed what had happened. And it had never happened before.

Without realizing it, I said in a whisper, "This was the first time we made love that I never, not once, had anyone else in my head." I was shocked that I had revealed that to Madison. He lay there silent. "I was with you, just you. Wow, this is what God intended. It's amazing." Tears began to roll down my face, dampening his chest. He still said nothing. He just hugged me tighter.

The next day I just had to tell someone who would understand. Yeah, I called Nonnie. I explained the whole event, leaving out some details.

"That's amazing, Lynnette. I'm so happy for you."

"I felt bad for Madison. He must have felt horrible hearing that we had never been alone while making love before. I'm afraid I hurt his feelings."

"Did you talk to him?"

"No. We just went to sleep and said our usual 'I love you' to each other."

"I'm sure if you talk to him you will find out that he's not upset with you. He's probably happy for you, and maybe a bit sad that you've had to struggle for so long."

"You're probably right."

"I have to warn you, though. It may not always be like that.

The mind will take time to process and practice not allowing anyone else in. You will need to be kind to yourself when others invade your mind."

"Okay, but I have hope, real hope, that Madison and I will only grow closer. God is so awesome! After all this time, He still keeps giving to my family and me."

That evening, Madison and I talked about the previous night. And of course Nonnie was right. Madison explained that that was how he felt every time with me, just him and me, intertwined in mind, body, and soul. The dissociative disorder will never go away, but now my mind, body, and soul are all together. I have hope.

Intimacy was now not only possible, it was happening. I was beginning to get back what the abuse had stolen and ripped away for so many years. There are still moments when I have to remember to keep working. I understand now that I will always have to work at staying whole and not let the past evil try to sneak in. I'm willing to fight, and I know others who love me are willing to work through everything with me.

It was an amazing event on an ordinary day. Thank You, Jesus.

Chapter 46

TRUE FORGIVENESS

*O*nce we addressed the majority of my issues, Jenny and I agreed that the time had come for me to confront my lack of forgiveness. I knew this step would be rough because, for years, the words I spoke never matched my actions and the only person I had fooled was myself. I had never truly forgiven those who had abused me or those who hadn't protected me. After Dad's arrest, any forgiveness I claimed was for the sake of the family unit. But the reality was, I hadn't forgiven any of them.

As therapy progressed, I realized that the dissociative disorder had clouded my ability to properly assign blame and process deep-seated anger. But the anger I carried went well beyond my abusers to include Ernie, Madison, and, especially, my mother. (Yes, you read that correctly—abusers, with an s. I'll explain more soon.)

Jenny tasked me with writing a letter to each of my abusers and anyone else to whom I held a degree of anger. She insisted I handwrite the letters without making corrections or stopping until I had nothing left to say. I knew this exercise would challenge me, as I had never spoken *my* truth to any of them. Because of my intense fear of abandonment, I had conditioned myself to edit words in my mind before I spoke them out loud. Because this would be the first time I'd truly spoken from the heart, I obsessed about the emotional upheaval this exercise might bring.

I labored over the letter to my dad.

Dear Dad,

It's not often I want to let you know how I feel about you. But lately you've come to mind. Therapy has a way of doing that—whether we want it to or not. I love you, Dad. I always have and always will. Maybe that's why it hurts so much when I wish you dead—vanished from my life. I accept the fact that what you did to me was part of a sickness inside of you. Though I now realize it had nothing to do with me, a part of me will always feel used and dirty. You stole a part of me that I'll never get back. You robbed me of my tender innocence and, equally horrific in my mind and heart, acted as if you had no remorse when you were doing it. I hated you for what you did to me because I will never again hold the innocent little girl you tore out of my heart. She is forever tainted by what happened.

I longed only to be loved—loved by my biological father, Ernie, by my mother, and by you. Yet you all hurt me. I hope you never knew about the abuse I suffered at the hands of others. I don't think I could ever look at you the same if I believed you stood by and did nothing while others hurt me. That's why a part of me hurts when I see Mom. She knew, but she chose not to believe, not to act, not to defend. As much as I'd like to blame Cathy—and I did as a child—I know she was only trying to save herself by leaving, as was Robert when he fled and Mary when she hated me for lying about you. They were victims too. They still are. I know that now.

I can't possibly know the pain or regret you have to live with—or whether you even experience them—but there are times when I wish you could shoulder the pain I have to carry every day of my life. I wish upon you the guilt and disgust that I have to push from my mind and heart every time I am with my own husband. By no fault of his own, he has to pay for your sins and the hurt from abandonment and neglect. I am surprised by how patient Madison is with you and how loving he acts toward you when you don't deserve it.

OTHER LETTERS BRING HEALING

Without a doubt, my father was the first and primary abuser. Those terms mean different things to me. Being the first abuser meant he stole my innocence. Being the primary abuser meant his offenses repeated over a period of years and made me vulnerable to the advances of others. I apologize to you, dear reader, for not having mentioned other abusers before now. I also apologize for being so vague now about the circumstances surrounding additional abuse, but I learned through the process of my dad going to jail that I don't need the legal system to intervene where God's justice is needed most. I felt—and still feel—that nothing could be gained by identifying others. Plus, I feared the likelihood of additional fallout after everything my family and I went though following Dad's arrest.

Though I couldn't bear to add pain and stress to my already fragile family, it doesn't change the fact that other people I trusted sexually abused me too. Without a doubt, being abused by my dad opened the gate to other abusers. I think I became sort of a target for it, as though I carried a sign that read, "Come after me. Others have." I never established clear boundaries because I didn't feel that I deserved to be treated with respect and tenderness. At the time, I believed that giving in gained me favor, and I used it to my advantage—even if that "advantage" was only to feel more loved and accepted. Though the others were never prosecuted (or formally identified) in order for me to experience healing, I still had to deal with the violation, hurt, and pain of their abuse. Ultimately, I had to forgive them—not for their sake, but mine.

The letter to my mom was littered with "why: questions: "Why didn't you love me and protect me? How could you pick Dad over me? Didn't you see that I just wanted you to love me and not feel like you were merely putting up with me? I wanted to feel special and treasured. I wanted to feel like I belonged. I wanted to feel like it wasn't my fault that your life was destroyed. I wanted—and still want—to feel like you don't blame me. I wanted you to see *me*. Don't you see everything I did, every concession I made, was so that you would love me and be happy? But no matter what I did, it was never enough. I needed your affirmation and your love, but you always fell short in making me feel worthy."

My letter to Ernie also contained a plethora of questions: "How could you give us kids away like we never mattered? Why didn't you want us or come back for us? Did you know how much it hurt me when you said you would come pick us up but then never showed up? Why didn't you rescue me, as my heart longed for you to?" It took years for me to finally come to grips with the abandonment issues I suffered from Ernie's inability to be the father I desired. But in time I learned to see Ernie as a man, not as a misguided, inadequate father. By understanding that, I finally learned to release my father-daughter dream and forgive him.

The anger I felt toward Madison was less about him and more about what he expected of me. In my mind, it seemed like he wanted so much from me. He longed for things I felt ill equipped to provide. He didn't do anything wrong specifically, but because I still struggled with feeling unworthy, his belief in me added more pressure than I could handle. In the letter, I peppered him with questions as well. "Don't you know how hard this is for me? Don't you know I would change if I could? I want this gone just as much as you. Don't you see how hard I'm trying? Don't you see how much I love you?"

THE LETTERS

During my appointment with Jenny the following week, we gathered the letters and a plastic bat and drove to the summit of Palmer Park. After making sure we were alone, I read the letters aloud, one by one, and then proceeded to hit the letters with the bat, as if I were hitting each person and each painful memory. Next, Jenny told me to forcefully rip up the letters to Dad and my other abusers. I picked them up one by one and shredded them to pieces. The intense physical act of beating then tearing up the letters ushered in a complete and cleansing emotional response. Racked with sobs, my chest heaved as I struggled to draw a deep breath. My face hurt from being contorted, and wiping salty tears from my cheeks made them raw. After what seemed like hours, I sagged to my knees, spent. I glanced around to see tiny bits of paper littering the dirt and grass around me.

But then I noticed something quite curious. I had not beaten nor ripped the letters to Mom and Madison. Jenny suggested it was because subconsciously I felt more hurt than anger toward them. I crumpled Mom's letter and stuffed it into my pocket. I decided to give Madison his letter with the hope that he would understand me better after he read it.

Jenny gathered the confetti-like shards of paper while I sat in exhaustion. There was nothing left unsaid. No tear remained. Nothing—just nothing. With little time to spare, I took a few deep breaths, got in my car, and drove us back down the mountain. Completely processing the experience would have to wait. I needed to put on my mommy hat and pick up the girls. But what occurred at Palmer Park felt good. For the first time, I actually experienced a freedom beyond being allowed to feel. I had been allowed to *express* how I felt.

The next Sunday, I went to church and quietly gave it all to God. "It's all Yours, Lord. I'm done. I don't want to be angry anymore. I'm weary of holding onto hate. I don't want to hurt anymore." When I spoke those words, I felt the most incredible sense of relief and peace I had ever experienced. *"It is finished"* now reigned where anger once stood. I could truly feel His love and presence fill my heart and soul.

With the bitterness and anger now gone, it was time to begin working on authentic relationships with my family. Where fake forgiveness had once reigned, now came the time to demonstrate true forgiveness. With one big difference, this time forgiving was *my* choice. Forgiveness this time would be done for *me*—not anyone else. Once I released all the anger, bitterness, pain, and guilt, I was able to see how I'd let others hurt me. I established clear and appropriate boundaries, and with pain no longer clouding my view, I was able to start making significant, necessary changes in all of my relationships.

As I continued to work with Jenny, I began to understand those around me. Where once I saw mean, bitter, strong, or weak people, I now saw people who had been hurt as well, people with their own history, deep-seated issues, and vulnerabilities. In time, I began to see their character and strengths rather than just the person who had failed me as a child.

My perspective was now one of an adult instead of the wounded child I had been for so long. I began to ask honest, sometimes difficult questions and enter into genuine conversations with them. A pivotal moment occurred when Nonnie talked to me about letting go of *my* expectations of who *others* should be and merely accepted them for who they are.

"No matter what you want or what you wish, Louise will never meet your expectations. This is not to say your mom doesn't love you or that she doesn't try, but more that you aren't giving her a chance to be Louise."

"I don't understand. I only want my mom to be a better mom, like you. For example, you call your kids often. You don't wait for them to call you."

Nonnie signed. "That's my point exactly. Louise isn't me. She communicates differently, and for different reasons. Her life experiences were different from mine; her children are different from mine. Yet you keep expecting her to jump over the bar you've set, labeled Linda. That isn't fair, fair for her or fair for you. She will keep failing, and you will keep yearning for something that is never going to happen."

I felt anger welling within me. "So what am I supposed to do, just let her not be there for me? Not share with her when I'm disappointed in her lack of communication or love?" When I heard a stern tone to Nonnie's voice, I knew I'd overstepped.

"That's not what I mean or what I said. What you can do is afford her a little grace. You know enough about her childhood that you should feel empathy knowing that she come from a broken family like you and what that might have done to *her* inner child. Lynnette, when are you going to give her a chance to love you the way *she* knows how?"

Her words stunned me into silence. I had never taken into consideration what it did to her when her father left her or what pain she endured when Ernie left. Nor did I think about how at just thirty-three years old she had to handle her whole life coming apart when the abuse came out. I never asked her why she didn't call her mom, family, or friends for help. I had no idea what inner strength she mustered up to pull my siblings, dad, herself, and me through that. Meanwhile, I sat in my self-righteous chair demanding and then condemning when she didn't do things the way I wanted.

As tears rolled down my face, I asked in embarrassment, "What do I do now? She hates me. I've been nothing but a shame and a disappointment. I've been mean and condemning to her and to dad."

Her voice softened. "I know for a *fact* that she loves you and is extremely proud of you. Just try to love her for her. Try putting yourself in her shoes before you lash out. Start talking to her. Give her the grace you wanted and received."

The conversation went on for another half hour, and by the end, I had a new understanding of my mom. While our relationship didn't improve overnight, I did start talking to her beyond the surface conversations. I asked questions. She smiled and a conversation would grow. I tried the same with my dad. We were all new at this, but we were making every effort.

Identifying where new, healthy boundaries needed to be implemented with my parents and with others was challenging. In the past, I had no boundaries. If they said jump, I would say how high. In therapy, Jenny helped me recognize that part of the dysfunction of the family unit was due to lack of healthy boundaries. I would have to be assertive and kind in order to set proper boundaries with my family and with others.

In the beginning, I struggled with saying no; learning to do so took intentionality and practice. The new boundaries were not only healthy to the overall relationships but also for me. They helped develop a genuinely compassionate and serving heart toward my parents and others. Accepting them for who they were began to show in all areas of the relationship. With my parents and other family members, I was no longer conducting myself as a needy child but as a responsible adult who was investing in each of them. In turn, they, too, invested and opened up in ways that allowed us to build healthy relationships.

BETTER MOM NEEDED

Extending true forgiveness helped me to realize that I had been living as a victim, and my immediate family was paying the price for it. My emotional instability caused inconsistency in my behavior, and my daughters suffered. My impulsive behavior often frightened them. I knew that needed to change.

In order to gain greater stability in our family, I needed to take the first step toward establishing emotional control and identifying the root of any anger I felt. It was critical for me to have proper expectations of the girls at their respective ages. Mine had been far too high, which put undue pressure on them. When bad days came, I had to learn to say to them, "Sometimes Mommy has a bad day, but that doesn't make it your fault." When necessary, I made sure to apologize to them. "I'm sorry for exploding and saying mean things. I was wrong. Mommy needs a timeout." I made sure they knew what I had done wrong and asked for their forgiveness.

My daughters were quick to respond with "It's okay, Mommy."

Then I would have to explain to them that it wasn't okay. "People are not allowed to hurt you just because they hurt. But thank you for your forgiveness. I will try harder."

Consistent affirmation was crucial to their emotional health. I made every effort to humanize myself to my children—unlike what I experienced growing up. During my childhood, my parents never apologized for their abuse—assaulting us verbally or beating us when they were drunk. Rather, our entire family swept such incidents under the carpet. I didn't want that dysfunctional dynamic for my kids. When I talked to my mom about this, she explained that she wasn't taught to be a vulnerable mother. Her role models were strong, quiet, take-it women. Mom also told me she wished she had talked to us kids when she was sad, scared, and overwhelmed. Doing so would have made a huge difference in our family. She said she was proud of me for being so open and vulnerable with my girls.

Chapter 47

DEEPENING OUR UNDERSTANDING

I couldn't believe it was almost Thanksgiving, our third in Texas. My parents-in-law would be coming to visit from Colorado, and my parents were coming over as well. I was almost finished with the first draft of the book. I just needed to talk to all my parents one more time to polish up some details.

I was able to talk to my parents when they came for a visit. Halloween had just past, and Mom knew that I'd saved her some of the leftover candy. I loved spoiling my parents when I got the chance with little gifts. I found Mom and Dad in their usual place, outside on my back patio, smoking cigarettes. I wanted to ask them both a personal question, so I asked my girls to stay inside. We chatted a bit, and then I explained to them that I was almost done with the book and wanted to ask them a few questions.

"Sure, honeybun, ask away."

"First you, Mom. How did you do it? I mean, I did the math. You were only thirty-three when everything with Dad and me came out. How did you handle it all? I remember being thirty-three, and I don't think I could have handled all that you went through." (As I write this part, I'm brought to tears. Tears for all the hurt caused by others and by me to my mom who did her best to love and only wanted to be loved in return. Tears for all the years I wasted hating my mother for being herself. And tears for how far we have come, together. I'm just overwhelmed with emotions.)

Mom's smile reminded me of a mischievous child who knows a secret and is about to share it. She simply said, "One day at a time."

"Really? It couldn't be that easy. How did you know you could make it? Did you know?"

"Now that is a different story. I think that the turning point for me was when we were all driving back from the police station. You kids were in the backseat, telling each other what had happened at the station when we were taken away separately to talk to the officers. I was numb. I remember praying quietly in my mind. I asked God, 'What am I suppose to do?'

"It's not like He answers you with words. I felt a peace in my heart, as if He was telling me not to worry. Saying, 'I have you. I will help you. You and I will walk through this.' It was the most calming, reassuring, comforting feeling. And I know me, calm isn't my forte. So this was all Him. It felt almost serene.

"When I got out of the car, I was home. I knew what I was going to do. I knew how I was going to act. I told your father what I felt, and he agreed to follow my lead. That's when they sent us to Linda. She was like the star in the dark sky. She said almost every thought I had that God had said to me that day. It may sound unreal, but she did. She did everything she said and more."

Dad and I were wiping away tears. "Wow. Why didn't you ever tell me that before?"

"First, you never asked, but mainly because you were never ready to hear it ... until now." Her voice was soothing and her eyes gentle as she imparted wisdom that only a mother who had experienced all that she had could give.

My mother knew me so well. After all these years, talking

with my mother changed once I learned to see *her*, not the person I wanted her to be, but the gift God gave me. She's very compassionate. She's loyal and kind. Growing up, it seemed as if she didn't want me or my siblings, but really she was just a young, busy mom who happened to be an introvert. She also had her own hurts, scars, and childhood to overcome. She had choices when we were conceived, and she chose us. It was undoubtedly hard. Her first marriage crushed her heart and left her a twenty-something single mother of three children, all under the age of four. As my biological father walked out of our lives, she was left to do what she could and what she thought was best for us.

Not a game player, she did love watching us play. Not a baker, she would eat, with a smile, the half-baked goodies we made. Not a hugger, she never turned down a hug. As a child I saw only all the things she didn't do, but now I see all the ways she gave love and continues to do so. By no means is she like me, but now I see how I am like her.

We had some deep conversations about the past. Our perspectives were different, of course, but she said she's sorry she made mistakes or that we thought she didn't love or want us. She just didn't know how to express her feelings. Now she sends me texts with words of encouragement, compliments, pride, and love. At times, a bit of bitterness will sneak in as I think to myself, *Where was all this kindness when I needed it?* Thankfully, I'm able to reread it and see her love and devotion was always there. Maybe it was harder for me to notice as a child, but Mom always, always, always loved my brother, my sisters, and me.

"Dad, what about you? Why did you stay? It would have been much easier on you, and at the time I wanted you to. How did you handle it all?"

"Well, you answered part of it. At the time you may have wanted me gone, but your mother and I knew that you would always feel that way. You see, she and I had many, many long talks about you kids. We talked about all the should-haves, would-haves, and could-haves, but we also talked about the future, all the pros and cons. I told your mom that I wanted to stay and fix everything. But at the time, neither of us could definitely say we were going to stay together. So we put you kids first. We decided to get through the courts and the therapy and do what we had to do for you kids."

"Then what? Did you have a turning point?"

"I was sitting drinking a cup a coffee at the counter in a local diner. There was a guy sitting next me, and he says, 'I can see you have a problem.' I looked at him. 'You will get through it and things will be fine.' I looked at him and he went into detail as to what my problem was. He said, 'Your children will be fine, and you have a good plan.'

"Your mom and I just discussed earlier that morning about what we were going to do. I didn't know this guy. I never had seen him. I went to dinner at that diner several times after that, but no one knew him and he never come back. It was eerie. I was almost spooked, but I took it as a sign from God. It was so strange. I can't think of any other reason for the guy talking to me when I didn't say a word to him. He was just specific about the issue being with my kids. Not work or wife or anything else."

I stopped rocking in my chair as I listened to Dad's story. His eyes were moist, but his voice was steady. He recalled the events as if it were yesterday. Mom had a slight smile on her face as she looked at me. I was just soaking in all that God had done to keep our family together. Angels everywhere. Dropping in to speak words of encouragement and wisdom. The Holy Spirit filling each of us with hope and love exactly when we needed it most. Although my family didn't talk about God, or give Him any true importance throughout our lives, He never failed us. Never.

Talking to my dad is relaxed now. As a child, I kept wish my father would come and rescue me. As an adult, I know my heavenly Father never left me and neither did my Dad. Oh, he could have. I didn't make it easy, at times none of us did ... and rightfully so. Yet he worked, waited, and patiently loved us all.

He worked to rebuild our relationships. He didn't give excuses. He apologized. He didn't run out on us. He proved his love. My dad … he's a good man. He was hurt. He had his own issues, and yes, they came back to haunt him and hurt his children. But as he says, when the rubber hit the road, he met us where we were and kept working.

After years of working on our relationship, my parents and I now enjoy a deep respect and love for one another. True, we don't agree on everything, but we are now able to talk without hurt, blame, or bitterness. At times they make me laugh so hard at the silly girl I was. They remembered it all. Things I don't remember. Unfortunately, the DD takes some of the good memories too. Yet my parents are always willing to share those stories. Although my childhood was indeed horrible at times, and we may have been poor, but we never went without because behind-the-scenes sacrifices were made. There were many fun and loving times also. I get so mad at myself for only remembering the bad times, but it can't be helped. Thankfully, my parents don't hold it against me. They just retell stories of ice cream sundae dinners, drive-in movies, ice wars, water fights, aboveground pools, crazy pets, family trips, and this little curly haired girl who made them smile all the way deep down inside.

Chapter 48

REVEALED

When I look back on where I was as a child, teenager, twenty-something, and young adult, I can scarcely believe the growth that has taken place. Much like the exquisite pearl I mentioned at the start of this memoir, God has covered me with His love, support, strength, and protection through many hardships and trials. But even greater than that, He's enabled me to find beauty in my struggles, to forgive and love unconditionally those who harmed me, and to embrace His truths and apply them to my messy life.

I have become one of those pearls. Not a cultured one, grown in a safe, sheltered environment, but one with flaws—garnered from a life that has endured much in order to gain much. Though I wouldn't necessarily choose every one of those struggles if I had the opportunity to do life over again, I realize now what the Lord has taught me through each one. Today I'm stronger for having suffered because I know more fully His sacrifices, mercy, and grace. And I wouldn't want to have missed out on any of those lessons learned.

And the day came...
when the hurt turned to understanding,

when the pain turned to grace,
and when the love overflowed like pearls of wisdom
given to me from my heavenly Father
on the day my eyes and heart opened to see His forever,
never-failing, always-present, great love for me.

Acknowledgments

This was a journey of obedience. I truly believe I was called to write this story of forgiveness and restoration. The story began decades before calling came to write the book, therefore before I get to far I want to thank the tireless and selfless efforts of the therapist I had, all of whom walked with that broken little girl as she grew into the woman I am today. Some names were changed for the book; however, therapist everywhere should know that *they matter more than they may ever know.* So, thank you "Paula," Linda, "Jenny," and Diane.

Friends of Encouragement came with throughout the years.

The early years: James A. and Scott. Thank you for the love.

My CS friends Crystal, Jenn, Stacey, Laurie, Marcy, Missy, Moina, Laura, Donna, Carmen, James S., Lisette, Yvette, Natalie, and Jeanne. Thank you all for loving me through the years of painful growth and for seeing me hidden behind the hurt.

The first draft, the time line of all the pain would not have been written if not for my beloved friend, Michelle Hoffman. As a co-writer, she handled me with care as I lived through the pain again in vivid details. For over a year, she patiently and lovingly pulled the history of abuse and hurt out, while ensuring I was left stronger for it. Thank you isn't enough.

To the best editor a new writer could have, Leslie Wilson. Yet another year of working with a new writer to pull the best story out, thank you. You showed me how to see the audience and provide them the hope I have during the dark time in the book. You're perseverance and devotion to me went above and beyond. I truly treasure you.

To my Texas friends and Lighthouse family, thank you for welcoming my family and me and for helping us on the journey of life with Christ.

To a beloved friend who came to help me, just because God asked her to. Jode, Thank you for way too many drafts for the cover of this book.

The Westbow Press Team: Jon, Kayla, Scott, and Pete have been amazing. If anyone thinks they have a story to tell and want guides and patience, then Westbow Press is the company to use.

Also, I'd like to thank EVERYONE mentioned in the book. Thank you for letting me telling my story and your part in it. It takes a village, and mine is the best. I love you all.

A special thanks to my family and extended family that have lived with me through it all, thank you: Steve & Sandie, Betty & Clark, Ernie, and my extended family of aunts, uncles, cousins, and in-laws. You all make my life full.

This book would not have been possible if not for my parents and my siblings. Mom and Dad, God gave me you both. Thank you for being role models. Both of you took responsibility for your actions, put the family first, and did your best to help us all. Your dedication, patience, forgiveness, and love gave our family the opportunity to grow even stronger together. I love you both.

Robert, God gave me you. Thank you for your love and support. Your words of encouragement and discernment have brought strength to our family. Jennifer, thank you for loving my brother through it all.

Mary, God gave me you to be my best friend through life. Thank you for listening to Him and believing in me. Lloyd, thank you for loving my sister through it all.

My step-sister, God gave me you. Thank you for loving me, and know we love you always.

Finally, to the three people who have changed my life. These three have shaped me into a woman I am proud to be.

To Madison, for seeing my potential and loving as Jesus loves me, unconditionally. Without your forgiving heart, I don't think I could have forgiven. You are the Heart of my Heart.

To my oldest, MacKenzie, thank you for teaching me to be a mom and listening to Jesus when He called us to fellowship. Your faith changed our family.

To my middle, Bowen, thank you for being with me every minute of everyday to remind me of love and the cost of fear.

To my youngest, Alexandra, thank you for being the brave girl I always wanted to be. Your faith has brought out the best in us all.

Blessed Lord, thank you for love, hope, and forgiveness. All the glory be YOURS.

CPSIA information can be obtained
at www.ICGtesting.com
Printed in the USA
LVOW10s1131130117
520875LV00001B/1/P

9 781512 752151